Identifying Race and Transforming
Whiteness in the Classroom

"With complexity and caution, this collection of essays illustrates a range of personal, pedagogical, and political changes made possible when critically addressing White privilege in the classroom. Virginia Lea, Judy Helfand, and the contributors to this volume have produced a helpful and insightful resource—long overdue—for teaching against racial injustice."

—*Kevin K. Kumashiro, Center for Anti-Oppressive Education; Author of* Against Common Sense: Teaching and Learning Toward Social Justice

"*Identifying Race and Transforming Whiteness in the Classroom* is a stimulating and thought-provoking set of essays by a diverse group of educators. The book focuses on how we can actively transform perspectives on whiteness that result in inequities and injustices in ourselves, in our curriculum, in our pedagogy, and, ultimately, in U.S. society and across the world."

—*Ann Berlak and Sekani Moyenda, Co-authors of* Taking it Personally: Racism in Classrooms from Kindergarten to College

Identifying Race and Transforming Whiteness in the Classroom

Studies in the
Postmodern Theory of Education

Joe L. Kincheloe and Shirley R. Steinberg
General Editors

Vol. 273

PETER LANG
New York • Washington, D.C./Baltimore • Bern
Frankfurt am Main • Berlin • Brussels • Vienna • Oxford

Identifying Race and Transforming Whiteness in the Classroom

EDITORS Virginia Lea
Judy Helfand

PETER LANG
New York • Washington, D.C./Baltimore • Bern
Frankfurt am Main • Berlin • Brussels • Vienna • Oxford

Library of Congress Cataloging-in-Publication Data

Identifying race and transforming whiteness in the classroom /
edited by Virginia Lea, Judy Helfand.
p. cm. — (Counterpoints; vol. 273)
Includes bibliographical references.
1. Discrimination in education. 2. Whites—Race identity.
3. Critical pedagogy. I. Lea, Virginia. II. Helfand, Judy.
III. Series: Counterpoints (New York, N.Y.); v. 273.
LC212.I34   371.829—dc22   2004011057
ISBN 0-8204-7068-6
ISSN 1058-1634

Bibliographic information published by **Die Deutsche Bibliothek**.
Die Deutsche Bibliothek lists this publication in the "Deutsche
Nationalbibliografie"; detailed bibliographic data is available
on the Internet at http://dnb.ddb.de/.

Cover design by Sophie Boorsch Appel

The paper in this book meets the guidelines for permanence and durability
of the Committee on Production Guidelines for Book Longevity
of the Council of Library Resources.

© 2004, 2005, 2006 Peter Lang Publishing, Inc., New York
275 Seventh Avenue, 28th Floor, New York, NY 10001
www.peterlangusa.com

Printed in the United States of America

Contents

Part I. Cultural Forms of Whiteness

Part II. Rethinking Self, Rethinking Whiteness

Part III. Ways of Knowing

Preface

Racial identity, racism, and the social categories we inhabit often consti-
tute major barriers that prevent us from acquiring the personal knowledge
needed to teach. Unless we question how we were raised, the conventions
and values we embrace and live by, and the social order that attributes
power and status to certain physical characteristics while denying them of
others, our ability to teach, to guide, and to inspire will be limited. To
prepare our students to enter a world where racial hierarchies are entrenched and unquestioned, where racial justice remains elusive, and where
racism and bigotry are pervasive even if disguised by a post–civil rights
social etiquette, teachers must understand their place in that world. We
must recognize that none of us are neutral or outside of the lines that divide the haves from the have-nots. We are all implicated in these divisions,
and unless we can come to terms with how we have been positioned, our
ability to work across these divisions so that we might undermine and disrupt them will be impaired.

Identifying Race and Transforming Whiteness in the Classroom is an opportunity to learn from others who have committed themselves to this
introspective struggle. Through the narratives of these experienced educators we gain insights into personal journeys taken by others as they pur-
sued a path of critical self-discovery so that they might be better able to
transform at least a small part of the world through their teaching.
Through their struggles, triumphs, and travails, we learn what it takes to
engage in educational work that is transformative and that succeeds in
crossing divisions related to race and class.If we read closely, we may also
get a sense of what it might take to have this change occur on a much
larger scale.

Books by themselves do not change social reality, and the reality of
schools serving the poorest children in America is almost always one of
deprivation and scarcity. I would not suggest that by reading this book a

teacher will be better prepared to work in America's forgotten schools or to teach successfully across social boundaries. But for those who are willing to confront their own baggage—their deeply held personal biases, their unrecognized privileges, and the various ways in which we are all implicated in the oppression of others—this book may serve as a catalyst to embark on the path of personal transformation. Those willing to take this path will find valuable lessons and insights in this book.

Pedro A. Noguera, Ph.D.
New York University
January 2004

Acknowledgments

Life never seems to afford many of us enough time to realize our ideas. We usually need the support of others to turn our ideas into realities. For my part, this book would not have become a reality without the support of a large number of people. They include Judy, my coeditor, lady of deep wisdom, warmth, and extraordinary editing skills seminal in bringing this book to fruition; all of the authors who generously contributed to the book, all inspired and insightful, a few of whom were my close friends as I went through a Ph.D. program at the University of California at Berkeley; Pedro Noguera, always supportive and encouraging, who was my advisor while I went through the Ph.D. program, and wrote a preface for the book; Asha, generous spirit—I have no doubt that we will meet again; and Babatunde, Lichelli, Tanya, and Mayana, my family, always my muses, whom I love like life—tolerating me while I worked myself crazy to complete my part in the book before my tenure year. To these special people and to the many others who have touched my soul and helped it to grow, I thank you.

Thank you Virginia for inviting me in and stimulating, challenging, and laughing with me on this collaborative, creative journey into a book and friendship. Thank you Pam for giving us space to work and for believing in our collaboration and affirming its value. Thank you to all the authors for opening yourselves to us in the intimacies of editing. And thank you to the editors and writers of the dozens of books I've read and learned from while working on this one, who reaffirm my belief in the power of words to connect, inspire, heal, and change.

Grateful acknowledgment is hereby made to copyright holders for permission to use the following copyrighted material:

P. J. Hallam, *Crossing Borders through Authentic Assessment of Classroom Discourse*, used by permission from the Center for Language Learning, adapted from the *Primary Language Record* which was developed by the Centre for Language in Primary Education. The Listening and Speaking Grid is a component if the Learning Record, produced by the Center for Language and Learning.

Ariel Luis, No ID, cutloose, Volume 1, 2002. Davis, CA: Ill-Literate Press. Available from http://www..ill-literacy.org. Reprinted by permission of the publisher.

INTRODUCTION

Parallel Journeys to Identifying Race and Transforming Whiteness in the Classroom

Judy Helfand and Virginia Lea

In this introduction, we begin with a personal journey back through our lives to see more clearly where our current thinking, feeling, and acting about race and whiteness was given birth, to trace its evolution along the paths of our parallel life experience, and to gain political clarity on how we embody and practice race and whiteness today. The dialogical nature of our process became for us a way of gaining greater awareness of the impact of race and whiteness on our lives. We are examining what we previously accepted as normal, seeing all knowledge as texts to be closely examined, including the texts that bear our own names. We are asking ourselves, "How do we become the social and cultural worlds in which we grow up?" and "How do we transform ourselves if these worlds are oppressive to even one of our students and colleagues?" We believe that it is possible, although extremely difficult, to change the direction of the interwoven personal and professional paths along which we are traveling, as long as we have the assistance of allies acting as lenses on our racism, our whiteness, and our antiracism.

Nineteen Sixty-Eight

JUDY: It's 1968 and I've just graduated from University of Berkeley School of Education with a lifetime secondary credential, qualified to teach Social Studies and German. My first real job is at a junior high in West Oakland teaching what were then called "educationally handicapped" students—mostly students who were such extreme behavior problems in their classrooms that they were felt to need special attention. When our class of graduating student teachers began the spring job search, most were looking for jobs in the largely white suburban towns outlying Oakland, but I wanted to work with "underprivileged" children from the "ghetto." I am inspired by Herb Kohl (1968/1990), who has just published 36 Children, *and is teaching at Berkeley. On the basis of the class and his book—and the political spirit of the times—I am convinced that all the black children in Oakland Unified School District are in danger of having their spirits crushed by the racist and classist educational institutions they attend. I will be part of a movement of like-minded, young, dedicated teachers who will save them by revealing to them their own innate worth and capabilities so that they conquer the basics and, armed with academic skills of reading, writing, and analytic thought, go on to success despite the fact that the schools are stacked against them.*

I do understand that as a white woman who grew up in comfort and privilege amid other white people and who attended elite colleges (Reed College and Berkeley), I will have to bridge the gap between my students and myself. But bridging that gap means showing that I'm not one of "them"—the war mongers, the capitalists, the racists, the "man." By building a classroom that is not based on authoritarianism, using alternative teaching methods, demonstrating that I care about my students and take "their" side against "them," I will win the students over. From this won-over position, they will stop fighting learning and flourish in my classroom.

Looking back at that younger me, I marvel that I could have been so right and so wrong. I was right in thinking the schools were crushing the spirits of the children. But I had no understanding of the role of the schools in the broader picture of systemic racism. I didn't see that placing me, a first-year teacher with no experience and no training in working with children with learning problems (which were likely at the root of many of their behavioral problems), was an institutional statement that these children were throw-aways. More importantly, I didn't see how I was romanticizing, turning myself into the great white savior. Good intentions were all I needed.

VIRGINIA: It's 1968 and I am a white teenager, a long way from her native England. I am studying at San Francisco State University and working in a carpet store to make ends meet. I am living with my boyfriend, a musician, who is also a teenager struggling to survive a long way from his New Jersey home. We go into a café on Market Street to buy an ice cream. It is Fleet week and the fleet is in. A white sailor with a southern accent says to my boyfriend, as he orders cones for the two of us: "Pretty white girl! Too bad she's with a nig-

ger!" My boyfriend turns to the sailor and exclaims, "I don't believe you said that!" "Oh, I said that," the sailor replies. "And if you want me, I'll be over there!" "You won't get over there," my boyfriend shoots back. And the two of them are suddenly on the ground, fists flying, crunching up against bodies, urged on by a hungry white crowd.

Then we all hear police sirens. Somebody has called in the authorities and I feel relieved. My boyfriend disengages himself. But instead of facing his foe with a sense of impending justice, my boyfriend grabs my arm, urging me to set off in a hurry down the street. I resist. "Stand your ground!" I say. "You've done nothing wrong." But far from releasing the hold he has on my arm, my boyfriend's grip intensifies. As he precipitates me down the street, he calls out, "Man, have you got a lot to learn. You see what your people are like." I am shocked, as much by his words as by the violent incident. "What do you mean, MY people?" I scream between gasps for breath. "That racist pig is not MY people."

It would take me a long time to understand what my boyfriend meant by his words. In spite of the dominant rhetoric, justice in the United States, and in Britain for that matter, has never been colorblind. For most of its four-hundred-year history, the colonial project in what is now the United States of America has ensured the privilege of the few by legalizing the indentured servitude and the slavery of the many. Because of this legal framework, one's racial status gradually became essential to one's experience of freedom or lack of it. In her book, Playing in the Dark: Whiteness and the Literary Imagination, Toni Morrison (1992) describes what she calls "the parasitical nature of white freedom" (p.57). As race became a critical aspect of identity, people developed clear, stereotypical expectations of others whom they saw occupying the other category across the racial divide, across what Du Bois (1965) called "the problem of the color line" (p.209). In this paradigm, I was white and experienced the same white privilege as the white sailor, whether I wanted to acknowledge it or not. In this, we were a people. The law would be more likely to support my interests than my boyfriend's, and experience had taught him not to wait around to see if this generalization would be borne out in a particular instance!

Academic writing is usually seen as requiring distance and objectivity from the author. We choose to bring ourselves into the work because we believe that our scholarship is deeply informed by how we have experienced the world. We have begun with these stories from 1968 because we see them as pivotal occasions in the development of our identities, and because they illuminate much about where we came from. However, they are far from being the only critical moments in lives full of contradictions and tensions. Understanding our lives growing up, making sense of who we are today, requires compassion for our efforts to answer to the demands of different, often conflicting cultural worlds. Knowing now that all histories (and her-stories) are made up of selected memories (Hall 1993), and that identities, like all knowledge, are socially constructed and multiple (Hwu 1998), we choose particular memories to share, aware of their changing nature.

Growing Up

JUDY: My own schooling began in Panorama City, a new housing development built after World War II. Today I know that the lending policies of the FHA and VA prevented people of color from buying homes in these new developments (Brodkin 1999; Conley 1999). Then, I never questioned that all my neighbors, all the children in my school, were white. I was exposed to anti-Semitism in around the third grade and after that experience believed I was the only Jew in the school. Just the other day, I discovered that my yoga teacher attended the same school at the same time. She is also Jewish. She experienced anti-Semitism in the form of rock throwing and name-calling. This feeling of difference, and my awareness of the holocaust, was one counter to my general feelings of safety. I knew it was possible that some day I could be dragged away by the American equivalent of Nazis. But it was a small part of my consciousness. The boy-girl divide was more of a daily irritant. I was athletic and fiercely competitive and hated "girls'" games. Any time I could, I would push my way into the boys' handball, kickball, or tetherball games.

Within this white world of upwardly mobile working-class and middle-class families, I grew up free to ride my bike to visit friends or visit the dairies and horse stables that bordered the housing developments. My mother might occasionally take my sister and me with her to a nearby older neighborhood to buy eggs or pick up the ironing, which she left with the "ironing lady" when she started teaching elementary school. This neighborhood appeared shabby and cluttered. I absorbed a sense of its being strange and foreign—different from my own in a "less than" way. Or the whole family might go to East L.A. to visit my father's relatives in a working-class Jewish neighborhood. I remember when a bagel factory near my great-aunt's changed hands and became a tortilla factory, as a growing Mexican-American population gradually replaced the older Jewish one. But no one helped me put what I observed into an analytic framework. My parents' friends were all white, mostly Jewish, and all lived in neighborhoods much like our own.

In fourth grade (1956), our family traveled overseas for three months. Traveling through Europe I got a feeling for history, of how old some cultures are. I also absorbed the reality and horror of World War II when I saw the de-struction in Germany and the evidence of bombs and bullets in France. We visited Jerusalem, where we had relatives, and traveled all over Israel. In some places our Israeli relatives carried machine guns because of the perceived danger. Although I am not clear on how, I'm sure that the experience of other cultures, people, languages, and geography affected my development. Even though the experience was largely European, with a little Jewish and Arab Israeli, it was far removed from my new, white, suburban neighborhood at home. I had seen a wider world.

We moved when I started seventh grade to a semirural area on the edges of the San Fernando Valley. Years later I learned that my parents chose the location because then I could have a horse—something I had wanted since I knew what horses were. In my new school, I had a few Japanese-American and Korean-American classmates, who stood out as different. Later, I realized that some of the students were Chicano, but at the time I was unaware of their ethnic heritage and history of oppression in Los Angeles. I simply saw them as "white like me." There was also a small group of Jewish students, so I no longer believed myself to be the only one and felt a sense of connection and identification with the other Jewish students solely on the basis of our shared Jewishness. I had no class consciousness, probably did not even have "class" in my vocabulary. Although I was aware that our family had more money than most of the other families, I still assumed that money was not a problem for any of my friends. Tracked into the top classes, my social interactions were primarily with the same thirty or forty students out of several hundred in my grade throughout that six-year period of secondary school.

It was the middle of the civil rights movement, but I knew little of it. Communism was the big topic for political discussions at home and in school, at least in my circle of friends. Of course, throughout junior and senior high school I did learn more about the wider world and was aware of the racial and ethnic diversity in L.A. In part this diversity was represented by the tourist destinations of Chinatown and Olivera Street, where diversity meant "foreign" food and souvenir shops. Otherwise, I associated racial and ethnic diversity with the existence of poor people and "slum" neighborhoods. But the poverty and decaying neighborhoods didn't mean much to me, other than to serve as evidence that there was something wrong with the U.S. capitalist system. I thought that in a fair world, everyone would live at the same standard as I did. It certainly didn't occur to me that I might have more than my fair share. In today's vocabulary, I took my social and economic position as normative.

VIRGINIA: In addition to limiting our vision of alternative ways of thinking, feeling, and acting, part of the problem of culture is that it both offers us a shared understanding of how to solve the problems of our own lives and often suggests solutions that advantage "people like us" while oppressing outsiders. This has often been the case with my own native English cultural elite as they imposed colonial solutions on others, while defining these solutions as benign. But, as Paulo Freire (1970/1993) tells us, oppressive, falsely generous solutions limit our ability to be fully human. In my view, class, gender, and race, including whiteness, are tools that people use to bring about such oppressive solutions. They were tools used in my maternal cultural web from which, as an adolescent, I could see no escape. The world seemed to be so fixed, relationships of power so entrenched. In desperation, I railed, emotionally, and thus unacceptably to the dominant culture against the low wages currently paid to service and factory workers. At the same time, although I was certainly unclear about the ways in which my father and his family benefited from the economic and political acts of white men over centuries that had laid the groundwork for the unequal world in which we lived, I did manage to glimpse that my parents were able to provide for my sister, brother, and I in relative comfort because of this exploitation.

When I look back now on my life, I first see a young person, deeply immersed in an upper-middle-class, white, English country society. I see a young girl of stark contradictions, who shared some of the same ways of thinking and acting as her family and friends, and yet whose emotional commitments and political leanings pushed her to the edges of this cultural web. I see someone who felt and even behaved as if she were an outsider, while receiving and acting on the privilege of whiteness. I see someone struggling with emotional tensions that resulted from the contradictions of her life: loving countryside and physical freedom, and the unconditional support of parents; loathing a growing realization that most of the world outside of her web did not share such social, cultural, and economic advantages, including freedom from want and freedom from physical restriction; and suspecting that the two were somehow interconnected.

In spite of my economic, and (white) symbolic and cultural capital (Bou r-dieu 1994), much of my time with others was spent trying to find ways of feeling positive about myself while resisting the powerful, conservative values and normal ways of behaving that surrounded me. I gradually developed a highly confused sense of who I was, and came to expect confrontation in my contacts with other people. And then the summer before I was sent to a boarding school on the south east coast of England, at the beginning of my thirteenth year, I experienced a literacy event that changed how I would "read" myself, my boarding school and indeed, the world (Freire 1970/1993). I learned about my part-Arab heritage.

I remember feeling disconcerted but did not realize just what an impact this knowledge would have on my identity until we began to study the Crusades at school. Not only were we presented with simplistic, stereotypical constructions of Arab peoples but also these constructions served to present the English as the civilized half of a dualism that has not changed to this day. A shared consensus among elites viewed British colonial rule over the "Orient" as entirely warranted. Arabs had been constructed as a people unable to effectively govern themselves (Said 1979). This "orientalism" was a form of racism. It involved constructing and disseminating an image of a people based on limited, and often distorted, "facts," treating this picture as if it represented the truth about the people, and then taking action against the people based on this picture. As I write, the American elite, their leader a descendant of the English, is building on this historical tradition of orientalism in its own empire-building Middle East policies and in its rationale for aggressive intervention in Iraq. At the same time, Nelson Mandela (2002) and others argue that this ideology obfuscates the economic motivation—in this case, the desire to control access to oil reserves—that drives the United States international policy in this region.

Orientalism at my boarding school was encoded in our textbooks, which included primary texts about the Crusades from the perspective of the elite Europeans of the Middle Ages. I learned about the Arab, infidel "them" and the benign French/English, Christian "us." I remember balking at the idea that the Arab infidels—men, women, and children—deserved their deaths at the hands of the crusaders. I could not accept this "truth." I was beset with dissonance as a result of my newly found Arab identity bumping up against the Englishness that I also embodied and in which I was immersed. And, as so often happens in situations of conflict and confrontation (Bourdieu 1994), I was presented with a choice between "orthodoxy"—conforming to the dominant English cultural script—and "heterodoxy"—embracing a counterscript that meant a self-imposed marginalization. It would have been much easier to squeeze myself into the former. But I could not. I had come to empathize with the Arab Other, and as Stuart Hall (1993) tells us, once we have experienced "the flash of recognition, the continuity of the broken and ruptured tradition . . . symbolic reconnection is made" (p.9). There is no regaining of the consciousness one once had before this recognition.

As Lillian Roybal Rose (1995) tells us, culture can both empower and oppress. Within our cultural webs, we may both love our parents and/or caretakers and other nurturers and depend on them for comfort and a sense of belonging. Yet we may observe social interactions or be called on to behave in ways that appear to us as unjust. For white children, socialization into a white supremacist system may come with hidden psychological costs, a cutting of connection with those deemed Other, and a burying of innate senses of fairness and justice (Thandeka 2000). Growing up, we may glimpse that our economic comfort is often at the expense of others outside of our web. Many of us who are white and upper to middle class, buoyed by the individualistic ideology of the Puritan ethic that allows us to measure our worthiness by what we achieve and not by how we have achieved it, decide to suppress the fleeting urge to do something about the structural injustices that have given us a leg up on others. We are able to block out of our view of the world the evidence that some people benefit from and others are subjugated by the economic structure within which we all live. Few of us are given the analytic frameworks we need for making sense of what we observe and experience. Many middle- and upper-class white children live such segregated lives that there is little chance for experiences that might clash with life as they know it. Nonetheless, for some of us, the dissonance is felt internally, causing us to find ways to struggle against the enveloping web, despite our inability to fully articulate the reasons for doing so.

Navigating out of the "Mainstream"

VIRGINIA: We "cannot go back through the eye of the needle" once we have acknowledged another sense of self (Hall 1993, p.11). But we can and sometimes do remake ourselves as members of real, imagined communities. I took from the lesson on the Crusades a small and inadequate piece of the pain that my Arab sisters must have felt as the crusaders cut their infants from their bellies. (How telling that George Bush equated the United States intervention in Afghanistan against Al Queda and the Taliban as a "Crusade.") It was at this point in my life that I first began to recognize the power of racism as a means of oppressing a people. Yet, I still did not see my own whiteness.

I was deeply unhappy at being sent away to boarding school. I could not accept the explanation given me by my parents that the act of removing me from a world that I loved was in my own interests. I wanted to go to the local state school, while my parents believed in my being "educated" with others from the same class background as myself. It was the acceptable cultural thing to do. It would allow me to take my place in that segregated, white, upper-middle-class world. At my boarding school I could not avoid confrontation with the dominant cultural world. In this "total institution," (Goffman, 1961), there was no escape from the oppressive daily rituals and relationships, teacher-centered pedagogy, and Eurocentric curriculum carefully designed to control the all-girl student population and socialize us into a certain way of thinking, feeling, and acting.

I began my career at the school by resisting the rigid rules and regulations that were imposed on students. At the end of my first semester at the school, in spite of being placed near the top of my classes except in Scripture and Geography, the headmistress wrote in my report: "Now that Virginia is beginning to settle down, I hope she will try to be more obedient and not talk in the wrong place or at the wrong time."[1] Similar remarks accompanied my academic reports for the next three years, including the acerbic, "Virginia is finding the process of growing up very difficult. If she would try to exert more self control and be more cooperative, she would find grown ups more sympathetic." And the next semester, the headmistress told my parents that "Virginia has been too uncontrolled and uncooperative. She has far too many bad marks for disobedience and thoughtlessness. . . . I am sure that occupation with hard work would help her to solve her problems and give her greater satisfaction and more direction to her life."

It was vaguely apparent to me even then that I was being asked to assimilate to an arbitrary standard that was sucking the life out of me. School was about control, represented by mean, arbitrary rules and regulations, made up by an invisible elite, and disseminated by a willing group of women who lived on the school premises. For example, we, the students, were not allowed to talk in the corridors; we could not wash our own clothes, including our underwear; we could make no choices as to what we ate unless our parents wrote letters of request; and most importantly, we could not express any ideas that deviated from the established school norm. We were supposed to come to accept this cultural territory as our own and defend it against all comers. The norms and values of the school would be the cultural scripts that would inform our out-of-school and future practice. The torch of upper-middle-class English female whiteness would be passed to us.

Although we came from very different backgrounds, I can empathize with bell hooks's (1994) experience as a child. She was bused to a white school where "we soon learned that obedience, and not a zealous will to learn, was what was expected of us" (p.3). This was true of my boarding school, and its relentless ideological efforts were successful in my case for a while. After three years, I began to conform: "Virginia is still rather noisy at times but generally speaking less emotionally and is easier to deal with." But at the same time, my grades dropped drastically. I was no longer near the top of my classes. I even decided to stay on at the school for the lower sixth form (eleventh grade) in order to become head of my house, although at the same time I had a sense that my beliefs and ideas had been and would continue to have to be outrageously compromised. When the position was given to another, I knew that my past as a rebel would not be easily dispensed with. I had been named, and the name had stuck. I would be allowed to be a loyal lieutenant but never a leader. I was still a loose cannon.

I survived boarding school but failed to get into an English university. Nevertheless, my privilege allowed me the option of coming to the United States as an au pair (maid) to a senator. In turn, this disastrous relationship allowed me to research and finally study at university—first Colorado College and then San Francisco State, during which time I had the pivotal encounter with race that I describe in this Introduction.

JUDY: Although I took my social and economic status as normative, I did not take myself as normative. The older I got, the more I saw myself as oppositional. Jewish as opposed to the assumed norm of Christianity. Smart in math and science as opposed to the expressed norm of girls as incapable in those fields. Wanting something fluid and exciting as opposed to the rigid confines of marriage and children after graduation. I was opposed to conservative, mainstream American beliefs and behaviors even though I didn't really know why or know what to replace them with. I felt myself to be different and sought out a place where difference might flourish, choosing Reed College for that reason. For a sheltered, middle-class white woman in 1963, it was a big step.

College opened up a new world. I plunged into the freshman Western civilization course, reading philosophy for the first time. Challenged and stimulated on an intellectual level, I was also eager to experience "grown up" activities such as drinking, smoking, and sex. I truly believed myself to be at an antiestablishment institution and failed to notice that (a) I was still surrounded by middle- and upper-class white people and (b) we were being taught the ideologies and methodologies that underlay the system we thought we stood outside of. I was receiving a Eurocentric education while being told I was learning about universal principles. When I transferred to Berkeley after two years, not much changed in that regard. I did become involved with the anti-war movement and supported the Black Panthers, but really had little understanding of imperialism or racism. I felt myself to be transformed since I had left home—and in many ways I was—but it was not a radical restructuring of my world view, which remained white and middle class. This was the young woman who obtained her teaching credential and walked into a classroom in West Oakland in 1968, sure she could make a difference in children's lives.

Schooling may be analogized to a powerful, fast moving "mainstream." Strong currents push to the banks of the stream any barriers to the efficient passage of a fleet of ideological vessels called *methodization*, which carry us in a single direction downstream (Bartholome 1996; Doll 1998). The fleet is lead by great schooling ships, fitted out in lavish ways. Behind are schooling vessels with lavish upper decks and dismal decks below water level. In the rear, rickety schooling ships in danger of sinking struggle to stay afloat. For our delectation, the vessels also transport, amongst other "normal" fare, such legal mandates and educational practices as high-stakes testing and packaged curricula that categorize knowledge and behavior in rigid ways. With their lavish provisions, the lead ships are best able to choose different forms of this fare. As we are transported, we are all—students, parents, teachers, and administration—methodized on the decks and in the holds into seeing a particular view of the horizon. Most of us do not see beyond the banks of the stream. A hegemonic mist hangs over the distant hills and valleys. Unable to disembark, we imbibe the ideological food and water that is available on board. It is "educational" nutrition that keeps the convoy in a particular configuration and therefore resonates with most of the teachers, administrators, and parents on the lead ships and on the upper decks of the secondary vessels. And even on the rickety ships, many of the teachers and administrators believe that they are making good headway along the "mainstream."

In other words, schooling is an almost watertight system that maintains the status quo. But, it is not 100 percent watertight. If a critical mass of passengers on the ships of methodization were able to catch a glimpse of a tributary, of a horizon, of an alternative way of moving along the educational water, they might join together to scuttle the ships, or sail them down tributaries into different waters. In those alternative waters, they might be able to build different, more democratic and equitable socioeconomic and political relationships defined by agreed upon definitions of equality and social justice. In fact, a number of passengers have always struggled to construct a different, more equitable way of traveling down the waters of life. We will be in good company if we join them and help the other passengers to see themselves within the complex web of power hierarchies we all inhabit and that are sustained by whiteness. We can encourage each other to build critical thinking skills and the ability to acknowledge the multiple points of view that exist and that can be imagined.

The Work in Progress

VIRGINIA: What I see now is that my particular lack of acceptable restraints and the rules and regulations of the school, were different sides of cultural whiteness. Whiteness is a system of advantage, but it is not fixed. Whiteness morphs. It is part of a system of race that adapts to socioeconomic, political, and cultural change to assure privilege to white people in general and all people, to some extent, who embrace its cultural norms and values. My protest in my boarding school stemmed largely not from a pragmatic, idealistic, or rationalistic attempt to benefit people who were being oppressed, but from a self-centered interest in surviving with my own naïve, confused identity and cultural privilege intact. However, through the act of resisting I did come to identify with the many people in this world who are oppressed by those subtle and not so subtle, powerful socializing mechanisms of school and society that maintain inequalities.

Since this time, my attempts to develop an identity within which I could breathe once again as I did as a child, and at the same time contribute to changing the schooling processes that silence and oppress our children, have been mixed. Achieving these goals depends in large part on transforming my own whiteness. In this, I am a proverbial work in progress. I became a teacher as much to be present in my own children's lives as to be an educational activist. I remember marveling at my ongoing contradictions. How could I once again tread the halls of a school, now as a teacher, still feeling the dread that had accompanied my childhood and adolescence? I was idealistic, but it would take many pivotal encounters, particularly with my women of color friends and colleagues, until I could begin to see more clearly the ways in which my own whiteness impacted what I did in the classroom, in spite of my best intentions. Some of my most influential friends were met while I undertook a doctorate at the University of California at Berkeley, one of the institutions that Judy attended. Others challenged me as I engaged in alternative educational change projects and life travels in England, France, Algeria, Canada, and California. And the boyfriend who had such a powerful influence on my whiteness as a teenager continues to impact my life as we share the struggle for social justice as husband and wife.

Now a teacher educator, I am engaged in developing practices, inside and outside of traditional classroom settings, that help K–12 students, student teachers, and practicing teachers to recognize their own whiteness. I am committed in my personal and professional life to finding ways for us all to become more aware of the social and cultural scripts that shape what we do in the classroom, and in situations like the one I encountered in 1968.

JUDY: Today I can look back and see how unconscious I was of my white privilege and my class privilege, how unaware I was of my oppression as a woman, how my desire for social justice was thwarted by not knowing what to do to make a difference, and how my exuberance and love of life led me to individual pursuits of pleasure and adventure. After one year of teaching I left the country for world travel and exploration. Today, after years of community activism, self study and, eventually, graduate school, I can work toward social justice with more consciousness than I brought to bear in 1968.

The situation in public elementary and secondary schools has only become more dire in the intervening years. Social policy seems to be moving toward abandonment of urban public schools to those too poor to afford private education. De facto segregation allows middle-class and some working-class white students to attend majority white schools in suburban areas with more school funding and more community resources (Conley 1999; Steinhorn & Diggs-Brown 1999). An increasingly white teacher force is ill equipped for contemporary challenges of educating students in public schools. But for the many educators who do care, who, as I did, want to make a difference in children's lives, resources exist. Self-reflection, research, and analysis by scholars and educators can help us prepare for the challenges and enter classrooms with more than our good intentions.

Why This Book?

We—Judy and Virginia—are white middle-class women who live now as we have throughout our lives the advantage of being placed in a white racial category in our personal and institutionally defined relations with others. We came to our collaboration on this book, not with a desire to increase this advantage by centering our whiteness, but with the clear understanding that even though many of us see ourselves as fighters for social justice, most of us will, however unwittingly, contribute to reproducing unequal opportunities and outcomes for our diverse student populations unless we identify race and transform whiteness in our classrooms.

As upper-middle-/middle-class white children, we attended "good" schools and supposedly received a "superior" education. We did not encounter within our early schooling the tools required to make whiteness visible in our classrooms, nor the theoretical frameworks within which to examine the inequities and injustices that we observed and experienced. However, our early education did provide us with the credentials required to find gainful employment, as well as some keys—such as literacy—we could use for self-education later. But until we undertook that education, our efforts to struggle against the web, to sail against and beyond the "mainstream," were ineffectual.

The stories we recount exemplify the role of schools in the maintenance and construction of *whiteness,* a term that has come into increasing usage over the past ten years. The intense current intellectual and theoretical interest in whiteness encompasses a focus on whiteness as a social construction. Seen in this way, whiteness is a constellation of social practices, knowledge, norms, values, and identities that maintain a race and class hierarchy in which white people disproportionately control power and resources. Educational institutions serve as one of the primary systems for constructing whiteness. At all levels—social, economic, political, and cultural—they sustain racism and white supremacy within the United States.

To return to the schooling ships, those rickety vessels carry a preponderance of working-class and poor students of color along with poor and working-poor white students. The disaster of urban schools is well documented and the racism of the educational system starkly revealed by many studies (for example, see Kozol 1996; Maeroff 1999; Noguera 1995). And as the editors' stories illustrate, while the lead ships serve to equip their mostly middle and upper class white students with the skills required to utilize and maintain their race and class privilege, they are doing little to equip those young people with the skills required to build a democratic system based on social justice—not white supremacy. The current interest in whiteness helps us see that we need to transform schooling for *all* students.

Social justice educators have recognized that to teach for social justice we need more than efforts at devising new, multicultural written curricula. While the work of Grant and Sleeter (1998) Slapin and Seale (1998), Christensen (2000), and Shor (1987), among many others, is extremely important, we need to heed the call of Pinar (1998) to rethink the notion of curriculum. The research of Doll (1998) and others helps us to recognize the historical role that curriculum has played in efforts to socialize and control our students. Yet, official authorities have required us to present curricula as legitimate, fixed, and universal bodies of knowledge in written/illustrated form to our students in the classroom.

We see the "classroom" and its "curriculum" as part and parcel of our own internal geography. The curricula that we willingly adopt in the classroom (as opposed to the curricula that is imposed on us by law) are external reflections of the "paths" that we are pursuing in our private as well as professional lives. We are driven along these paths by certain norms, values, beliefs, and emotions that are responses to our past experiences. These norms, values, and beliefs often closely imitate the social and cultural worlds in which we grew up, went to school, developed our identities, and currently study, live, and work as adults, even when we think we are "living" a million miles from these worlds.

If we take curriculum as the interplay between these bodily held norms, values, identities, and practices of the educator *and* students, and the official syllabus, texts, and other classroom resources, we can approach our curriculum with more confidence as a potentially dynamic and liberating *process*. In other words, in opposition to current demands for uniformity and control in the name of accountability, the curriculum can become whatever all parties involved in the learning process want it to be.

However, even this approach to the curriculum will not become the practice of social justice unless we recognize the connections and disconnects between our current practice, our intentions, and our deeper, often less than conscious social and cultural assumptions. Culture is complex and messy, and we are our cultural expressions. The more our internal social and cultural landscapes, with their peaks and valleys, are shrouded in the whiteness that defines many of our society's institutional policies, procedures, and laws, the more we are likely to be implicated in reproducing the race, class, gender, and other hierarchies in which we live our lives. While holding to ideals and envisaging practices of equality, freedom, and justice for all, we often nonetheless socially reconstruct whiteness through our teaching practices, our choice of readings and work assignments, our classroom structures, and the many small daily interactions with students that usually remain invisible to us and go unremarked. While many teachers carry a commitment to educating all students from all racial and ethnic backgrounds according to their needs, and making each student feel valued and empowered in the classroom, these good intentions are often unrealized.

Interrupting the reinforcement and continuation of whiteness is possible but requires attention, commitment, and a lot of work. We are able, if motivated and possessed of the tools, to identify the ways in which our thinking, feeling, and acting mirror those dominant cultural norms, values, and beliefs that gave rise to and lie behind the unequal socioeconomic structures in which we are lodged. In other words, we can look closely at the ways in which we may reflect the formal, dominant cultural world. We can move away from an individualism that sees people as "islands," insulated from the influence of how others see us, and from the ideology that rains on us through institutions, such as school, the workplace, and the mass media (television, video games, and the movies).

Our Process

Over the two years we have been working on this book, we have often discussed the process, monitoring how the book was emerging within the very systems we hoped to critique and change through the chapters collected here. In this section we share some of our thoughts and feelings about our process.

JUDY: In starting work on this section my first thought was "Why did Virginia ask me, another white woman, to work on this with her?" I know I have editing skills and am familiar with book production. And I have a deep interest in whiteness. But I still cling to the belief that, as a white woman, to truly "interrupt whiteness," I need the critique and insights of people of color.

VIRGINIA: I think all of us who receive privilege from looking white, expressing dominant cultural traits, and experiencing relative socioeconomic advantages, need the critique and insights of people of color if we are to see beyond and work to change our familiar. However, while I work on other projects with colleagues of color, I think this current book works with Judy and me, both of us raised for much of our lives in white enclaves, performing the editorial roles. Why? I confess that I first asked Judy because, while I admired her extensive knowledge and her insights about race and whiteness, she was present in a way that my friends of color could not be at the time. I met Judy when she sought me out at the state university at which I work as a potential adviser for one aspect of her MA thesis. My university is, like many teaching institutions, a place that affords little time for enriching conversations and research with one's peers. Judy and I found the time to talk on several occasions about the paper she was working on, and I was taken by her forthrightness and commitment to antiracist practice. I was taken by the potential of a further collaboration.

I also asked Judy to work with me on this book because of her hunger to grow and be changed by our contributors, and to validate and include diverse voices. In addition, I learned early on that she had editorial skills that I lacked. In my experience, the partnerships with the most enlightening outcomes are those in which the partners have complimentary traits and abilities. I have experienced Judy and our partnership in such terms. I have wondered why Judy responded to my invitation to participate in this project.

JUDY: When Virginia asked me, I was enthusiastic. The collaboration would necessitate further meetings and discussions with Virginia, who challenged me in my thinking and was always interested in the kind of reflection that engaged the body and spirit alongside the mind. I knew she would go a long way toward satisfying my desire for meaningful conversation on whiteness. Also, I did have time for a new project and loved the prospect of engaging with as yet unknown contributors.

The first response to our call for submissions came almost entirely from white women. This paralleled my past experience in projects where white leadership desires multicultural participation. But unlike with much of my past experience, I found Virginia in full agreement with me that we needed to ask again and take the time to find authors writing from a variety of social locations in regard to race and ethnicity. I believe that somehow the words we use, no matter how much we want to invite those from different social locations, will resonate with those most like ourselves. I also believe that, drawing on collective and personal experience, people of color have little reason to trust their words to white editors. Taking time to solicit more submissions did result in contributions from a greater diversity of authors. Yet this process has reaffirmed my belief that to build alliances across axes of difference always requires extra effort from those toward the privilege end of the axis.

JUDY and VIRGINIA: We also asked ourselves why we had so few contributions from men. We knew that teaching at the secondary and elementary level was and remains primarily a woman's profession. And teacher educators also tend to be women. But beyond that, Judy wondered if men in academia see a book edited by women as having less status than one edited by men and have less interest in contributing. And Virginia noted that our two male contributors are men of color. If there were more men of color in the profession, would our contributions from this quarter have been higher?

JUDY: As we prepare this manuscript for production I realize that I have been pulled further into the orbit of academia than I originally intended. In our early discussions I remember arguing for a book that would be valuable to elementary and secondary classroom teachers who might be put off by books written in academic language and style. Yet we are being published by an academic press not widely distributed in bookstores. Although I know anecdotally that many readers are discouraged from reading books with citations in the text, we requested APA style in our call for submissions as being "standard" and thinking we could change later. But now it seems like too much trouble. This is one of the ways in which whiteness works—as the path of least resistance.

Early on, Virginia learned that in order to be sure that this text would "count" toward tenure, her name should appear first. While I had no hesitation in agreeing to this, it does bother me because our names will not be in alphabetical order and many will read it as if I contributed less to the process. This requirement of the university where Virginia is seeking tenure maintains whiteness by enforcing and valuing individual effort over collective effort. If I had also been seeking tenure, it could have been problematic and divisive, actively discouraging collaboration.

VIRGINIA: I know that if I were in Judy's position, I would share her feelings that resulted from my asking her if she would agree to my name appearing first on our book. My request was a response to the scarcity model of socioeconomic practice, eloquently described by Elena Featherston, a contributor to this volume, and embraced by the academy. The scarcity model in respect to tenure says that only a few spaces must exist in the hallowed halls of tenure or the value of that state is diminished. A colleague at my university advised me that my tenure prospects would be greatly enhanced if I made sure that my name came first on the book. I remember agonizing over talking to Judy about it because I felt our contributions were of equal value. Yet I also felt that without the relative security of tenure, my voice as a scholar and activist might be compromised.

How much of my response was due to my own whiteness? In working on this book, I have become so much more aware of how much my life has been shaped by whiteness, even though I have seen myself as trying to move outside of that symbolic, cultural, political, and socioeconomic space. I have been in some kind of school since I was four years old! I have been impacted by the competitive expectations that arise out of the dominant social institutions in capitalist socioeconomic systems—especially the United States and Britain of today. Capitalism requires that we think in terms of scarcity if it is to be maintained. In other words, capitalism requires whiteness.

There is another critical question: Was it really necessary to have my name come first on this book to meet my tenure demands? Maybe not. There is not enough space here to go further into the issue of tenure, but its relationship to whiteness is important. Suffice it to say in this space that, with great emotion, I ended up saying to Judy that I hoped we would work together on a second project on which Judy's name would come first! Now, as I review this process, I wonder how collaborators could creatively present their names so that neither the one nor the other is perceived as coming first.

In this first project, we believe we have created a space in which a diverse group of educators feel confident about introducing and sharing their narratives about identifying race and transforming whiteness in the classroom. In the following we introduce their chapters.

Identifying Race and Transforming Whiteness in the Classroom

Many insightful people have taken the journey toward identifying race and transforming whiteness in the classroom. However, although their work is critical, and often informative and inspiring, it is far from complete. Whiteness, embodied and institutionalized, has a way of suffocating and diverting attempts to create more egalitarian, socially just cultural, socio-economic, and political arrangements.

Refusing to be suffocated or diverted, the writers collected in this volume have embarked on their own individual and collective journeys to identify race and transform whiteness in the classroom. They share the belief that the classroom is one of the primary forums through which white privilege and the cultural forms that whiteness takes may be reinforced and resisted, and they seek ways of contributing to this resistance. Resistance includes identifying and attempting to transform white privilege or to undo colonization, and identifying and attempting to transform the cultural scripts that many if not most teachers and students have been expected to perform in the classroom and beyond, these scripts being blueprints for the current hierarchical and unjust social scene. Resistance is supported and carried out through the innovative classroom practices the authors have developed to support these processes of identification and transformation.

The writings reflect the cycle of *vigilant praxis:* The personal work is prerequisite to implementing new practices in the classroom. The effects of challenging and interrupting whiteness in the classroom are made apparent as we consciously engage with ourselves and others in accessing what happened. We then return for more reflection on how and why both we and our students continue to inhabit this dominant ideological world. Cycling through reflection, implementation, and assessment we re-view how we engage in antiracist teaching so that we can develop more effective activities to interrupt and contest whiteness. In this way we continually build on our experiences, revealing the hidden ways in which we embody whiteness and unconsciously impose that whiteness in the classroom. This is what we mean by *vigilant praxis.*

In writing of their own vigilant praxis, about interrupting race and transforming whiteness in their classrooms, the authors have provided (1) accounts of personal reflection and transformation; (2) insights into the cultural forms of whiteness; (3) suggestions for embracing ways of knowing that value difference and connectedness and for creating genuine harmony that recognizes and includes conflict; and (4) descriptions of how they developed classroom practices suited to the work. While most chapters attend to all four of the areas mentioned, one area is usually of primary concern. In introducing the work, we have used these four areas as an organizational tool.

Rethinking Self, Rethinking Whiteness: Personal Accounts of Transformation

Laurie Lippin (chapter 7, "Making Whiteness Visible in the Classroom"), Sherry Marx (chapter 8, "Exploring and Challenging Whiteness and White Racism with White Preservice Teachers"), and Kelly Maxwell (chapter 10, "Deconstructing Whiteness: Discovering the Water"), offer us powerful accounts of their own journeys as white people to personal transformation. For example, Maxwell narrates her own process of discovering whiteness as a norm and the removal of her cultural "blinders," which allowed her to begin to see the full picture and to admit her white privilege. People of color struggle with embodied whiteness also. Carlos Aceves (chapter 1, "The Xinachtli Project: Transforming Whiteness through Mythic Pedagogy") and Leny Mendoza Strobel (chapter 12, "Teaching about Whiteness When You're Not White: A Filipina Educator's Experience") describe their own process of decolonization. All of these authors work at helping white students undertake their own journeys and share what they learned about effectively facilitating the identification and transformation of whiteness in the classroom.

Identifying the Cultural Forms of Whiteness

Elena Featherston and Jean Ishibashi (chapter 4, "Oreos and Bananas: Conversations on Whiteness," P. J. Hallam (chapter 5, "Crossing Cultural Borders through Authentic Assessment of Classroom Discourse: A Freirean Approach") , Eileen O'Brien (chapter 11, "'I Could Hear You If You Would Just Calm Down': Challenging Eurocentric Classroom Norms through Passionate Discussions of Racial Oppression"), and Leny Strobel (chapter 12, "Teaching about Whiteness When You're Not White: A Filipina Educator's Experience") offer us great insight into the ways in which whiteness has impacted their lives and the lives of their students through the traditional, Eurocentric curriculum. These authors are far from being a homogenous group, and Featherston, Ishibashi, and Strobel, as people of color, are able to contribute their own experiences of race as a social construct designed to control people and allocate them to positions in the existing social hierarchy. Hallam and O'Brien, as white people, focus more exclusively on the cultural forms that have been institutionalized in the classroom and how these forms create culture shock, alienation, and resistance in many students of color and low-income students.

Embracing Ways of Knowing That Value Difference and
Connectedness and Creating Genuine Harmony That Recognizes
and Includes Conflict

It is our sense that all of the authors do or would acknowledge their own multiple and sometimes contradictory race, ethnic, gender, sexual, and ability experiences, and embrace a theoretical approach that values the connectedness of living beings. With this sense of the possible in mind, they seek to create experiences so that their students may develop identities and practices that will enable them to find personal meaning and motivation in their educational and wider cultural, socioeconomic, and political endeavors. For example, Rosemary Christensen (chapter 3, "Teaching within the Circle: Methods for an American Indian Teaching and Learning Style, a Tribal Paradigm") meets this goal by drawing on her Native cultural knowledge; Carlos Aceves (chapter 1, "The Xinachtli Project: Transforming Whiteness through Mythic Pedagogy") calls upon the mythic pedagogy of his Mexican ancestors; Gary Lemons (chapter 6, æWhen White Students Write about Being White: Challenging Whiteness in a Black Feminist Classroomæ) introduces his largely white students to Black feminist scholarship; and Grace Mathieson (chapter 9, "Reconceptualizing Our Classroom Practice: Notes from an Antiracist Educator") brings black civil rights experiences into her classroom. Pauline Bullen (chapter 2, Naming Race and Racism as a Problem in Schools"), along with Aceves and Christensen, moves us to understand more fully the alternatives to Eurocentric ways of conceptualizing relationships and traditional Eurocentric curricula.

Developing Educational Practices That Support These Efforts

While the authors in this book differ on their definitions of whiteness and their approaches to *transforming* the impact of race and whiteness on the lives of students in schools, they are all engaged in a vigilant praxis and committed to transforming whiteness in their classrooms. Their foci are political, cultural, and socioeconomic. Instead of embracing a "one size fits all," top-down, rigid methods-oriented approach to teaching, the final weave of their ideas offers the reader a number of antidotes to the race and class hierarchy that characterizes the modern school. Coming from diverse backgrounds, the contributors provide diverse perspectives on the role of race and whiteness on this "failure." All their contributions include stories of actual classroom experience—K–12 and college—embedded in critical, theoretical frameworks. They tie an investigation of whiteness to practical and essential concerns with social justice and the dismantling of racism and white supremacy within the classroom and school.

Visibility, Connection, and Emotion

Stepping back from the editorial process to consider what more might be emerging from the dialogue of voices we inhabited, we found three concepts weaving through the collection: visibility, connection, and emotion. Considering each contribution through its relationship to these concepts provides another window into the work. Visibility is especially associated with whiteness, as various authors address the *in*visibility of whiteness to white folks in particular. Maxwell calls whiteness "the water we swim in," and others such as Featherston & Ishibashi, Marx, and Mathieson draw attention to the normalcy of dominant cultural whiteness. Naming whiteness as invisible is the first step to making it visible. Thus begins a process described variously as decolonization (Strobel and Mathieson), critical consciousness (Hallam), interrogating identity (Lippin), critical cultural therapy (Marx), critical race consciousness (Lemons), and applying the four Rs—re-search, re-cognize, re-spect, and re-tell (Featherston & Ishibashi). However named, the authors are stressing the importance of knowing oneself as a racialized being, of understanding one's relationship to the dominant culture, and of beginning the process of transformation that allows one to actively deconstruct racist ideology.

As attention to whiteness makes the hegemony of European cultural thought and behavior visible, other cultural ways of being and thinking become visible as well. Aceves, Christensen, and Strobel, in particular, describe how they claimed their own indigenous cultures and are using their relationship to their own cultural ways of learning and construction of knowledge to the benefit of their students. Aceves writes of the Xinachtli Project, which uses a mythic pedagogy based in the oral tradition of the indigenous Mexicans to create a meaningful learning environment for Chicano students. Also based in oral tradition is Christensen's Circle Teaching method that reflects Indian values, psychology, and philosophy. Lemons and Mathieson, who bear very different relationships to black feminism, make black feminist thought the center of their curriculum, Lemons in working to develop critical race consciousness in college students and Mathieson to create an inclusive fifth grade classroom. Hallam also writes of using cultural practices outside the dominant practices of whiteness where oral language becomes a focus that helps transform her multicultural classroom from the "banking" model described by Freire to one in which all students are engaged in liberatory education.

The second concept, *connection,* underlies both the teaching methods introduced in many chapters and the ways in which educators sustain their own personal journeys and strengthen their practice. Many authors stress the need for students to exchange stories with each other and engage in critical dialogue in order for learning to occur. For example, Lippin describes how she does this even within the confines of the academy where she may have over one hundred students in her undergraduate classes. And Aceves and Strobel point out that we need to move beyond dualisms, that it is not sufficient to define oneself in opposition to the "Other," nor can learning take place without the contributions of everyone's truths. Connection also emerges in relation to history, as several authors mention the need for white students to connect with the history of white supremacy and genocide in the United States, as well as with the history of resistance by white people. A core value of Christensen's Circle Teaching is connectedness, and she describes how students work in groups and learn to cooperate and depend on each other.

Connection for Marx emerges in the critical cultural therapy that she engages in with white preservice teachers working with English language learners, using observation and dialogue to help them move from unconscious racism to awareness of whiteness and white racism. In her discussion of research done with black educators in Toronto public schools, Bullen makes clear the role of racism and white supremacy in blocking many of the connections within educational institutions that white teachers may take for granted. But she also names the important community connections and support networks that empower these teachers to continue their efforts to turn aside Eurocentric thinking and engage in antiracist practice however they can.

Finally we come to *emotion,* which several contributors find key to the transformative learning described above as decolonization, critical race consciousness, and so forth. Featherston & Ishibashi and O'Brien remind us that white cultural norms value intellect over emotion, that "objectivity" is based in separating emotional knowledge from intellectual understanding. For these authors passion and emotion are seen as essential to a learning community. Addressing the role of anger in challenging Eurocentric classroom norms, O'Brien describes how in her classroom the legitimization of anger serves to decenter whiteness and disrupt other hierarchies of power. Strobel describes a similar insight in her own classroom when she realized that only through honest expression of thoughts *and* feelings can the compassion required to really hear each other occur. Lemons also reports on the importance of emotion when he describes how his students tap into the emotional current around fear of dialogue on race and their anxiety about the internal changes such dialogue might ignite. Further, his students write of the emotional and spiritual transformation they experience in his classes. He describes the willingness of white students to embrace black feminist thought as a testament to its liberatory power and capacity as an agent of inner healing. Addressing the role of emotions in learning for grade school children, Aceves talks of the emotions box used in his classrooms by which students can ritually express and release emotions and in the process learn from them.

Following the threads of visibility, connection, and emotion through the work collected here provides snippets of the creativity, practicality, theorizing, and ruthless self-reflection the authors have gifted us with in their contributions. Many other rich themes can be found in the following chapters. Given the complexity of each chapter and the complex interrelationships of each with the whole, we abandoned our efforts to create thematic sections. The chapters are arranged alphabetically by author. We trust that you will encounter what you need to help you identify race and transform whiteness in your own practice.

Notes

1. My mother kept all of my report cards from which I am quoting.

References

Bartholome, L. I. (1996). Beyond the methods fetish: Toward humanizing pedagogy. In P. Leistyna, A. Woodrum, & A. A. Sherblom, A. A. (Eds.), *Breaking free: The transformative power of critical pedagogy* (pp. 229–52). Cambridge, MA: Harvard Educational Review Reprint Series no. 27.

Bourdieu, P. (1994). Structures, habitus, power: Basis for a theory of symbolic power. In N. B. Dirks, G. Eley, & S. B. Ortner, (Eds.), *Culture, power, history: A reader in contemporary social theory.* Princeton, NJ: Princeton University Press.

Brodkin, K. (1999). *How Jews became white folks and what that says about race in America.* New Brunswick, NJ: Rutgers University Press.

Christensen, L. (2000). *Reading, writing and rising up: Teaching about social justice and the power of he written word.* Milwaukee, WI: Rethinking Schools.

Conley, D. (1999). *Being black, living in the red: Race, wealth, and social policy.* Berkeley: University of California Press.

Doll, W. E. (1998). Curriculum and Concepts of Control. In W. F. Pinar (Ed.). *Curriculum: Toward new identities* (pp. 41–75). New York: Garland Publishing.

Du Bois, W. E. B. (1965). The souls of black folk. In *Three Negro classics.* New York: Avon Books.

Freire, P. (1970/1993). *Pedagogy of the oppressed.* New York: The Continuum Publishing Co.

Goffman, E. 1961. *Asylums.* New York: Anchor.

Grant, C. A. & Sleeter, C. E. (Eds.) (1998). *Turning on learning: Five approaches for multicultural teaching plans,* 2nd edition. John Wiley & Sons.

Hall, S. (1993). Negotiating Caribbean Identities, *Walter Rodney Memorial Lecture,* Centre for Caribbean Studies. Warwick: University of Warwick.

hooks, b. (1994). *Teaching to transgress: Education as the practice of freedom.* New York: Routledge.

Hwu, W. S. (1998). Curriculum, transcendence, and Zen/Taoism: Critical ontology of self. In W. F. Pinar (Ed). *Curriculum: Toward new identities* (pp. 21–41). New York: Garland Publishing.

Kohl, H. (1968/1990). *36 children.* New York: Penguin.

Kozol, J. (1996). *Amazing grace: The lives of children and the conscience of a nation.* New York: Harper Perennial.

Maeroff, G. I. (1999). *Altered destinies: Making life better for school children in need.* New York: St Martin's Griffin.

Mandela N. (2002). Nelson Mandela: The U.S.A. Is a Threat to World Peace. *Newsweek.* Available: http://www.msnbc.com/news/806174.asp

Morrison, T. (1992). *Playing in the dark: Whiteness and the literary imagination.* Cambridge, MA: Harvard University Press.

Noguera, P. A. (1995), Preventing and producing violence: A critical analysis of responses to school violence, *Harvard Educational Review, 65* (2).

Pinar, W. F. (Ed.) (1998). *Curriculum: Toward new identities.* New York: Garland Publishing

Roybal Rose, L. (1995). Healing from racism: Cross-cultural leadership teachings for the multicultural future. *Winds of Change* (spring).

Said, Edward W. (1979). *Orientalism.* New York: Vintage Books.

Shor, I. (Ed.) (1987). *Freire for the classroom: A sourcebook for liberatory teaching.* Portsmouth, NH: Heinemann.

Slapin, B. & Seale, D. (Eds.) (1998). *Through Indian eyes: The Native experience in books for children.* Berkeley, CA: Oyate.

Steinhorn, L. & Diggs-Brown, B. (1999). *By the color of our skins: The illusion of integration and the reality of race.* New York: Dutton.

Thandeka (1999). *Learning to be white: Money, race, and God in America.* New York: Continuum.

PART I

Cultural Forms of Whiteness

1

Teaching about Whiteness When You're Not White: A Filipina Educator's Experience

Leny Mendoza Strobel

On June 12, 1995, I wrote in my journal:

> Yesterday I may have finally resolved the meaning of my recurring dream about divorce. I have been reading bell hooks' Black Looks where she talks about decolonization and dealing with "white terror." Of course, I thought, my dream is about divorcing "white terror" and its control of my life. The dream is about learning to rise above the fear, to think beyond fear, to leave it behind. Leave the system behind. The "voice" said to me yesterday: in order to decolonize, you must recognize the white terror, examine how your life revolves around this terror. How can you remove its fangs?

I teach college students and stand in front of classes of mostly white, middle-class, suburban students several times a week. Even as a consciously decolonized person, there is still a part of me that is afraid to displease and afraid to offend white folks. I persist in teaching in spite of this fear because I believe that the issue of whiteness and its symbolic power is something that we all need to face squarely and unflinchingly, because beyond this fear lies our healing and reconciliation as well as our potential to become a truly radical democratic society. But it is something we cannot bypass. We can only pass through.

So, how do I, a nonwhite teacher, teach about the social construction of whiteness and white privilege? I believe that one must first decolonize before taking on this responsibility. In this paper, I write about this process of decolonization that has helped me deal with the issues of whiteness and white privilege in the classroom. I tell the following story as a way to illuminate how transformative practice in the classroom, for me, must proceed from the deep structures of feeling, as informed by theory and practice.

I will always be grateful to other writers and scholars who have walked the road of decolonization before me. I like Homi Bhaba's (1990) definition of decolonization: to remember the dismembered pieces of the past in order to make sense of the trauma of the present. I am also indebted to the work of bell hooks (1984, 1992, 1993), Gloria Anzaldua (1987), Toni Morrison (1992), Alice Walker (1967), Minh-Ha (1989), Carlos Bulosan (1946), and many others whose writings about their experiences illumine mine. Their works give me courage and the permission to also name my own experiences. When I realized that I could name and speak of my fears that come from the overwhelming power of white symbols over my life, I knew that this dream was pointing to my own freedom. But it is the Brazilian educator, Paulo Freire (1970), who gave me the language with which to speak and write.

In one of my earlier published essays, I wrote about a childhood experience in the Philippines that, in retrospect, I now mark as the moment when whiteness claimed me. In this essay I write about my father, who is a devoted and very proud Methodist, as proud as his father, who was converted to Methodism by the first American missionaries who came after U.S. colonial rule was established in this nation. He refused to participate in the Catholic/colonial culture of our community in its celebration of fiestas, which, according to my father, is really about the worshipping of saints and as Protestants we do not worship them. As you can imagine, our house was the saddest-looking house when fiestas and other holidays came around. This is an excerpt from that essay.

> Things changed the day my sister, who had been teaching Filipino culture at the dependents' school at Clark Air Base, asked to bring to the town fiesta a Yankee from Maine, the school's administrator. Perhaps it made my father glad that this very important white man was interested in my sister. Although my father relented cautiously about breaking a family nontradition, he soon found himself making plans to roast one of the pigs he had been raising to supplement his income and pay our tuition. That year Junior the pig was sacrificed in honor of the white man.
>
> I was assigned to make sure the house was clean, especially the toilet and the toilet bowl. When no amount of muriatic acid would erase the yellow-stained bowl, my sister handed me a copper penny and told me to use it to scrape the stain. For hours, I sweated on my knees, scraping the yellow. This left a mark in my soul that I wouldn't understand for many years. I learned then that yellow isn't good enough. Only white will do. (Strobel 1993)

I wrote this essay a few years ago as I was struggling to get a handle on the relationship between my Filipino colonial history and how I experience whiteness. When I began to look at my colonial history, I realized that the symbols, images, books, and stories that were imposed on us and that told us what it meant to be civilized and Christian were written by white philosophers, historians, anthropologists, and missionaries. In this body of knowledge, they were able to equate being white with being a universal human, and part of universalizing the white experience is by calling it the human experience. It wasn't until I came across the writings of other people of color and how they experience whiteness that my own distinctions became clearer.

Being a Christian at that time, it was difficult for me to come to terms with what I was realizing because it also meant learning how to question the difference between a Western system of theology and the core meaning of the Christian gospel. Thus, in one of my dialogues with God, I wrote in my journal:

> I have been angry with the white missionaries and white people who robbed me of the opportunity to know You on my own terms. I have felt this fakery I have lived by, this cultural Christianity; and part of that cultural Christianity includes the oppression of dark people, their being judged as inferior people. All my life I've lived feeling inferior to white people, beholden to them for their intelligence, affluence, productivity, and cultural creations. After I became a Christian I wanted even more to become like them, for to be like them is to be like You. I do not believe that any longer. I need to sort out this narrative that has given me so much deep-seated fear and shame. Help me to come home. Help me to become a whole person.

I returned to the academe partly as a way of resolving the sense of alienation and nonbelonging that I felt. In my studies, Fanon (1963), Freire (1970), Nandy (1983), and other postcolonial scholars helped me to understand how my perception and understanding of the world and the people in it is always colored by ideology and power relations between groups of people. In my book, *Coming Full Circle: The Process of Decolonization Among Post-1965 Filipino Americans* (2001), I dealt with these questions: How does one become a whole person if all that you have assimilated and believed in was a result of your having received negative projections from the white people who claimed and asserted their power over you? And if you are not who the oppressors say you are, who are you? What is a Filipino without and outside of the definitions that were imposed by colonial narratives? These are the sorts of questions I struggled with in trying to understand my experience, and one of the directions I took was to learn more about what the Filipino scholar Vince Rafael calls "white love."

Because the Philippines was the first and only formal colony of the United States, the form of colonization that the United States brought to us was called "benevolent assimilation." Vince Rafael (2000) describes it succinctly:

> Colonization as benevolent assimilation was deemed as a moral imperative, as wayward native children cut off from their Spanish fathers and desired by other European powers would now be adopted and protected by the compassionate embrace of the U.S. As a father is bound to guide his son, the U.S. was charged with the development of native others. . . . Because colonization is about civilizing love and the love of civilization, it must be absolutely distinct from the disruptive criminality of conquest. The allegory of benevolent assimilation erases the violence of conquest by construing colonial rule as the most precious gift that the most civilized can give to those still caught in the state of barbarous disorder. (p. 21)

This is the reason why when we think of the genocides committed by the United States, the Philippines does not come to mind easily because many Filipinos fell in love with their colonizers and fell into the trap of self-negation. This white love created historical and cultural amnesia that perpetuates our collusion with white supremacy. By contrast, the narrative of the U.S. nation erased from its own memory this experiment in colonization and imperialism. Consequently, I propose that decolonization is rupturing this amnesia and healing the psychic and epistemic violence of colonial encounters. And, because colonization damages both the colonizer and colonized, the parallel process that I am seeing emerge among white folks is the process of deconstructing whiteness at the cognitive and affective levels.

In the mid 1990s when I came across the writings of people of color and white women who were studying whiteness, I felt relieved that others now recognize the need to challenge whiteness as a powerful symbol of privilege. Peggy McIntosh (1988), in her widely circulated essay "White Privilege, Male Privilege," provides a definition: white privilege is like an invisible package of unearned assets that one can count on cashing in each day but about which one was meant to remain oblivious. These privileges are conferred not because they have been earned but merely on the basis of one's skin color. As a white woman, she then made a list of the personal privileges that accrue to her without having to ask or earn them. McIntosh says that what she saw as attendant to being a human being in the United States consisted in unearned advantage and conferred dominance. She said,

"I did not see myself as racist because I was taught to recognize racism only in individual acts of meanness by members of my group, never in invisible systems conferring unsought racial dominance on my group from birth." Ruth Frankenburg (1993) in *White Women, Race Matters,* arrives at a similar conclusion: social structures and institutions are racialized and those who engage in antiracist activism must look at their own whiteness from the perspective of having been socialized and constructed by racial ideology. These are two pivotal works that I have since assigned in my ethnic studies courses. Even as this discourse is more widely circulated in popular culture and in academic texts today, there are still white students who are shocked to learn that such privilege exists and they are its beneficiaries.

I was glad to read bell hooks's writings on decolonization and on whiteness in *Black Looks* (1992). She writes that when people of color study and interrogate whiteness it must be more than about victimization or powerlessness. She emphasizes that loving one's blackness is an act of political resistance, an antiracist commitment against structures of domination. These structures of domination can both be gross and subtle, the media being the more dominant system that reinforces white privilege. Of late, it seems that capitalism will sell just about anything . . . and difference based on skin color sells. Commodification of ethnicity sells, as in our interest in the "primitive and exotic" and, according to bell hooks, the exotic and primitive, the "nonwhite other" often serves as a spice to the blandness of white culture. Difference is therefore seductive as an encounter with the "other" but these encounters never require that one relinquish forever his/her dominant positionality. hooks writes that the mutual recognition of racism, its impact both on those who are dominated and those who dominate others, is the only standpoint that makes possible an encounter between races that is not based on denial and fantasy.

Maria Lugones (1990) also theorizes that the travel of nonwhites into white spaces is often unplayful and painful, whereas the travel of white people into nonwhite spaces is playful and freely chosen. Lugones, a Latin American writer, expands on the theory of playful and unplayful traveling in psychological terms. By citing her own inability to love her mother, whom she experienced as manipulative and exploitive in relation to her servants and her own children, and subservient to the men in her culture, Lugones realized that it was only by understanding her mother's history and cultural conditioning that she was able to love her mother again. Extending this analogy to her relationships with white women in the feminist movement, she says that the failure of white women to identify with the sort of unplayful traveling that women of color must do within white feminist culture comes from this lack of knowledge of each other's history and cultural conditioning.

In my attempt to practice a new way of relating to white people, I contacted a white woman in Sonoma County who conducts "Understanding Whiteness" workshops. When I called her five years ago I asked her if she would be willing to dialogue with me on the effects of the symbolic power of whiteness in my life. At that time, she declined to meet with me by saying that she and the white women she works with are not ready to dialogue with women of color because white women still have so much inner work to do. About two years ago, she called me and she wanted to talk. As a consequence of that talk, we encouraged each other's antiracist work. I introduced her to my department chair and then she was able to teach the "Understanding Whiteness" workshop as a course to undergraduates at the university where I teach. She also decided to embark on a graduate program that would focus on the study of white culture and white identity. She asked me to be the chairman of her committee.

We tried to create a mixed-race academic discussion group on whiteness in our community. During the first meeting, a white woman spoke of her awareness of her whiteness as a symbol of oppression and domination, and she had tears in her eyes as she spoke of her guilt and she looked at me directly as if asking me what she should do. I told her that by asking me, she is giving me her burden, which I am not able to take away from her. I told her that I am also struggling to resist my tendency to make white people feel comfortable by telling them what they want to hear. The white women in the group were surprised to hear that women of color often have to make white people comfortable or that we often remain silent in order to protect ourselves from being chastised for having mistaken views about race or for using race as an excuse. We talked about the role of guilt. One of the white women said that guilt is often a way to avoid talking about whiteness, that it's important that guilt be examined and eventually released. It was agreed that any action that is taken from a position of guilt will eventually undermine antiracist work. The work needs to go from the personal into social and institutional practices that can decenter white supremacy. I think our honesty and our willingness to listen to each other, more than any solution that we could come up with, was probably more healing than our original purpose of having an academic discussion of the topic.

I am aware, however, that this is a very difficult project to undertake simply because whiteness and its symbolic power and the privileges it confers to white people has not been discussed as publicly as we seem to be doing today. People of color, of course, have always spoken of whiteness, of white folks, but often in whispers and away from the ears of white people. And many people of color just as easily buy into the ideology of white supremacy because they may see its overwhelming power in all aspects of their lives and the culture around them. Our internalized racism runs very deep and only a conscious process of decolonization could unravel our complicity and then suture and heal this form of oppression.

Dualism as Root of Divisive Ideologies

"That's just the way it has always been; whites have always been on top"—both my white and nonwhite students still say so without them realizing that this is an essentialist way of thinking. Essentialism is the perspective that reality exists independently of our perception of it, that we perceive the meaning of the world rather than construct that meaning. From this perspective, there are real and important essential differences among categories of people. Social constructivism, by contrast, takes the position that reality cannot be separated from the way a culture makes sense of it—that meaning is constructed through social, political, legal, scientific, and other practices (Rosenblum & Travis 2000).

In the classroom context of discussing the difference between essentialist and constructionist views of reality, I demonstrate how this ("that's just the way it is!") statement can be rewritten from a constructionist perspective. For example, Charles Mills's (1997) first sentence in his book, *The Racial Contract*—"White supremacy is the unnamed political system that has made the modern world what it is today"—locates white supremacy within an historical time frame and geographical site. The statement also can be rephrased (which is Mills's thesis) as: While white supremacy may have dominated the last four hundred years, it is possible that the future will be transformed as white and nonwhite persons withdraw their consent from the racialized social contract that has put white supremacy in place. Withdrawing consent can be possible when we understand what Mills calls "the epistemology of ignorance" and "white moral cognitive dysfunction" and how this has come to be. Therefore, the statement: "that's just the way it is, whites will always be on top" can be shown to be a social construct rather than a fixed truth about the nature of our differences.

It has become my classroom practice to help students move from essentialist to social constructivist ways of thinking. Usually, when white students in my classes are confronted with the U.S. history of imperialism and colonialism, their response is: "I do not have anything to do with the past. Don't make me feel guilty. I am not racist." When we discuss Mills's *The Racial Contract*, the students realize that the social contract that they buy into ("all men are created equal," "the right to life, liberty, and the pursuit of happiness," and other liberal and humanistic values) is implicitly a racial contract because it was never meant to apply to nonwhite subjects. The only way genocide, slavery, colonialism could be justified and rationalized was because the social contract was written by and for white subjects. These white persons, who represent those who have moved from the "primitive state of nature" to a "civilized state," then had to help others who were still in the "state of nature" to become "civilized" like them. The state and its polity and judicial systems established a moral code that defined the rights and duties of civil society. Categories of persons (those who have become civilized) and subpersons (still in a state of nature) were constructed and became part of the narrative of civilizing missions via colonization. By 1935 almost 85 percent of the planet had been touched by one form of colonization or another by Europe's colonial powers and, later, the United States.

The answer to the question: How can white people act in racist ways (slavery, colonialism, genocide are racial wars) while sincerely believing in the morality of their actions? is answered by the social contract. The social contract gave us concepts that legitimized the racial order (whites on top, blacks on the bottom). In this ordering of races, whites will come to assess how well they're doing based on how nonwhites are doing (not well); which then results in the cultivation of patterns of affect and empathy for nonwhite suffering (See, we are doing you good by teaching you how to overcome your laziness; how to develop your natural resources, how to develop your economy, etc.).

In other words, the social contract starts with the nonrecognition of nonwhites as being fully human; being less human, they therefore are in need of the civilizing influences of those who are already fully human. Mills writes that this evasion and self-deception becomes an epistemic norm because to disagree is to turn the white world upside down. How can colonialism happen if there's already a recognition that the colonized nonwhites are as human as white folks? So in revealing the social contract as a racial contract, Mills is saying that it makes it easier for all of us to withdraw our consent from it and refuse to be complicit in the political and economic system that perpetuates it. One fine point he further makes: there is a distinction to be made between "whiteness" and "Whiteness": "white" is the color of one's skin, "Whiteness" is a political and economic world. The social contract can become a universal moral document if steps are taken to make its own dark racial shadow visible. To recognize it as such, it would become easier to withdraw our consent when it only serves its white beneficiaries.

To my students, this framework is illuminating and liberating. It is as if someone has turned the lights on for them. This cognitive framework enables them to see the political world and its structures and institutions and their location within them. In my classroom experience, such cognition has been helpful in dealing with feelings of defensiveness, guilt, and shame. It also shows them a way out of the "epistemology of ignorance." There is a way out of our dualistic "us" versus "them" thinking.

Other materials that have been helpful in introducing a different view of the story of humankind on Earth are through the novels of Daniel Quinn, *Ishmael* (1992), or the *Story of B* (1997). Through these novels, I am able to introduce the indigenous worldview (and, additionally, from a Filipino perspective) as a way of showing that the indigenous worldview is becoming more and more salient as global awareness about (un)sustainability of life on earth is entering the U.S. culture's mainstream. In my courses, I have found it useful to show the linkage between white supremacist beliefs and values with global capitalism; and in response to this totalizing view, I present the practices of resistance of people on the planet (postcolonial subjects, indigenous peoples, the poor and disenfranchised in affluent nations) against what they experience as marginalization coming from the West (the United States and its allies). These novels provide a historical context from which white students can then begin to locate and position themselves in relation to nonwhite peoples on the planet. Additionally, the novels help to distill the implicit value assumptions in Western ideologies of "development," "progress," "American Dream," "capitalism/free trade." This constructivist way of thinking lifts the burden of shame and guilt from students but also replaces it with a keen sense of responsibility; it leads to empathy.

The path to empathy is difficult at first. I believe that the failure of white students to identify with the experiences of people of color is deep-seated. Most of the white students I teach have been socialized and educated to think of themselves as autonomous human beings with the limitless opportunity to be all they can be. They also believe that our democratic system works equally for everyone, so it doesn't occur to them that people of color might not feel or experience their life in the same way that white folks do. When I talk about American history from the perspective of those who have been marginalized and what has been selectively included and excluded from the narrative of the nation, they become defensive when asked to deal with what this past has produced—our deep racial divide being one of the more obvious results. Deep-seated cultural conditioning disconnects them from this past, and even though this disconnection is now slowly coming to consciousness and beckoning to be healed, too often students respond by seeking to avoid blame and its accompanying guilt and shame. But in those instances when confronting the past leads to a sincere effort to understand how a nation's history of producing "others" also produces social and political differences that privilege one group over another, then healing can and does occur. Dialogue opens up guilt and shame give way to acknowledgment and a reexamination of personal practices in need of transformation. Many of my students speak of being able to see how discriminatory practices continue to exist unchallenged in their places of work, or in the classroom, or in their homes. One student told a seminar that she has had to painfully admit to herself that her father was a member of a white supremacist group when they lived in a small all-white community and that a group of men (her father included) made sure that no people of color moved into their neighborhood. Being able to accept this as her father's position enabled her to enter into a dialogue with him. The result of the dialogue is that her father is now aware that his daughter has a different concept of race relation than he does. While this may seem like a very small step, it is a step toward creating dialogue around a topic that we dare not discuss with those who are closest to us.

It is dialogical processes like these in the classroom that enable white students to narrow the gap in their psyche when the topic of whiteness is brought up. At the abstract level they may be able to blame the culture's materialism or foreign policy or the capitalist system or patriarchy, but when invited to locate themselves within this society's structures, there is a discomfort and a sense of powerlessness to transform these institutions. But those who do look at their lives might begin with soul searching by interrogating their grandparents' and parents' racial attitudes and perceptions and how these are passed on from one generation to the next.

Whiteness, Interrupted

There are stories that are told over and over again and images pervading the media that shape our perceptions of people of color in terms of danger or pleasure, or in terms of their position as inferior and in need of white people's civilizing tutelage. Danger when they are perceived as threats to one's privileges, the encounter as pleasure when it involves experiencing something new and different. Patronizing when we insist that people of color serve the needs of white people for self-affirmation via the negation of the other. I tell the following anecdotes to my students to illustrate this.

Scenario 1: A few years ago I received a white missionary's fund-raising letter. (He was in the Philippines and writing to his U.S. supporters. Incidentally, when I was growing up I only saw white missionaries.) I knew this missionary from my days in the Philippines and had donated to his mission work for many years, while I was still in the Philippines and even when I was already in the United States. In this letter he wrote: "I know now why the Filipino has no self-esteem. It is because they never hear the words 'I love you' spoken to them by their parents." He then went on to explain why he needs to teach Filipinos how to become more verbally articulate in their expressions of love for their children. My very deep gut reaction to this letter was anger because I have never felt unloved by my parents even though those words were never uttered to us daily. I felt angry that this missionary assumed the mantle of authority on Filipino self-esteem. I felt angry that he was using this story to raise money by playing on his supporters' pity for poor Filipinos with low self-esteem. By negating Filipinos, he was then able to make himself feel superior, and it made him feel good and innocent because he wanted to raise the self-esteem of Filipino children.

Emotions are very good teachers. My anger at this letter made me believe that I knew something in my guts that revealed the truth about me as a Filipino. Even though it took me some time to articulate what this truth (that we are not unloved) is about, it did teach me how to question narratives that are imposed on us by a supposedly superior culture. In fact, I now believe that my work all these years was an attempt to reply to this missionary letter. Who are we as Filipinos if we are not who they say we are? Thus, in my work and writing, I foreground Filipino knowledge and indigenous concepts of the interconnected and interdependent Self, concepts of honor, freedom, equality, deep empathy, concepts of interdependence and connectedness, concepts of courage and conviction as an articulation of an answer to these questions. Come to think of it, this articulation is what also gives me a sense of a ground to stand on and roots to hold on to. bell hooks is right, we must learn to love our brownness as an act of resistance against domination . . . but now I can also add that loving one's brownness is also an act of courage that enables us to reach across racial barriers.

When I wrote to this missionary to critique his letter, he wrote back with profuse apologies but refused to acknowledge that his motives were anything but noble and loving toward the Filipino people. (Why do they always say: You lovely people!?)

Scenario 2: Recently, one of my students, Jill, asked me about a novel by the Filipino American author Jessica Hagedorn. The book, *Gangster of Love* (1996), is about the way the lives of Filipino Americans are shaped by the intertwined history of the United States and the Philippines. Jill's boyfriend is Filipino American, and she thought the book would give her insight into his culture.

Jill was especially interested in the mythic creatures, the *aswangs* and the *tikbalangs*, mentioned briefly in the book. When I asked why, she admitted that she was fascinated by their exotic mysterious nature, their "otherness." Asked if she knew about the relationship between the United States and the Philippines—especially that the two countries had been at war and that the United States had colonized the Philippines until 1946—she admitted she did not.

I told Jill that to read this book is to ask herself: What do I, a white, middle-class woman from the Midwest, have to learn from Hagedorn? What do I know about U.S.-Philippine relations? What do I know about Filipino American lives? What do I, a fifth-generation American, know about the immigrant experience, about what "others" (nonwhite, non-European) must do to belong to U.S. culture? What does it mean to be an American? Is being white and being American the same? How about being human and being American?

I suggested to Jill that asking these questions might reveal the links between her personal history and that of Hagedorn's characters. Such a shared background would open up two possibilities. First, she could use it to critique the ideologies that shape U.S. hegemony and dictate the different paths for people's lives. She could ask where the breaks in the common human thread have occurred, how individuals are complicit in creating and preserving them, and what she and others might do to reattach those severed ends. Second, the newly discovered links between herself and the characters could open an inner dialogue that would uncover parts of herself as yet undiscovered. From this she could get to know herself better, love herself better, and love her boyfriend better.

Jill took up the challenge. She explored the questions, let herself be changed, relinquished her defenses, and entered the dialogue.

In the classroom, I encourage the sharing of personal stories like these that demonstrate how whiteness can be interrupted. This deep level of sharing, however, requires a space of safety, respect, and empathy.

Beyond Dualism

In a recent dialogue with an African colleague, we talked about our shared postcolonial subjectivity and our relationship to whiteness. I told him that I have been wondering how my preoccupation with whiteness and its symbolic power and its twin, male power and privilege, has perhaps fixed me into the solidity of being a postcolonial always, an "other." I told him that for years now I have been mulling the pull that my intuition seems to be calling me toward: to move away from the solidity of this position as "Other." M says that we cannot get away from it because we are not white, we are Third World persons, and that it is still our ethical, political, and human responsibility to speak against societal structures that marginalize, exclude, and exploit all those who are positioned as we both are. We ponder our positions as academics, as "Third World" scholars in the "First World" with advanced degrees, as positions of privilege. We consider our middle-class status signified by our cars and his suburban condominium and my suburban tract home in expensive Sonoma County as signs of privilege. Are they?

I asked him if he ever feels the need to question this space that he has accepted in the margins, feeling somehow tokenized, a badge of exceptionalism. *Not all black men are goons and pimps. Not all Africans are from the jungle and are primitive.* We are so aware of the grammar of modern life, how it locates us and fixes us, and how it condemns and limits us to positions of resistance and of always having to be the one to defend "our communities" or educate the "center."

I told M I am tired of my oppositional subjectivity. Decolonization began as an oppositional space for me, and it was a necessary and strategic space that I engaged, and it then enabled me to reconfigure my own identity. But now I am asking: What do I do after I decolonize? I want to crossover and embrace my "other." I want to love white folks. I love them already.

This is what I am learning now, thanks to Buddhist concepts. What is my "wild mind" when it is no longer attached to the subjectivity imposed by racial ideology, history, and social constructs? What work will pay me when I no longer want to teach from this position? Without anything to resist, without having anyone or anything to rely on for security and certainty (which theories provide), on what ground should I stand?

After years of academic sojourn, I am beginning to realize that the very dualisms (colonizer/colonized, white/nonwhite) I have resisted have solidified into more dualisms. *Us versus Them, Inside versus Outside, Center versus Margin.* The hardening of these positions shuts down parts of the heart, parts of my self. As much as I have been fixed by master narratives of the past, I now also fix this oppositional stance toward my "other." It was and still is, many times, useful to understand the world in this manner and to act on the basis of positions we have chosen between two opposing positions. But there are also limitations.

Coming from an evangelical Protestant background, leaving and deconstructing this past liberated me from one set of constructs: Western theology. I turned my back on the religion of my childhood once I saw it in the light of the cultural baggage that came along with it. This enabled me to embrace my recovered indigenous spirituality that is grounded in animist and shamanistic beliefs that basically affirm the goodness of the universe and of the soul even in the face of impermanence and openness to the unknown. If only I wasn't conditioned to believe in human nature as sinful and in need of redemption and salvation, the trust in impermanence and the open life might not be too threatening. The search for something to attach to, for a story to tell, and a new language of telling leads to other paths.

This other path, Buddhism, offers concepts beyond language and thought and ventures into the nonconceptual realm (all is emptiness). I wonder how my postcolonial angst can be transformed without an "other" to blame, to fix, to escape from, or escape to? What would the politics of my everyday life look like? What happens when the enemy "without," which bell hooks calls the "white supremacist capitalist patriarchy," becomes the enemy "within"? The controlling, punishing master is no longer outside myself but (if one were honest enough to admit) also within.

What if the master on whom I have projected so much anger, hurt, and pain is revealed not as an enemy or a benevolent master but a wounded soldier in the same war I have been fighting? And both of us now face each other with wounds open and festering. In this war, I realized that the spirits and voice of my ancestors have been unheard in the din of bullet words and glances. My footfall has become heavy and my sighs too deep for words. Buddha came through my grandmother's spirit to rescue me just when I was about to cave in. A window in my mind opens and a new vision appears, and letting go of thoughts and ideologies, becomes much more facile. You are healed now, my Lola whispers, you can now let go and move on with all that you have recovered and reclaimed of your Filipino soul. You were always whole, and didn't know it, she said.

This is how the paradigm of Western dualist thinking melted for me. With Love and, with it, clarity and compassion. During my academic sojourn, my mind was relentless in building up its arsenal of theories and concepts, the more the better to defend my newly formed Filipino counternarrative from the further assault of bigger and better dominant narratives. The narratives of colonialism and imperialism and white supremacy still carry their weight in the real world, I realize. Today, add even new ones: postcolonialism, postmodernism, globalization, nomadism, border-crossings, transnationalism, diaspora. I resist the elitism of academic language, but I can't avoid the challenge of finding new frames for looking at my world.

I can position and locate myself in these various contexts, and I have the language to do that. In my teaching, I have the opportunity to translate these theories into living tools that students can take with them in their daily lives. These are new ways of seeing and thinking beyond modernist dualistic paradigms—this is what I tell them. Lately, however, I have been feeling the need to make changes in how I see this world. The word "resistance" has less appeal to me, as if my bones have grown tired of being pulled in two opposing directions. It keeps the wounds from healing if the skin is constantly pulled apart. What would happen if I approach the wounded soldier and offer him my salve? What would the place of both our "becoming" together look like?

This question seems to be pointing to a new theme: reconciliation. My own inner movement toward reconciliation is, to me, a return to the nondual nature of reality, which is a very Filipino way of being. It is as if this reconciliation within is being made possible by a certain death: the death of one's tenacious clinging to ideologies. Even assuming that ideologies have their hegemonic power in the lives of people, it is really those who are able to transcend ideologies who are most compassionate. Being compassionate, they are able to cross borders of all kinds with a minimum attachment to ego or self-consciousness.

Still, I struggle in my attempts at this nondual, compassionate, reconciliatory position because I have no control over how other people might locate me, and based on their perceptions and beliefs about Filipinos, they might make certain demands or conclude some things about me. Must I let them determine who I am or can I trust that dialogue and encounter would or could result in a transformative moment for both of us? Maybe the dualistic tendency to push our being-ness into an either/or position is not a reflection of who we are but of the context we live in? I realize that in my classrooms, the students also have to deal with the same dilemmas when they encounter me.

I attempted to try my new resolve at reconciliation with my teaching credential students. In one exercise I asked the students to discuss their social geography as they were growing up to tease out the racial patterns in the choices their parents made. We were hoping that from this exercise they would become aware of how racial attitudes are passed on generationally. Then we discussed the McIntosh list of privileges and asked the students why it is hard to give up the benefits of whiteness even as white people are hurt by it.

Their responses: A white male student said that he doesn't "get it," because he hasn't experienced his whiteness and maleness as positions of privilege. A white woman said that she is aware of racism and has spoken and acted against it, but she rarely thinks of her whiteness as somehow a position that is hurtful to herself and others. Another white male angrily asserted that his life has nothing to do with any kind of privilege; it all has to do with hard work and therefore he deserves everything he worked for.

Soon a heaviness and darkness enveloped the room. Defenses were up, hurt feelings were showing in tight jaws, flushed faces, taut bodies, tired and limp arms, and teary eyes. We were barely polite by then. They said they don't want to feel guilty for not having had "diversity" in their lives, for choosing to live in "safe" (read: white and suburban) neighborhoods, for choosing to raise their children away from "bad" (read: ethnic and poor) neighborhoods. These, too, are privileges, I told them. And privileges are just that. We acknowledge that as a result of institutional, cultural, and political configurations in U.S. society, they are able to have these choices without seemingly harmful consequences to themselves.

In my attempt not to locate myself as "other," I told them that I accept and acknowledge my own privilege as a woman of color. I tell them I feel just as privileged as they are, and maybe to some extent even more powerful in some ways (I am the professor, after all!). Except in certain places and contexts where I come face to face with racism and people who would put me in my category as their "other," only then do I become aware that my privileges are severely limited. I spoke of my sadness as I recalled the effects of the symbolic power of whiteness in my life; how I've worked hard to divorce it, to remove its fangs so it will no longer suck my blood and energy. Only then did a moment of recognition, a moment of communion, a transforming moment become palpably possible. In this brief classroom encounter, I saw the possibility of compassion made possible by the honest expression of feelings and thoughts that refused to pigeonhole the participants into "us" versus "them." We are all wounded soldiers in the same war, in need of healing and reconciliation.

In class, I told the angry white male student that I acknowledge his poverty and difficult life growing up. I also reminded him that as a teacher, when he stands in front of children, the children will read him first as a white male and they will project all the symbolic meaning of whiteness and maleness that they have learned from the dominant culture onto him; that the children will not know immediately what his personal story might be. I told him it is up to him to make his story available to his students as a way of bridging the many gaps that were already in place even before he stepped into the classroom.

The student responded with relief (ah, so you understand me after all!) and a newfound realization: Whiteness as a symbol of privilege as constructed by social ideologies, and whiteness as the color of his skin. He knew from then that he can no longer afford to reduce all of his life experiences to "individual hard work" and that he would now have to navigate the waters of symbolic meanings and their interpretation in various contexts. Perhaps he would even feel less threatened when the "Other" talks back and offers him a challenge to go beyond dualistic and essentialist ways of thinking.

End Thoughts

We have now entered a new millennium and with it come new arrangements in our communities. In California, there is no longer a white majority. The global migration of people will continue to challenge the racial hierarchies within a global capitalist system. We are becoming more and more conscious that whites are only a small percentage of all the people on the planet. We are becoming conscious of the disparity in the distribution of power and resources in a finite global environment. There are so many new lenses that are now available to us for looking at our relationship with each other. And when things change, it makes us nervous because there are no guaranteed outcomes. But within a radical democratic practice, we can only trust that our dialogue between all participants will move us all toward an understanding of our common future and common good. Therefore what I want to close with is a paraphrase from the Russian philosopher Mikhail Bakhtin: We will never know who we are just by looking at the mirror, he says. We must allow other people to tell us who we are from their own locations and positions. And from there create dialogue. Create Art. Create Love.

References

Anzaldua, G. (1987). *Borderlands: La frontera, the new mestiza.* San Francisco: Aunt Lute Press.

Bhaba, H. (1990). Interrogating identity: The postcolonial prerogative. In D. Goldberg (Ed.), *Anatomy of racism* (pp. 183–209). Minneapolis: University of Minnesota Press.

Bulosan, C. (1946). *America is in the heart.* New York: Harcourt, Brace.

Fanon, F. (1963). *The wretched of the earth.* New York: Grove Press.

Frankenburg, R. (1993). *The social construction of whiteness: White women, race matters.* Minneapolis: University of Minnesota Press.

Freire, P. (1970). *Pedagogy of the oppressed.* Translated by Myra Bergman Ramos. New York: Bergin and Garvey.

Hagedorn, J. (1996). *The gangster of love.* New York: Houghton Mifflin.

hooks, b. (1984). *Feminist theory: From margin to center.* Boston: South End Press.

hooks, b. (1992). *Black looks: Race and representation.* Boston: South End Press.

hooks, b. (1993). *Sisters of the yam: Black women and self-recovery.* Boston: South End Press.

Lugones, M. (1990). Playfulness, "world"-traveling, and loving perceptions. In G. Anzaldua (Ed.), *Making face, making soul: Haciendo caras: Creative and critical perspectives by women of color* (pp. 390–402). San Francisco: Aunt Lute Books.

McIntosh, P. (1988). *White privilege and male privilege: A personal account of coming to see correspondences through work in women's studies.* Wellesley, MA: Wellesley College Center for Research on Women.

Mills, C. (1997). *The racial contract.* Ithaca, NY, and London: Cornell University Press.

Minh-ha, T. (1989). *Woman, native, other: Writing postcolonialism and feminism.* Blooming-ton:Indiana University Press.

Morrison, T. (1992). *Playing in the dark: Whiteness and the literary imagination.* New York: Vintage Books.

Nandy, A. (1983). *The intimate enemy: Loss and recovery of self under colonialism.* Delhi: Oxford University Press.

Quinn, D. (1992). *My Ishmael.* New York: Bantam Books.

Quinn, D. (1997). *The story of B.* New York: Bantam Books.

Rafael, V. (2000). *White love and other events in Filipino history.* Durham, NC: Duke University Press.

Rosenblum, K., & Travis, T. (2000). *The meaning of difference: American constructions of race, sex and gender, social class, and sexual orientation,* 3rd ed.. New York: McGraw Hill.

Strobel, L. M. (1993). A personal story: On becoming a split Filipina subject. *Amerasia Journal, 22*(2), pp. 3–54.

Strobel, L. M. (2001). *Coming full circle: The process of decolonization among post-1965 Filipino Americans.* Quezon City: Giraffe Books.

Walker, A. (1967). *In search of our mother's gardens:* Orlando, FL: Harcourt Brace Jovanovich.

2

Crossing Cultural Borders through Authentic Assessment of Classroom Discourse: A Freirean Approach

P. J. Hallam

When I completed my teaching degree at UC Berkeley in 1976, the work of Brazilian educator Paulo Freire (1972) strongly influenced my instructional stance. As I prepared for my first full-time teaching job in a Las Vegas, Nevada, junior high school, I had some awareness of the racism and oppression facing many of my future students. Las Vegas was, and still is, a multicultural city that offers an abundance of "entry level" jobs. I thought that Freire's approach would help me reach students, so I carefully packed dittos of Freirean "problem-posing" activities and other ideas that I viewed as potential tools for improving students' intellectual and academic skills through critical dialogue.

The structural limits embedded in the social institution of education soon hammered my ideal of being a teacher who provided a "forum open to the imaginings and free exercise of control by learners, teachers, and the community" (Freire 1972). As with many other first-year teachers, idealism was replaced by a struggle to get through each day. Overcoming institutional barriers such as traveling from classroom to classroom every fifty minutes, instructional materials limited to old SRA kits, and a "Well, nobody helped me!" philosophy for inducting new teachers drained my time and energy. At the end of my first year, I reviewed my dittos of Freirean ideas and despaired.

In subsequent years, I did manage to implement many aspects of Freirean philosophy, such as respect for students' ethnic and cultural differences, but my teaching practices still did not break through many traditional barriers. On reflection, I knew that I was what Freire (1972) termed a "banker." In the "banking" method of education, learners receive deposits of preselected, ready-made knowledge. I recognized that I spent more time "banking" than I did helping students analyze prevailing mythologies in order to reach new levels of awareness. "Banking" was hard to resist. I felt comfortable using it, as I had experienced it as a middle-class, white student growing up in suburban communities.

When I returned to California to teach in 1985, my self-perception as a "banker" became more acute when I was hired to teach sixth grade humanities to students in a low-income, multiracial community and my self-assessments highlighted shortcomings, especially with reaching African American male students. Fortunately, educators at this school prioritized increased academic growth of nonmainstream students and offered many staff development opportunities on such topics as team teaching, sheltered English, cooperative groups, hands-on learning, Family Learning Nights, reading and writing workshops, and integrated disciplines. I took advantage of these opportunities, but the knowledge and skills gained in these courses did not provide enough momentum to enable me to substantially digress from "banking." Continued limited engagement in academic learning on the part of many students, African American male students in particular, ultimately provided me with enough glaring evidence to force me out of my comfort zone.

In my fifteenth year of teaching, I finally began using Freirean instructional practices and began crafting an approach that did push my students and myself into critical dialogues that crossed cultural borders and enhanced academic learning. The key to this long-awaited success was an emphasis on oral language.

An emphasis on oral language—it sounds so easy. Every teacher knows that oral discourse is central to learning. Teachers often encourage students to talk, to answer questions, to participate. What was so different about this approach?

Assessment is the tail that wags the dog in education. This is evident in ways that are hugely obvious, such as the use of large-scale test scores to bribe and punish educators. It also affects teaching in less obvious ways, in ways that we barely notice. For example, look in any language arts teachers' grade book. What percentage of grades are on aspects of oral discourse? Very few, if any. Then again, why do teachers even use grade books? Why do teachers think that student achievement, especially in language arts, can be meaningfully documented in tiny little squares? In the

American scientific-oriented approach to learning, this is common practice. Student growth is commonly documented by dividing subjects into discrete topics and then evaluating them with single numbers or letters. It is nearly impossible to create evaluation data that can fit into tiny squares when the subject is as ephemeral as oral language. Thus, assessment of oral language is largely a matter of teachers' implicit knowledge. What I found is that when it becomes explicit, a whole new side of education is opened.

To document how switching to a new approach to oral language and assessment transformed "banking" into "critical pedagogy," I will articulate the theoretical underpinnings of oral discourse and crossing cultural borders, share my experiences that lead to this revelation, report on how my relationship with students, especially students of color, changed radically, and analyze difficulties that arise when engaging in this kind of instructional practice. This is a hopeful story, one that illustrates how stepping outside the traditional assessment paradigm can significantly improve the educational contexts of nonmainstream students and their mainstream teachers.

Theoretical Rationale

My instincts as a teacher told me that language was the key to engendering change. This is not surprising when viewed from the theoretical underpinnings of literacy learning. In one of the most widely accepted views, the Vygotskian perspective, language is central to human life because it is a tool for learning. Vygotsky (1978) explains, "The specifically human capacity for language enables children to provide for auxiliary tools in the solution of difficult tasks, to overcome impulsive action, to plan a solution to a problem prior to its execution, and to master their own behavior" (p. 28). From the beginning of life, language transforms experiences, such as pointing, to knowledge, that is, pointing often results in having an object placed in your hands and thus promotes internal recognition of the meaning, "I want that."

At home and in other nonschool environments, toddlers learn their culture's rules and conventions for conversation and social discourse. For example, they learn turn-taking rules (Sacks, Schegloff, & Jefferson 1974). By the time they enter kindergarten, children have had experience with learning how long participants should wait for their turn to talk, appropriate ways to change topics, techniques for including new members in the conversations, and how to end conversations. They also have been introduced to the concept of power structures in oral discourse because they know that they, as less powerful beings, children, are supposed to defer in conversations to more powerful beings, adults (Lakoff 1990).

The socialization of children's language continues in primary school, where new rules and regulations must be learned (Dyson 1993). The social context of traditional American classrooms is uniquely demanding. Where else in American society are large numbers of people told to be quiet for hours at a time, without barriers to hearing and seeing each other (Cazden 1988)? Not at the workplace or in public gatherings. For this reason, oral discourse rules must be very constraining in order for traditional American classroom contexts to work.

Traditional classroom discourse is most often structured by an interaction pattern termed "IRE" (Mehan 1979). In this turn-taking sequence, teachers make an *inquiry,* "I," usually by asking a question where they know the answer; then teachers select students to *respond,* "R" and finally; teachers *evaluate* their responses, "E." Teachers control the entire process, determining what information should be highlighted, which students respond, when they respond, and how well they respond. This power differential is commonly maintained throughout classroom discourse practices, even in oral discussions, where more students respond and teachers' evaluative comments are minimized (Barnes, Britton, & Torbe 1990). Students' roles as recipients of information predetermined by the teacher are maintained, and thus student discourse in most classrooms is aligned with "banking" instruction.

Reflective Assessment

When I examined my practice, I saw the shortcomings of my overreliance on traditional "banking" techniques, especially the oral discourse practice favored by many white American teachers, the inquiry-respond-evaluate (IRE). For example, it constrained participation of students from cultures with patterns of oral communication that differed, such as African Americans (Heath 1983). It also minimized the amount of time for English Language Learners (ELL) to interact with native English speakers, an important aspect of second-language learning (Wong-Fillmore 1992).

These shortcomings became most clear to me when I discovered that I had very little concrete evidence on students' abilities in important aspects of oral language. Were persuasive students successful because they used evidence from the text we just read or did they rely on personality traits? Which students understood a concept well enough to apply it to a new situation and share their insights with others? Could students listen to others' opinions and modify their own, or did they strive to dominate conversations? The IRE and other teacher-lead discourse patterns did not provide opportunities for me to assess my students' abilities in these areas.

These insights became possible when I adopted a new approach to literacy assessment, the *Primary Language Record* (PLR) (Barrs, Ellis, & Hester 1989). The PLR was developed by teachers in inner-city London who wanted to draw out the best efforts of their students from diverse cultural backgrounds. Unlike American teachers who engage in this endeavor, their vision was not narrowed by the standardized testing paradigm that dominates American education. Their collection of ideas and strategies from successful teachers provided many avenues of assessing talking and listening that are ethnographic in nature. The systematic conferencing and observational note taking required by the PLR are not commonly encountered in American education (see Appendix A for a sample "Listening and Speaking" data collection page).

After field-testing many techniques, the British authors developed a format and guide for documenting students' growth in oral discourse that has proven to be culturally sensitive across many contexts (Falk, MacMurdy, & Darling-Hammond 1995). I used the PLR's theory, format, and strategies to challenge and change my approach to teaching.

An Initial Conflict and Dialogical Problem Solving

The PLR's format requires assessment of student discourse across a variety of contexts. This forced me to incorporate more paired learning, small group learning, and free-wheeling oral discussions. When students began to talk and control discourse more than I did, staying on topic was not a problem. Students dove into challenging material via literature circles and other such strategies. The PLR supported student engagement also because it prioritizes student self-reflection. Students wrote daily in metacognition journals and evaluated their growth weekly via summaries that went home to parents. When students had to consistently think about their progress and provide evidence to back up their opinions, they soon realized that on-task behavior was essential, so their motivation to participate increased naturally. The problems that did arise were because of the change in power structure.

When I became but one more participant in most of our oral discussions, students became more empowered. We began engaging in what Freire termed a "dialogical" approach to learning, which is characterized by cooperation and mutuality in the roles of teacher and learner (Freire 1972). In this method, all teach and all learn. This contrasts with an anti-dialogical approach, which emphasizes the teacher's side of the learning relationship and frequently results in one-way communiqués perpetuating domination and oppression. From the Freirean perspective, this change marked my first step in dismantling hierarchal, Eurocentric "banking."

When I withdrew from the usual IRE turn-taking convention, I also created a void. In my classroom, where about 20 percent of the students were African American, 20 percent Asian American, 30 percent European American, and 30 percent Hispanic, this void was readily filled by African American students. Our perspectives on this turn of events varied considerably. African American students enjoyed themselves and sometimes their enthusiasm resulted in heated arguments as they vied for the floor. Some non–African American students wrote in their reflection journals that they considered African American students' conversational domination rude and inconsiderate. In some students' journals, African American students were called "turn hogs" and the students urged me to step back in and "get control."

For my part, I was delighted that African American students were so involved. As a white teacher, I was amazed at how much energy was tapped when students engaged in a discourse style that was comfortable to them. I also felt at a loss as to how the resulting conflicts could be mediated. Like the students who complained, I did not have a clue how to gain entry into their stream of thoughts and opinions. I also wanted to feel included, not excluded. On a very small scale, this situation provided myself and other white participants a taste of what it was like to be on the outside of the "discourse comfort zone."

From a theoretical standpoint, conflicts such as these naturally occur when multiple interactional styles are allowed. Our situation actually provides a classic example of confrontation between two commonly encountered styles in American discourse, "involvement" and "considerateness" (Tannen 1984). The African American students' style is most closely aligned with the "involvement" style. They were using typical involvement devices such as emotional connection, interest, variety of pitch and speed, colorful vocabulary, variety of syntactic forms, and frequent overlapping and "back channeling," such as "Oh, yeah," "You go girl!" and "Thank you!"

Many of the rest of us relied on a conversational style at other end of the spectrum, "considerateness," a style favored by European Americans and American educational practices. Considerate-style speakers use devices such as waiting for pauses between turns, steady articulation, few back channels, and little overlapping or interrupting. From a linguistic perspective, the conflict between styles we were experiencing in our classroom was a particularly difficult one. Robin Lakoff (1990) elaborates the inner dynamics of the power struggle that occurs when these two discourse styles conflict:

> When a conversation includes both types of speakers, each tends to make derogatory assessments of the other: to a considerateness user, an involved speaker is aggressive; and indeed, the former may have trouble getting and keeping the floor in company with involved speakers. On the other hand, involvement users often see considerate speakers as boring and uninterested, and if the former perceive themselves to be riding roughshod over them, rationalize that the latter didn't have much to say anyway. In such mixed groups, involvement users certainly hold a conversational advantage: they do most of the talking and choose most of the successful topics. But in the long run, they may lose power because they are perceived as not good people, as too difficult to deal with. (p. 50)

As a white teacher, I had been modeling and enforcing the considerate style for years, and it was not until I started using the PLR varied contexts grid (Appendix A) for assessing oral discourse that I had the opportunity to realize the importance of recognizing and valuing students' differing discourse patterns. Until I experienced it myself, I had no idea of how frustrating it is to have a conflicting discourse style given preference over my own. At this point, I began to really cross a "cultural border" inherent in school structures (Giroux 1992). I began to understand how much privileging the European style of discourse contributed to the silencing of African American students.

This frustration provided me with an opportunity to utilize the Freirean "problem-posing" approach. In "banking" classrooms, our conflicts based on the power dynamics of turn taking would have gone unexamined. The considerate style of the dominant majority would have continued to be privileged at the expense of African American student participation, or, if I left my thrill of increased participation of one group unexamined, the African American style would have dominated at the expense of considerate style users.

Instead, we entered into critical dialogue (Freire 1972). This kind of exploration is characterized by depth in the interpretation of problems, scrutiny of findings with openness to revision, and attempting to avoid distortion from preconceived notions when analyzing them. Students wrote in their journals about their frustrations, this time without loaded terms, such as "turn hog," so that we could discuss the situation from a problem-posing perspective.

In subsequent discussions, African American students shared that they were used to just saying out loud what popped into their heads because that is what they did at home and at church. The African American students in our class called this "shouting out," and they wanted to use it more in school.

Some non–African American students expressed how it was hard to deal with a turn-taking pattern where speakers did not have to designate when and who would speak next. Many of us were unfamiliar with turn-taking conventions based on participants' evaluation of who was the wittiest, most insightful or, sometimes, loudest. We also were surprised to learn that the African American students in our class sometimes based turn taking on the speakers' ability to assess audiences' reactions. If others were paying attention, then the speakers continued until someone else managed to draw attention away from them.

At the other end of the turn-taking spectrum were Asian American students who were concerned about their lack of participation. Their journal reflections indicated that they wanted to contribute more but felt that they did not have anything of value to say. In private conversations with students who had recently immigrated from Southeast Asia, I encouraged them with a method commonly used by middle-class, white teachers: I said that of course their thoughts were important and they should not be afraid to share them. Their responses to me revealed that it was not a matter of being shy or lacking the courage to speak aloud. Rather, from their cultural perspective, only adults or people with much living experience were wise enough, worthy enough to contribute to discussions on classroom subjects. So they postponed participation until they felt they had wise and insightful comments to share that were worthy of other students' time.

To address this issue, I shared with them examples of how others students' input based on their life experiences helped us understand a piece of literature or event in history, even though the students were not "experts" in the field. Because we were studying ancient China, I encouraged students to share some of their own background knowledge on this topic. Students responded by immediately bringing up how I mispronounce Chinese names. I got the feeling that they had wanted to tell me this for a long time. As a white teacher, this was an embarrassing moment. I could only imagine how annoying it must be for them to listen to their teacher hack away at their language. I had not bothered until this time to analyze my role as "the expert" in the class deeply enough to take advantage of alternate forms of expertise in the classroom.

Wanting to take advantage of a "teachable moment," I encouraged this initial foray by Asian American students into sharing their thoughts by openly soliciting their input while teaching about ancient China. Other students were more able to catch on to Chinese pronunciation than I ever was, but that is not the point. Over time, comments from myself and other students to Asian American students on the value of their contributions increased their comfort level to some extent. The door opened for increased participation by Asian American students and increased respect for their knowledge on the part of other students. Teachers cannot know everything about everything, so it is worth the risk for white teachers to cross cultural borders and explore other available pools of knowledge.

Through open discussion of the sources of students' discomfort, we eventually defined our own turn-taking strategies. Freire (1972) maintains that decision making by consensus is difficult, and we found this to be true. It took a few debates, sometimes heated, to come to consensus on the following rules for turn taking:

(1) In activities where turn taking is already structured, for example, literature circles and author's chair, all students had to follow prescribed rules of turn taking. Because these activities were based on egalitarian theory, their structured discourse conventions provided opportunities for all students to participate. This rule privileged students with considerateness style, but this had its advantages. It provided a structure for Asian American students to take risks by sharing their thoughts in a discourse style with which they were comfortable. It also provided opportunities for involvement style students to develop their skills with the dominant culture's discourse practices.

(2) In small, less structured groups of three to five, we used "free-wheeling" conversational rules. We acknowledged that African American and other involvement-style students would dominate these discussions until considerateness students took risks and developed more assertive and outgoing discourse practices. Students thought this was necessary so that they would do well in college and other situations where it is important to express opinions. Comments from students expressing empathy for the courage it takes to try new things helped us reach consensus on this rule. To elicit these comments, students taught me and encouraged me to use current (school appropriate) slang. This lesson amply demonstrated the concept of "try" and "risk taking."

(3) In large group discussions, we used "free-wheeling" style again for the occasional discussions on hot topics of interest to all. Mostly we used "popcorn" turn taking, where the current speaker selects the next one after a few minutes of speaking. We moved our desks into a big circle so that we could all see each other. Volunteers could raise their hands, and students

could "pass" when selected, but the speaker could select anyone. Asian American students knew they might be chosen, so this provided them with a format for trying out a comment or two. To deal with the difficulty they had holding back their comments, African American students indicated the importance and cleverness of their comments through body language. If they thought what they had to say was very important, they snapped their fingers or waved their hand emphatically; if it was absolutely the best comment imaginable, they jumped up and down beside their chairs while waving their hand emphatically.

(4) Students who were still learning English were not expected to participate as often, being as it was especially difficult for them to put their thoughts into English. Whenever possible, we paused for them to have their thoughts translated by bilingual students and then shared. We also were patient and nonjudgmental in that many of us had a newfound respect for the courage it takes to speak in a new language.

Although my role as participant in oral discourse was egalitarian in nature, my knowledge and abilities in instructional theory and practice meant that I still needed to guide students' learning. My observations and students' reflections after each discussion session provided us with evidence to determine the extent to which comfort and quality were maintained. I used this information when I had chats with individual students so that we could better understand how their discourse practices affected themselves and others. Sharing power in oral discourse and assessment provided the first real opportunities for the dialogic process and problem solving through critical discourse.

Language Variation and Liberatory Education

Increased usage of African American English Vernacular (AAEV), or Ebonics, by many students evolved as the other main source of culture clash. When I accepted our turn-taking rules, I relinquished the power to correct students whenever I saw fit, so I could no longer engage in the typical white, mainstream teacher practice of pointing out "double negatives" or asking students to conjugate the verb "to be" in their sentences. I was conflicted about how much AAEV should be used in our classroom, because, while I respected their home language, I also worried that without sufficient modeling of Standard English, students' facility with the "language of power" would be diminished (Delpit 1988). Furthermore, in parent conferences at the beginning of the year, an activity built into the *Primary Language Record* format, many parents had said that they wanted their children to improve their Standard English.

This conflict provided us with a chance to engage in a process central to the Freirean philosophy, "liberatory education" (Freire 1972). Liberatory education engages learners in challenging status quo and in changing the world. Students are discouraged from merely adapting themselves to social practices uncritically. Liberatory education's goal is to develop the skills needed to advance economic and personal empowerment through critical dialogue.

Critical discourse on the conflict between their community language and the language of power eventually allowed us to create an empowering alternative to status quo discourse practices. We decided that most of the time we would use what students called "college English" because that is what they needed to get into college, and most of them felt that education was a viable path for increasing economic and personal power. But, occasionally, we would use "Westside," the local version of AAEV, so named because the community members who speak it live on the west side of a large city. Essentially, this agreement formalized "code switching," or switching from one language or vernacular to another, depending on the context (Labov 1972). We decided that we would use Westside when transitioning from one activity to another and when discussing emotionally laden academic topics or current events.

This decision made it socially acceptable to use a community vernacular, a rule-bound variation of a language, in the classroom. The official sanctioning of students' community language increased respect for both languages because the social meanings behind language choices made the power of both languages more explicit. This decision and the learning activities that it led to, described in the next paragraph, provided students with the opportunity to replace internalized negative images of their language (created and imposed by the oppressor) with positive ones.

Students from many races in our school spoke Westside. But not everyone in the classroom was fluent in Westside. I, the white, middle-class adult, was an obvious example. Students new to the community, especially ones from immigrant families, were another example. These students had the courage to point out that they did not understand all the Westside words. To solve this problem, we made dictionaries out of lab books, just like our English literature vocabulary books. A few times a month, more often at the beginning, beginner Westside speakers shared words that were unfamiliar to us, and our more knowledgeable peers defined them for us. Eventually, fluent Westside students brought in lists of words that they knew were appropriate for classroom language, that is, not curse words, in anticipation of this activity.

We spent time talking about the entomology of the words. For example, "He yoked" (meaning he had a muscular body) came from the body-builder's practice of drinking raw eggs. Word histories were also recorded in our Westside dictionaries. Knowledge of the logical and intelligent creation of Westside vocabulary extended our perception of "slang" words to respected additions to our social interactions.

Because my perception of Westside is that it is largely based on AAEV, I continued the deconstruction of the "uncouth" myth of their community language by sharing what little academic background knowledge I had about the grammar of AAEV. Not only did this endeavor increase our respect for Westside, it also increased students' interest in verb conjugations. For example, their use of the verb form "be" in AAEV referred to an action that took place lots of times. When we looked at sentences where it sounded "right" to use the verb "be" unconjugated, rules governing its usage became apparent. Sentences with a continuous time frame, such as, "They be tired after playing basketball" sounded right, while "They be tired right now" did not. AAEV usage of the verb "to be" is rule-bound and not merely an avoidance of conjugating the verb "to be." Learning about the grammar of AAEV brought a new perspective that was especially empowering for African American students. As a white teacher, I realized how important this was and regretted that my knowledge of AAEV was so limited. Increased emphasis on the history of AAEV and its unique rules should be more prevalent in educational settings.

Students' pride in their community language grew also when I pointed out how the language is so exciting and, well, "hip" (to use an AAEV adjective) that advertisers constantly coopt words and phrases from AAEV. We could think of many such phrases off the tops of our heads. The irony that nonmainstream students who use AAEV are demeaned by society, while white men in suits who use it are richly rewarded, was not lost on the students.

From the Freirean perspective, these Westside language explorations and resulting insights exemplify "praxis" (Freire 1972). Praxis is the process of creating culture and becoming critically conscious human beings through a cycle of action-reflection-action. Characteristics of praxis include self-determination (as opposed to coercion) and intentionality (as opposed to reaction). Through analysis of their Westside language practices, students intentionally created new perspectives and uses for their language. This process increased students' pride and ownership of their community language and diminished the impact of negative social feedback about it.

The process of liberatory education through our dictionaries was not limited to African American students, however. One day, a student pointed out that we did not have any Asian words in our Westside dictionaries. The Asian students in my class said that they did not have a vernacular similar to AAEV or even slang words appropriate for use in the classroom, and were reluctant to make contributions. This impasse was broken in February, when the ubiquitous "Gung Hay Fat Choy" signs appeared for Chinese New Year. We added these "regular" (not vernacular) words to our dictionaries. Students decided we had to write them in Chinese script. Thus, Asian students who knew how to write in their home language became our more knowledgeable peers, walking around helping us write "Happy New Year" messages in Mandarin. Many of us had a difficult time with this "handwriting," and our respect for Asian calligraphy, and thus for these cultures, grew. As the year progressed, we added a few more Mandarin and Vietnamese words, which provided many non-Asian students and myself with the opportunity to appreciate the differences between the cultures.

Assessment and Liberatory Education

Using Westside in our classroom brought about a new level of cultural consciousness and served to create a level of supportive and motivated students never achieved before in my teaching. From a Freirean perspective, our journey is an example of the power of "participatory research" (Freire 1972). Participatory research helps people who are exploited and oppressed overcome symptoms of dependency and poverty by investigating and dismantling prevailing practices. Westside dictionaries and activities challenged traditional knowledge and provided an avenue for students to create new perspectives. Our process valued their stories and their voices and thus modified their definition of social equality in a positive and empowering manner.

I firmly believe that this change would not have happened if not for the assessment practices mandated by the PLR (Barrs, Ellis, & Hester 1989). The path to including Westside in my instructional strategies was paved by the PLR. The PLR's approach to language and assessment guides and enhances teachers' abilities to honor and build on the students' abilities with home languages. My students would not have had the opportunity to share their experiences if I had continued to rely on "inquiry-response-evaluate" discourse patterns and other traditional classroom discourse practices that strangle diverse discourse styles. My introduction of other discourse practices was prompted by the PLR's requirement for documenting talking and listening across contexts. Instructional practices that promoted liberatory education followed this change naturally after I relinquished authoritative power over turn-taking conventions. Students' capacity to use the power entrusted to them and to take on roles they had never had before were substantially aided by the PLR's emphasis on reflection.

The PLR's format requires students to frequently review their actions and examine their work products within a framework of clearly defined and developmentally appropriate expectations by providing developmental scales for reading and writing (see Appendix B). I extended this concept through the development of rubrics for other academic areas.

For example, we developed a rubric for oral presentations after talking about what made a good presentation good and what students needed to work on to improve presentations that were not effective (see Appendix C). After subsequent oral presentations, students assessed themselves and I responded to their self-assessments. Later, students assessed each other and I responded to both student assessments. My feedback was based on my abilities as a more knowledgeable peer. Sometimes hypercritical students needed feedback to learn when they were being too "picky," and sometimes hypocritical students needed feedback to learn that they needed to have evidence to back up their opinion of accomplishment. I listened to students and reviewed their evidence when we disagreed. Sometimes they provided information that changed my opinion and sometimes they did not.

The power teachers have over students did not completely disappear in our classroom, as my knowledge of learning was essential to their growth and as students at this age still need adult guidance to mature into socially responsible members of society. However, the PLR assessment practices were far more empowering to students than anything else I had ever encountered in educational practices. The few examples provided in the story of my journey reveal how drastically internal dynamics can change for the better if assessment practices promote student-centered and culturally critical instruction practices, rather than diminish them.

But to what extent are the lessons learned in our journey relevant to the educational world outside of my classroom? Why should educators care about the events in one isolated classroom? The final section of this chapter deals with these important topics.

Beyond the Classroom

The traditional American way to move effective instructional practices beyond the classroom is to "publish and promote." If I were to choose this approach, I would publish a glossy teaching unit with handy "Multicultural Personal Dictionaries" and then I would travel to large gymnasiums filled with teachers to proselytize the virtues of exploring students' community languages (for a modest speaking fee and travel expenses).

But, as with many aspects of traditional American educational practices, this avenue would miss the point. The real point is that teachers and students need to go on their own journeys exploring hot button issues of race and oppression based on their own particular contexts. The main components I used to become more aware of the hegemonic practices of white teachers and the steps for alleviating their negative aspects are already available to teachers. *Pedagogy of the Oppressed* (Freire 1972), the *Primary Language Record* (Barrs, Ellis, & Hester 1989) and America's version of the PLR, the *Learning Record* (Barr, et al 1999) are readily available. What teachers who have the willingness and courage to engage in this process really need is structural support. For example, teachers need time built into the day for investigating, for reflection, for contacting parents and involving them in their instructional planning.

Another needed structural support is a shift in assessment policies that places teachers and students at the center of educational assessment. Teachers know their students' learning best. They keep in constant contact with students, and skilled teachers' instructional plans are based on continuous assessment of students' learning. They also make the criteria for gauging the quality of student work visible and accessible. They help students learn to keep track of their own progress and set their own goals so that student engagement is maintained by tapping into intrinsic motivation (Berliner & Calfee 1996).

One major barrier to wider public acceptance of teacher-based assessment is the variability of teacher scoring decisions. This is a barrier that can be overcome. Techniques for increasing teachers' scoring reliability were developed in the 1980s when the Educational Testing Service developed methods that dramatically increased reliability in essay exam scoring (White 1994). As more and more districts in the 1980s mandated writing samples as part of their competency exams, these techniques became widely known and practiced. Increased numbers of educators became adept at developing rubrics and consistent at interpreting these rubric descriptors through calibration exercises. Teachers shared these techniques with other teachers and often integrated them into instructional practices.

The benefits of teachers learning how to score reliably, such as discussions on what learning in their subject area actually entailed, coming to consensus on what quality work looked like, and agreement on how students could demonstrate mastery, became more widespread. But current policies, such as the federal law No Child Left Behind (2002) undermine this progress by championing the role of large-scale, machine-scored, standardized tests. Structural support for teacher-based assessments and the honoring of teachers' professional knowledge is being diminished by current educational policies, despite increased evidence that enhancing it is profoundly beneficial.

Staff development on improving the reliability of teacher judgments of student work is a win-win proposition. Money spent on teachers' discussions and internalization of developmental milestones in learning enhances their pedagogy, and it increases their scoring reliability. It is far more cost effective than putting money into tests and enactment of policies that constrain curriculum and diminish teacher efficacy.

Evidence of this kind of structural support is provided in studies on teacher-based assessments. For example, studies on teachers who use the American version of the PLR, the *Learning Record* (LR), reveal that staff development on portfolio assessment promoted high levels of teachers' scoring consistency, increased engagement in instructional practices deemed most effective by research, and steady progress in student achievement (Hallam 2000, 2001). Investigation of performance-based science assessments developed by science educators also found that staff development on assessment and scoring promoted scoring consistency and student learning (Wilson & Sloane 2001).

The impact of teacher-based assessments on nonwhite students has not been explored fully, especially as public policies funnel huge amounts of educational funds into the production and evaluation of large-scale, machine-scored, standardized tests. However, initial explorations indicate that equity issues can be better addressed through teacher-based assessment than they are through machine-scored tests (Falk, MacMurdy, & Darling-Hammond 1995). Both kinds of testing rely on human judgment—machine-scored test questions and answers are written by humans; only the scoring is by machine. A key advantage of teacher-based assessments such as the PLR is that they are open and available for public scrutiny. Instances of bias or prejudice based on ethnicity can be brought to the public's attention and action can be taken to solve these problem areas. The same cannot be said for published large-scale tests, which are shrouded by secrecy.

The time and structural support needed for teachers and students to embark on their own journeys into uncovering barriers based on race and perpetuated through our current assessment practices are of crucial importance. In the current political climate, where state and federal policies support curriculum that dictates in detail how teachers should teach because politicians distrust the teaching profession, however, the exact opposite action is being legislated. In the struggle to reclaim our profession and achieve more progressive and just education, the power of liberatory practices should not be overlooked. Students as well as teachers, administrators, and parents can move forward through dispassionate analysis of status quo practices, engagement in critical dialogue, and creative solutions developed through collective efforts. In this chapter, I described how this kind of liberatory education, despite imperfections, had a profound effect on a teacher and her students. It is within reach of others to engage in similar efforts.

References

Barnes, D., Britton, J., Torbe, M. (1990). *Language, the learner and the school*. Portsmouth, NH: Heinemann.

Barr, M., Craig, D., Syverson, M., & Fisette, D. (1999). *Assessing literacy with the Learning Record: A handbook for teachers, grades K–6*. Portsmouth, NH: Heinemann.

Barrs, M., Ellis, S., & Hester, H. (1989). *Primary language record: Handbook for teachers*. Portsmouth, NH: Heinemann.

Berliner, D. C. & Calfee, D. J. (Eds.). (1996). *Handbook of educational psychology*. New York: Macmillan.

Cazden, C. (1988). *Classroom discourse: The language of teaching and learning*. Portsmouth, NH: Heinemann.

Delpit, L. (1988). The silenced dialog: Power and pedagogy in educating other people's children. *Harvard Educational Review, 58*(f3): 280–98.

Dyson, A. H. (1993). *Social worlds of children learning to write in an urban primary school*. New York: Teachers College Press.

Falk, B., MacMurdy, S., & Darling-Hammond, D. (1995). *Authentic assessment in action: Studies of schools and students at work*. New York: Teachers College Press.

Freire, P. (1972). *Pedagogy of the oppressed*. London: Penguin.

Giroux, H. A. (1992). *Border crossings: Cultural workers and the politics of education*. New York: Routledge.

Hallam, P. J. (2000). *Reliability and validity of teacher-based reading assessment: Application of "Quality Assurance for Teacher-based Assessment"(QATA) to California learning record moderations*. Unpublished doctoral dissertation, University of California, Berkeley, CA.

Hallam, P. J. (2001). *Learning Record Moderations: 2001 combined schools validity report*. San Diego, CA: Center for Language in Learning.

Heath, S. B. (1983). *Ways with words: Language, life, and work in communities and classrooms*. New York: Cambridge University Press.

Labov, W. (1972). *Language in the inner city: Studies in the Black English Vernacular.* Philadelphia: University of Pennsylvania Press.

Lakoff, R. T. (1990). *Talking and power: The politics of language.* New York: Basic Books.

Mehan, H. (1979). Learning lessons. *Harvard Educational Review* 48, pp. 32–64.

No Child Left Behind. (2002). PL 107-110. Washington, DC: US Department of Education.

Sacks, H., Schegloff, E. A., et al. (1974). A simplest systematics for the organization of turn-taking for conversation. *Language* 50, pp. 696–735.

Tannen, D. (1984). *Conversational style.* Norwood, NJ: Ablex.

Vygotsky, L. S. (1978). *Mind in society: The development of higher psychological processes.* Cambridge, MA: Harvard University Press.

White, E. (1994). *Teaching and assessing writing: Recent advances in understanding, evaluating, and improving student performance.* San Francisco: Jossey-Bass.

Wilson, M., & Sloane, K. (2001). From principles to practice: An embedded assessment system. *Applied Measurement in Education, 13*(2), pp. 181–208.

Wong-Fillmore, L. (1992). Second-language learning in children: A model of language learning in social context. In E. Bialystok (Ed.), *Language processing by bilingual children* (pp. 49–69). Cambridge: Cambridge University Press.

Appendix A: Listening and Speaking Data Grid

Data Collection   Secondary (Grades 6 to 12)

Name_____   Grade_____

 1. Talking & Listening: Observation Notes

Record below, the student's use of talk for learning and for communicating with others in English and/or other languages about that learning.

Include different kinds of talk (e.g., planning an event, solving a problem,, expressing a point of view, reporting on the results of an investigation, interpreting a poem...)

Teachers might comment on student experience and confidence in the social dimensions of talk (e.g., initiating a discussion, listening to another contribution, qualifying former ideas, encouraging others...)

The matrix sets out possible contexts for observing talk and listening. It may also be useful in suggesting a variety of contexts in which to assess reading or writing development. Observations noted below can be plotted on the matrix to record the range of social and learning contexts sampled.

Learning Contexts	Social Contexts			
	Pair	Small group	Student with Adult	Large group
Collaborative learning activities				
Dramatic/ visual interpretation				
Problem solving discussion				
Literary discussion				

Published as a component of The Learning Record™. For information, call or write the Center for Language in Learning, 10769 Woodside Ave, Suite 203, Santee, CA 92071. Phone (619) 596-3723; Fax 3725. Website address – www.learningrecord.org. Email – lrecord@cll.org. All materials © 2002, by the CLL.

Appendix B: LR Reading Scale 2, Grades 4–8

Becoming Experienced in Reading

1 Beginning Reader: Uses just a few successful strategies for tackling print independently. Relies on having another person to read the text aloud. May still be unaware that text carries meaning.

2 Not-yet-fluent Reader: Tackling known and predictable text with growing confidence but still needing support with new and unfamiliar ones. Growing ability to predict meanings and developing strategies to check predictions against other cues such as the illustrations and the print itself.

3 Moderately Fluent Reader: Well-launched on reading but still needs to return to a familiar range of reader text. At the same time beginning to explore new kinds of texts independently. Beginning to read silently.

4 Fluent Reader: A capable reader who now approaches familiar texts with confidence but still needs support with unfamiliar materials. Beginning to draw inferences from books and stories. Reads independently. Chooses to read silently.

5 Exceptionally Fluent Reader: An avid and independent reader who is making choices from a wider range of material. Able to appreciate nuances and subtlety in text.

Appendix C: Sample Rubric for Oral Language

Room 202 Oral Language Rubric

5: "The Best"

Uses hand motions and body language

Lots of confidence

Speaks clearly and loudly

Not too fast or slow

Right length

Interesting, on topic

Exciting, uses expression

Uses volume changes, loud/soft on purpose

Pauses and changes speed on purpose

Eyes on people, not floor

Uses visual aids, holds so can see, but not in front of face

Listens when others have turn

3: "Medium"

Uses a little expression

A few mistakes

Some eye contact

Voice changed a little bit, and not because lost place

Some confidence and control over volume

1: "Needs Helps"

Giggles too much

Holds paper in front of face and reads

Too soft, fast, slow, or low

Lip synchs instead of talking

Mixes up words a lot

Mumbles

No expression or feeling, boring

Adds unimportant things

Repeats what someone else said a lot

Turn hog

Doesn't participate much

3

"I Could Hear You If You Would Just Calm Down": Challenging Eurocentric Classroom Norms through Passionate Discussions of Racial Oppression

Eileen O'Brien

Many educators who desire to transform the hierarchies of race, class, gender, and other forms of oppression in their classrooms often focus on altering the *content* of their curriculum rather than on the *process* by which that curriculum is developed in the classroom space. Yet developing an inclusive learning experience involves not only decentering whiteness (maleness, etc.) in course material but also making space for nondominant modes of interaction and behavior as ways of processing that material. Here I want to explore how incorporating the emotional response of *anger* in class discussions of racial oppression disrupts the normative hierarchies of white dominance in classroom space. This disruption is not without its challenges, particularly for some white learners, but it ultimately creates great antiracist possibilities seldom tapped by unemotional approaches to oppression.

Several analysts of race, gender, and class oppression have critiqued the false dichotomies of public/private, reason/emotion, and mind/spirit (among others) as creations of those in power, used to devalue feminine, non-European, and working-class ways of being. As Marimba Ani points out in her book *Yurugu: An African-Centered Critique of European Cultural Thought and Behavior* (1994), the first step to objectifying (and thereby controlling) someone is to remove any emotional attachment to her/him.

Thus, being "objective" and therefore intellectually superior means disconnecting from all that is deemed emotional, according to dominant Eurocentric thought. To this end, everything that displayed such "objectivity" became labeled as civilized, while anything emotionally expressive was deemed irrational, uncivilized, and thus deserving of domination by those in power. This dichotomy between reason and emotion not only serves as justification for colonization and oppression, but it also functions to suppress any revolution against oppression. As bell hooks notes in her book *Killing Rage: Ending Racism,* "rage is not pathological. It is an appropriate response to injustice" (1995, p. 26.) Yet as long as emotions such as rage can be characterized by those in power as uncivilized and inappropriate, "it ensures that there will be no revolutionary effort to gather that rage and use it for constructive social change" (hooks 1995, p.18). It follows, then, that norms of classroom *behavior* that privilege "rational" intellect and devalue "irrational" emotion not only will continue to privilege members of dominant groups in the classroom but also will squelch the more revolutionary possibilities for liberation from emerging from such classrooms, *even if that course's curriculum reflects diverse perspectives.*

Although I will be focusing primarily here on anger as a legitimate (and integral) part of the process of decentering *whiteness* in the classroom, it must be clear that validating emotional expression in the classroom disrupts many other hierarchies of power as well. Many women know the admonition of "calm down" has been used to silence them in various ways. Similarly, the stigmatization of emotional expressiveness has been used to devalue the working classes. In discussing the "bourgeois class biases" that dominate mainstream pedagogy, bell hooks (1994) writes:

> As silence and obedience to authority were most rewarded, students learned that this was the appropriate demeanor in the classroom. Loudness, anger, emotional outbursts, and even something as seemingly innocent as unrestrained laughter were deemed unacceptable, vulgar disruptions of the social order. These traits were also associated with being a member of the lower classes. (p. 178)

Thus, the incorporation of emotion into the classroom process holds liberatory potential not only toward dismantling racial oppression but gender and class oppression as well, by creating a space where previously devalued forms of expression are legitimized as equally valid in the quest for knowledge.

The validation of anger and other forms of so-called inappropriate emotions in the classroom has particular implications for members of dominant groups. Hearing historically silenced voices speak out emotionally about their plight often gives members of dominant groups their first exposure to the lived realities of oppression. Because of the stigma described above, expression of raw emotion about oppression often stays within oppressed groups, where it is more likely to be taken seriously and understood. So a diverse classroom that affirms emotion can be an eye-opening experience for those whose privilege has heretofore insulated them from hearing such testimonies. Furthermore, members of dominant groups also may be dealing with their own anger on learning about oppression, even in the absence of "others" in the classroom with them. For instance, whites may become disillusioned with the educational system, feeling betrayed that they have been misinformed up until now about their nation's racist history, or white males may feel targeted and blamed as the "bad guys." Thus, those in privileged groups might appreciate the space to process these new emotions they are experiencing, and effective instructors can even channel this emotion into effective social change action. However, it is important to note that members of dominant groups still are accustomed to the privilege of being taken more seriously when their rage is expressed (O'Brien 2001).

Creating an inclusive classroom that affirms diverse modes of expression may sound simple, but it is actually an approach from which many instructors shy away. Our traditional socialization as educators teaches us to "maintain control" over the classroom, and we may take passionate outbursts as a sign of an unruly, undisciplined space that needs to be managed. In fact, encountering such settings has historically led even the most progressive instructors to retreat from fully inclusive classroom processes. Reflecting on the history of the incorporation of cultural diversity into academia, bell hooks (1994) writes:

> Many folks found that as they tried to respect "cultural diversity" they had to confront the limitations of their training and knowledge, as well as a possible loss of "authority." Indeed, exposing certain truths and biases in the classroom often created chaos and confusion. The idea that the classroom should always be a "safe," harmonious place was challenged. . . . Many professors lacked the strategies to deal with antagonisms in the classroom. (pp. 30–31)

Perceiving one's own "loss of control" can be a scary feeling, especially when mainstream pedagogical philosophies reflect a hierarchical teacher-student model, and any diversion from this hierarchy is a sign of professional failure. In my own discipline (sociology), even our more progressive national professional association held a conference session on "managing anger in the classroom," and when I submitted a paper affirming anger as a necessary and useful pedagogical process for teaching about oppression, this was politely deemed "inappropriate" for the session. Indeed, we are more ready to diversify the *content* of our curriculum than we are to confront the biases inherent in the *process* of teaching. Yet facing the racist, sexist, classist norm of keeping emotions out of the classroom is all the more relevant for those of us teaching in classrooms where topics like racism, sexism, and classism are the focus of the course content. It is urgent that we begin to share strategies for affirming anger in such classrooms, so that there are alternative models of pedagogy available for progressive instructors who desire traversing this tenuous terrain of challenging the status quo. Although a daunting task, its rewards are tremendous.

Sources of Personal Observations

I base this exploration of anger as a necessary part of the pedagogy of oppression primarily on my own observations at a small state college for the past three years teaching courses to undergraduates that deal with structures, identities, and relationships that oppress people. Although I have seen similar issues emerge across those years, and my examples may periodically draw from different semesters and courses, this paper will deal largely with a section of "Gender, Race, and Class" that met in Spring 2002. This was a cross-listed sociology, women's studies, and African American studies course comprised of mainly junior and senior undergraduates. Because our entire campus has less than 10 percent total "minority" enrollment, with barely 3 percent of that figure representing African Americans, my class was a more "diverse" environment than most of the students had experienced before. This class of twenty-nine students included six black students (five African American and one Jamaican; four women and two men), and one Mexican American male. There were seventeen white women and five white men. There were eight nontraditional students (this connotes students over twenty-five, who often are married/partnered with children) and four nonheterosexual students that I knew of (two of these were students of color, and two were white, although one was not openly "out" to the class). Our campus is comprised largely of first-generation college students, so most every student usually is working a job outside of school, with the nontraditional students often working full-time. Thus, my impression of the class background of the students is a fairly even balance between middle class and working class, although I do not have hard data for this. Overall, white females made up the majority of the class, but the students observed that the racial-ethnic and sexual orientation diversity in the classroom was more than they had experienced in most of their other courses. Although it was only a third of the class that provided this perceived "diversity," this handful of students happened to be more vocal and outspoken than most. I attribute this both to these students' individual personalities, and to the pedagogical philosophy I stressed throughout the course that affirmed diverse modes of expression.

I begin my courses by not only going over reading, writing, and participation requirements, but also by explaining my philosophy of teaching and learning, and asking students to agree to some ground rules for discussion. My teaching and learning philosophy was inspired largely by bell hooks's *Teaching to Transgress* (1994), and it is based on the ideal of a non-hierarchical "learning community" where teacher and students are colearners actively engaged in the pursuit of knowledge with each other. I let students know right away that they will not be lectured to, and that they need to take a very active role in the direction of the course. I also explain that there is a conscious philosophy of student empowerment behind this approach, lest my lack of lecturing be perceived as a lazy instructor's cop-out. Part of this philosophy is also a respect for one's peers and for the knowledge that peers can add to the discussion. This is especially important for a classroom that focuses on oppression, because as a white female I cannot provide them with equal experiential knowledge on all forms of oppression. (For example, I have not personally experienced discrimination based on the color of my skin.) Students have reported in evaluations that some of the most powerful learning experiences they have taken away from my courses have been those gleaned from the passionate participation of other students. They can read examples of discrimination all day long, but somehow hearing it "live" from a real person they sit next to every day seems to consistently have the greatest impact. This is true for both members of dominant groups and for members of oppressed groups, who report appreciating knowing they are not alone in what they are feeling or have experienced. For example, students talk to me about powerful learning experiences and credit them to the diversity in the room. Unfortunately, I rarely get students telling me how eye-opening the class has been in a homogenous classroom. Although I present this pedagogical philosophy in all sociology courses I teach, it is particularly essential for approaching oppression-related courses.

Along with this teaching and learning philosophy, I also introduce the students to some ground rules for discussion. As we read each rule aloud and discuss it, I leave it open to the students to revise, add to, or discard any part of the rules to make them their own, as this will be part of the contract they agree to for the semester. Although I will not list all ten of the rules here, there are two especially worth noting. One is to acknowledge that we have all been taught misinformation, both about our own group and about members of other groups. The implication here is that if I should be "caught" making a racist statement, and then someone in our learning community challenges that statement, we need to understand that this is not a personal attack. Rather, it is an attack on the system that has allowed the misinformation to perpetuate such that I, and many others like me, have come to accept it as truth. However, another ground rule states that we will be held responsible for not perpetuating misinformation once we have become aware that it is misinformation. That is, if we have just spent weeks going over evidence of institutional discrimination, and someone makes the statement that America is now an "equal playing field," this person deserves to be held personally accountable for the statement as opposed to excusing him/her by chalking it up to societal misinformation. I raise these guidelines to accentuate the afore-mentioned point that a course focusing on oppression in a deep and meaningful way cannot always be a "safe" or harmonious space. Yet it is still a community. As bell hooks writes: "Rather than focusing on issues of safety, I think that a feeling of community creates a sense that there is a shared commitment and a common good that binds us" (hooks 1994, p. 40). In agreeing to the ground rules, we acknowledge that the pathway may be rocky, but we are ultimately all in pursuit of certain common goals despite our differences and different starting points.

Tension in the Classroom

A wise professor on my dissertation committee once told me something I have never forgotten. He said that if his classroom did not become contentious, he was not doing his job. As a young graduate student, this comment stuck with me because I had been socialized into typical white middle-class female culture that taught me that conflict was a sign of distress and of failure. In fact, I still strive to avoid conflict in my personal life and relationships. Yet I have learned by teaching courses related to issues of oppression that the classrooms in which students seem most powerfully affected by the experience are always those characterized by emotionally intense discussions. Repeatedly I have observed that white middle-class female students tend to be the ones leaving class after the first heated discussion thinking something has gone horribly wrong, and I always revert back to that old professor's remark to help normalize the situation: "I'm not doing my job" if such conflict *isn't* occurring in my class. It is an approach that overturns mainstream white middle-class norms of etiquette, and thus is a deeply personal challenge for many white students especially.

The fact that we have dichotomized academic challenge and emotional/personal challenge in our society only adds to the unexpected/traumatic nature of that experience for them. They are being challenged in a way they never expected to be in a classroom, thus they are taken off guard and unprepared no matter how much I try to warn them from Day One.

Fast forward from day one to day fifteen. By this point in my Gender, Race, and Class course, we have built some sense of community; they have worked in groups, gotten to know each other a bit, shared personal examples and stories, and learned basic terminology. We are now beginning to discuss the manifestations of these various forms of inequality in specific institutions, beginning with the institution of education. We are dealing with the question of whether schools and teachers are doing all they can to promote diversity and multiculturalism in schooling. Students have just read critiques by parents and teachers of the educational system's lack of diversity and what still needs to be done. Enter two vocal class participants, Vivian and Roger. Although both are nontraditional students and come from working-class backgrounds, Roger is now married to a school-teacher, and his wife is supporting him while he goes to school full-time. Roger presents both himself and his wife as good white liberals—Roger quotes studies he heard on NPR, and beams with pride about his wife's struggles to understand her inner-city students who are predominantly students of color. Vivian, by contrast, is an African American lesbian mother, who could very well be the parent of one of the students whom Roger's wife teaches. She still struggles to make ends meet, both going to school full-time and working, yet still finds time to volunteer in the community with groups serving gay men, lesbians, and bisexuals of color. What follows is a paraphrased version of an interchange that took place between them during class.

Roger explains how hard it is for teachers to be supported by the school system as they struggle to serve their inner-city students. He says his wife has had to fight back stereotypes in her head that black parents don't care about their children when they don't show up for parent-teacher conferences, when the fact is many of them are working long hours and nonbenefited jobs that will not allow them to make the conference times. Vivian hears the statement "black parents don't care about their kids," and is enraged. She retorts with an impassioned rebuttal of that stereotype. Not only have black women historically cared for their own kids, but they also nursed white women's children at their breasts when white women apparently did not want that task. Furthermore, black women take care of each other's children, and become mothers to the whole community of children. Far from not loving their children, Vivian asserts there's a "whole lotta love" in her and in black women that surround her.

Vivian goes on to ask Roger what his wife has done to look inside herself and make herself more diverse. Has she attended the Puerto Rican festival, or gone to a black church? Vivian gives examples of some of her own community involvements and attempts to understand other cultures she did not know about, and asks if Roger's wife has done the same. Vivian also asks if Roger's wife has tried to meet the parents at other more convenient places and times. Whereas Roger states that his wife has met parents after school hours at Dunkin Donuts, he admits she has not attended cultural events. He had mentioned to me in private how much he thinks his wife would love to sit in on my course, but today he asks the class if they would like for her to come in as a guest speaker so they can ask her such questions themselves. There seems to be some interest.

Although this is the *substance* of the exchange between the two students, the text alone does not capture the interaction. Roger's style of speaking is an even-keeled, perhaps even monotone inflection, and he appears calm although quite engaged. Vivian's style of speaking is much more animated than Roger's, her head moves from side to side as she speaks and she uses hand gestures, even pointing in Roger's direction. I watch both of them carefully as the dialogue goes on, because I typically intervene if one person's point seems to be overshadowed or unheard. However, both parties appear not to be personally offended by the other, so when they have finished I interject related points and move us on with the issues they raised.

When class ends I normally have several students approach me to ask me questions, usually about written assignments and other technicalities. Today Roger happens to be one of those students, telling me when he will be submitting his journals. Again it is clear that his class discussion has enhanced him in a positive way, for he is not distressed about it and is focused on other things. However, as we walk out of the classroom together, I notice a gathering of several young white female students from class outside the door, whispering busily and intently with each other. One of them remarks to Roger as we pass: "I would not bring your wife in here because she'll just be attacked in class the way you were today!" Although Roger assures them that his wife is from Brooklyn and she enjoys heated debates and would not be intimidated by them, another white female goes on to say that she will never speak up in class because she doesn't want "what happened today" (which from her perspective was an "attack") to happen to her. I spend some time after class talking with this small subgroup of the class, but not as much time as I would like, as I must head to another commitment after class. I try to move them toward thinking of the interchange that took place in class as an exchange of ideas rather than a personal attack. I assure them (as does Roger) that he did not feel attacked, and explain that "I'm not doing my job" if we are not getting to the heart of these issues with some passion. But I know I have not done enough.

This is not the first classroom in which white students have expressed their concern to me privately that they do not want to speak out for fear of black students' "attacks" on them, or for fear of being called "racist" by them. I can recall no student of color ever calling a white student a racist, or any other name, during class, but this is the white students' perception. Prior to this semester, however, it has usually been an individual student expressing concern to me in her journal (it has notably always been a white female, in my experience). This gives me the time and space to construct a thoughtful written response to that student. However, my concern on this particular occasion is that there is a critical mass of students gathering after class reinforcing one opinion only without an alternative interpretation of the class dynamics, influencing each other to no longer speak up in class. Looking ahead I can see that, without intervention, the situation easily could end up disabling a substantial part of our learning community's participation if this group decides to simply shut down for the remainder of the semester. The learning experience could be thwarted not just for this group but for the entire class if the class discussion becomes restricted to only a select few willing participants.

Race, Gender, and Class Differences in Anger Perception

How my intervention will take place depends in large part on my perception as an instructor of the race, gender, and class dynamics of the situation, paying special attention to how my own social location biases how I will interpret it. These white middle-class women are turning to me, another white middle-class female, approaching me with what they assume will be a shared cultural understanding between us. Yet this subgroup of students is mainly focusing on the *racial* aspect of the class tension. In their perception, a black student has stepped out of bounds of appropriate classroom conduct by intimidating white students. They are expecting me, another white middle-class female, to concur with this perception, and do something about it so that the classroom is a more comfortable place for them. However, it is a privilege of whiteness to not have to take another racial group's perspective into account in order to survive in society, so they have not considered how unsafe it must feel daily to be one of a handful of students of color in a class where white students, however innocently and naively, utter hurtful stereotypes about your group. Furthermore, their perception of Vivian as attacking and intimidating calls forth all kinds of antiblack stereotypes that form the fabric of our society that teach whites to fear African Americans. Perhaps as a reader it might have been difficult to find anything too scary about Vivian's class remarks. But filtered through the color-conscious lens of our society, hearing and seeing Vivian's remarks, spoken in person by an impassioned African American woman, made a significant difference in how these white females interpreted it. I believe they were seeing someone they were taught to fear, so this emotional response overwhelmed any other conscious listening they might have done to the *substance* of what she was saying.

I have found repeatedly that a passionate point made by a writer of color in an assigned reading can be heard and understood by a white student in a way that the same point uttered by an impassioned classmate of color will not. That same insightful classmate's point is much more likely to be perceived by white students as a personal attack. For example, in this same class, we read a piece by Audre Lorde (an African American lesbian writer) who is angrily tired of whites always turning to her to be their educator on oppression, and asserts that it is the oppressors' responsibility to educate themselves, not the oppressed, who have enough extra burdens of their own. We read this near the beginning of the semester, and it gave rise to a stimulating discussion about whether it was the oppressor's responsibility, the oppressed's responsibility, or both, to educate others about oppression. Yet near the end of the semester, when a white student asked what should be done about racism, and a black student responded, "you figure it out," a white middle-class female wrote to me in her journal that African Americans were basically undeserving of help if they were going to be so "rude" to those who volunteered to help make changes. I reminded this student that her black classmate's point was identical to Audre Lorde's, that it was white students' responsibility to educate themselves about oppression. However, again it was not just an intellectual point this time, as it was filtered through this white middle-class female's interpretation of an impassioned black male student, whose physical presence she has been taught to fear.

As I have already mentioned, these feelings of fear and intimidation that white students experience in their classroom interactions with students of color are most often expressed to me by white middle-class female students. In the interchange between Roger and Vivian, for example, Roger did not feel threatened in a way that the white middle-class female students, imagining themselves in Roger's shoes, felt that they would be. Roger comes from a working-class background, and I have already established that societal dichotomy between the "polite" and calm middle-class norms of interaction and the "loud" and boisterous working-class norms. Many men are also socialized to more readily disconnect their emotions from the intellectual or public sphere. Thus, students like Roger may be less likely to see impassioned and angry classroom interactions as personal threats the way white middle-class females tend to do. Finally, racial stereotypes have also been sexualized, such that white females have historically more often been projected as innocent victims of black violence, particularly sexual violence. This only intensifies the fear response to African Americans in white women's minds.

Case in Point: Vince versus Susan

To further illustrate this gender difference, I want to contrast two journal entries, one from a white female (Susan) and one from a white male (Vince), both of which included emotional statements about Vivian's impact on them. Both were written at the end of the semester, but while Vince's writing reflected excitement and enlightenment, Susan's writing carried resentment, pessimism, and despair. Vince begins by describing himself as a "white male who grew up upper-middle-class in a predominantly white neighborhood" who, before taking this class, was "so naive" and did not realize until now that "this is not a perfect world." He writes:

> Vivian's stories and struggles in particular had a strong impact on me. Hearing what a black lesbian woman had to go through in this world really made me think. Some of the things she said shocked and amazed me. For example . . . she shared with us that she had to go around and collect pens and paper for school and how other people didn't really help her because of the way she is.

On the last day of class, I had the students make any closing statements they desired, and part of Vivian's remarks pertained to Vince. Vivian told the class she knows a lot of people in class did not like her, but she does not change herself just to be liked, and she just hoped she had some kind of impact on people so that when we meet someone like her again we will realize she is also human just like them. She stated what many of my students of color have told me over the years: white students who try to act like allies while in the classroom will often walk right by their classmates of color on campus and not speak. Yet Vivian was very moved when she passed by Vince on campus one day and he looked her in the eye and said, "What's up, Vivian?" Thus, clearly Vince's transformation was not just made up on paper for my benefit, for he was walking the walk beyond the classroom doors. Furthermore, Vivian sensed that not everyone in the class felt the same way, particularly members of the white female majority of the class.

Susan's sentiments represent some of that animosity that Vivian was sensing. Like Vince, she also identifies herself as previously naive: "Up until I took your class I tried to pretend like it [racism] was something that happened only in extreme ways (like the Rodney King situation ten years ago) but now I understand that it is part of everyday life." Yet she progressed to a point at which people of color's anger about racism was perceived as personal prejudice toward her as a white person: "I think the hardest thing about this class is to know that I am hated by people because of the color of my skin." Susan felt hated by Vivian, and, like another white student I mentioned earlier, felt affronted that blacks would seem less than appreciative toward whites who genuinely wanted to help: "Don't get me wrong, I understand the anger of the African American students in our class, and I know that they are 100 percent justified, but the majority of the white people would not have been in that class if we weren't concerned with educating ourselves and making changes." Unlike Vince's uplifting sentiments about the course, Susan ended this way:

> In closing I have to say that I am very disappointed in myself, because I let this class get to me so much that I am now horribly cynical about the African American race. Perhaps this is a step in the process, but I am scared of the feelings I am having. I don't want to feel this way.

As many teachers of race relations courses know, it is very typical for students to enter optimistically, and by midcourse reach a breaking point or plateau of sorts where they may be ready to give up or shut down. I will never forget the first time I taught a course about racism, and a student (another white female) wrote in her journal that she was sick of talking about race, and asked why we had to talk about race so much. (Imagine a chemistry student stopping mid-semester to exasperatingly question why we are still talking about chemistry!) Those of us who teach race relations and other courses on oppression know that our task is both an intellectual and emotional one, and we are often both educator and therapist throughout the semester. Yet I read Susan's journal entry with sadness that her plateau hit at the end of the semester rather than the middle, because I knew our time together was drawing to a close. We made plans to meet after the semester was over, however, so I could give her some additional readings to help her work through what she insightfully observed as "a step in the process" toward an antiracist identity.

Beverly Daniel Tatum has written extensively on stages of racial identity development, including how they affect students' digestion of oppression-related course material. When discussing white students, she points out that whites may begin as naive (the Contact stage), but then their naiveté is broken as they acquire information about inequality. Eventually during this acquisition process they may reach that breaking point, similar to Susan's mentioned earlier, which Tatum identifies as the shift from Disintegration to Reintegration. Disintegration is when that "perfect world" that Vince described gets challenged in their minds, and Reintegration is the process by which one incorporates that new information into one's current worldview. This can trigger several different emotional reactions, but unfortunately a more typical one is Susan's, where guilt is deflected back onto the "other" in a blame-the-victim ideology. "The guilt and anxiety associated with Disintegration may be redirected in the form of fear and anger directed toward people of color (particularly Blacks) who are now blamed as the source of discomfort" (Tatum 1992, p. 15). I planned to share Tatum's work with Susan, to reassure her that the difficulty with which she was learning about racism was not uncommon, and that there were several more antiracist ways of being white that would be positive and proactive if she could move beyond this "step."

As with all stage theories, progression is seldom linear, so it is no anomaly that Vince moved immediately to thinking about ways to solve racism without blaming blacks while Susan did not. What is instructive about the difference between the way Vince and Susan interpreted Vivian's passionate classroom participation is that each of their social locations determined how and what they would learn from the same person. When Vivian spoke out in class, she brought *experiential evidence* by voicing examples of discrimination, but she also brought the *emotion* that came with experiencing it. If Vivian had simply listed in a monotone voice her evidence, Susan and other white females in the class probably would not have felt threatened by her nor developed animosity toward her. Yet by the same token, neither would students like Vince have been so passionately moved by her examples. While our course was filled with both written and oral testimonies about discrimination, it was Vivian that impacted Vince's (and others') learning experience the most. So while a classroom that validates multiple modes of expression is not easy or safe, and requires interventions that the average professor may not be willing to take the time to do, it yields some amazingly powerful personal transformations that are seldom seen under other approaches.

Interventions

Although I have already described certain interventions I did with individual students to help move them through their emotional reactions, this particular semester's situation of a sizable group influencing each other with their resistance seemed to call for a more large-scale response. I did not want half the class to shut down without knowing alternative ways of moving through their discomfort. I decided to focus the next class discussion on anger as an appropriate response to oppression. This seemed particularly important to me in light of the white women's after-class response, which so clearly assumed Vivian had breached class etiquette and expected me to "breathe order" back into the room. I began by asking them to read silently a short piece by Paul Kivel entitled "Thank You for Being Angry" (Kivel 1995). Here is an excerpt from that essay:

> Relationships between people of color and whites often begin as friendly and polite. . . . But then the person of color gets angry. Perhaps they are angry about something we do or say. Perhaps they are angry about a comment or action about someone else, or about racism in general. . . . For a person of color, this may be a time of hope that the relationship can become more intimate and honest. The anger may be an attempt to test the depth and possibilities of the friendship. They may be open about their feelings, to see how safe we are, hoping that we will not desert them. Or the anger may be a more assertive attempt to break through our complacency to address some core assumptions, beliefs or actions. Many white people have been taught to see anger and conflict as a sign of failure. They may instead be signs that we're becoming more honest, dealing with the real differences and problems in our lives. . . . We could say, "Thank you for pointing out the racism because I want to know when it is occurring." Or, "I appreciate your honesty. Let's see what we can do about this situation." More likely we get scared and disappear, or become defensive and counterattack. In any case, we don't focus on the root of the problem, and the racism goes unattended.

After focusing the class on the usefulness of anger to alert us to the seriousness of oppression, I wanted to direct us to "the root of the problem." Clearly, the white women gathered after class were not discussing the manifestations of racism in the public school system, which is what Roger and Vivian's exchange was all about. What could have been a powerful learning experience about what still needs to be done to make schools multicultural, from both a teacher and parent perspective, was reduced to a critique of personal conversation styles and manners of a fellow classmate. So the subsequent class exercise I initiated asked the class to brainstorm things they learned from the last class discussion about racism and stereotypes, on the part of teachers and schools, which I recorded on the board. In other words, I wanted them to focus on the *substance* of the material that the passionate discussion provided us with, rather than just fixating on personality styles of the speakers. Because everything was so fresh, I was still immersed in some ways in the students' personal-level interpretation of the interchange—it still seemed like an individual difference in communication styles, and I didn't want to pick apart their personalities personally in front of the class. It wasn't until I had some time and space from the situation that I was able to process the cultural differences in communication that clearly resulted from Roger and Vivian's different social locations.

Another intervention occurred near the end of the semester, initiated by one of the students. As part of the learning community philosophy, I require each student to lead one day of class discussion, and Tracy, an African American student, guided us through a reading by a black feminist writer on issues of sexism within the black liberation movement. She broke the class up into race- and gender-specific groups—one for white men, one for white women, one for black men, and one for black women. Each group was asked to consider a different statement made by the author, and the most contentious statement became the one assigned to the white women. It was a critique of black men who fear the assertiveness of their black sisters, preferring relationships with white women with low self-esteem, who more willingly submit to being controlled by men. The white women in the group reacted angrily to the generalization that white women were passive, desired being controlled, and that those who sought interracial relationships did so from a place of low self-esteem. Some white women who had remained relatively quiet for the duration of the semester spoke out passionately against being stereotyped in this way. Although perhaps initially some of the white women felt attacked yet again by African Americans, Tracy skillfully pointed out that now maybe the white students in the class understood how it felt to be stereotyped. She felt that hearing them express their anger was a positive experience for our learning community in that perhaps it could be a point of solidarity between the blacks and the whites in the class.

Both Tracy's and my interventions affirmed that anger indeed is appropriate in the classroom, and in fact is a logical response to hearing stereotypes and misinformation about one's group. It serves to educate us about how deeply painful such stereotypes are. Tracy's intervention also came from a personal place of being tired of being seen as the angry black with a chip on her shoulder by all the whites in the room. She wanted her white classmates to connect with her common humanity, to demonstrate that anger at injustice was a common human response that they could share. Prior to being on the receiving end of prejudice, it had been easier for the white students to view anger in the classroom as a sign of African American unruliness, but now perhaps they had developed empathy and could move past the walls keeping them from hearing the *substance* of their black classmates' contributions.

Facing Being "Out of Control"

I have yet to see any significant body of writing that addresses how instructors can tap into anger and passion in classrooms exploring oppression-related issues and use it as a catalyst for growth and change. The strategies I described above were situation specific, and were developed with certain personalities and incidents in mind. Yet even though the specifics of the situations might have been unique, some themes are enduring. Each semester there are members of the learning community who, somewhere in mid-semester, view the classroom space as a disaster because it is not harmonious, in some form or another. Including myself as a part of this learning community, it is always a point of growth for me to remember that once this discomfort occurs, it means I am doing my job because we are finally getting deeply to the heart of the issues. Conventional pedagogical models that teach us to "maintain control and order" do not allow us to conceptualize success as a somewhat unsettled classroom.

Cutting even deeper growing pains is the realization that, as a part of the learning community, even I am not exempt from those feelings of discomfort. As a white instructor, I have been personally and publicly challenged by students of color. In one class, we were doing a privilege exercise in which all students begin at the same starting point, but are asked to take a step forward for each "privilege" (read from Peggy McIntosh's list of white privileges) that they believe they can count on, and the class typically ends up with darker-complexioned students toward the back and lighter-complexioned students toward the front. Keesha, an African American student, got more and more visibly dissatisfied with how the exercise was progressing, until she eventually stormed out of class. What was especially hurtful to me is that she ignored my pleas not to leave, and I had initial worries that my authority in the classroom had been undermined.

I telephoned Keesha after class, and she agreed to come into my office and meet with me before the next class. During our meeting, I discovered that Keesha left class out of frustration with the white students who refused to step forward when a white privilege was read aloud because they did not think it applied to them. Because we were already several weeks into the semester, Keesha's initial optimism about white students being able to understand oppression had been eroded, for she could not understand after all we had read and discussed why many whites in the class still did not believe the extent of racism's existence. Not unlike the white students described in previous sections, Keesha had reached a breaking point in the semester where she had begun to give up hope in the idea of racial harmony. I explained to her that, because whites had been taught misinformation all their lives about racism's existence, it was going to take more than a few weeks for them to get it. I also reminded her that everyone had different starting points. To inspire her with hope, I asked her to name any white students in the class she felt were moving toward antiracism, and she could name one or two she viewed as allies. Then I promised her that she would be able to add more names to that list by the end of the semester. Keesha came back to class and was an enthusiastic participator until the end of the semester.

Although my initial internal response to Keesha's leaving class saw her as disruptive and disobedient, I knew that perception was filtered through my own white lenses. I was able to look past my first response and say "thank you for being angry" by making a space for Keesha to tell me where her anger came from, taking my own advice that I would give students about getting to the "root of the matter" rather than stigmatizing personalities.

I would be challenged even more personally to take my own advice later in that same course when two different students of color "called me out" for having overlooked them before and/or after class when they were waiting to talk to me among other white students. We were discussing examples of how whites often do not even realize when they are discriminating (based on a discussion of Feagin 2000) and before I knew it, my own behavior was being scrutinized by the students. It was so easy to sit there in class and criticize all the discriminatory whites that Feagin cited in his book, yet when I became the class's next example of the unintentional discriminator, I felt my whole identity as a white antiracist called into question. My internal reaction was the typical white stance of defensiveness. There must have been some logical explanation for why I did not see them—were they standing farther back, behind someone or something else that obstructed my view? Here I was the "authority" on racial discrimination, as the course instructor, and I felt all the mainstream pedagogical pangs of my authority somehow being threatened and stripped away. Yet I managed to remind myself I was another member of the learning community, and asked myself as I would any other student to hear and validate the students' perception. My response was to tell the class this was another excellent example of how well-intentioned people may not realize how their behavior is being perceived, and that we must be ever-vigilant and mindful of falling into patterns of injustice that require great effort to struggle against.

Although initially mortified by this incident, wise colleagues pointed out to me that I had successfully created a space where students felt comfortable sharing these perceptions, that they would not have done so if they did not think I would hear them. Furthermore, although one of the two students of color who called me out that day dropped out because of deaths in the family and other health issues, the other student eventually became quite drawn to me. She told me she gained a great amount of respect for me that day because of my honesty. She brought me a pie for Thanksgiving, gave me a beautiful holiday gift, and opted to do an independent research project with me the following semester. In the first moments of that class discussion, I could hear that common white female response inside of me, not unlike that of my students: "Oh my gosh, she hates me, she thinks I'm a racist!" It took all the strength I could summons to hear the *substance* of their comments, to understand how much they hurt when their common humanity was ignored, and to affirm their perceptions of me as yet another part of that system we had been analyzing all semester.

I raise these examples to demonstrate that affirming passion and emotional expression in the classroom is not easy. It is scary and unsettling not only for students, but for instructors as well. In intervening to make contentious experiences catalysts for growth and change, one must be ever mindful of the race, gender, and class dynamics that impact both how emotions are expressed and how those emotional expressions are perceived. An instructor of color seeking to affirm emotion and passion in a learning community may confront similar issues, but they are likely to manifest themselves in different ways than I have described here. For example, an African American instructor may face the additional stigma of being perceived by the white students as a co-conspirator with "black rage." Thus, while the white students expect to me to restore order, and write openly in journals about antiblack stereotypes, an instructor of color may not experience that same level of frankness from their white students. Conversely, students of color might expect automatic solidarity and support from an instructor of color, and feel hurt and betrayed if such comfort does not immediately come to pass. Gender and class differences, in both instructor and student composition, will undoubtedly produce more variability in outcomes and possibilities of such an approach. But if one is committed to the hard work necessary for incorporating emotions into classrooms where racism/sexism/classism are studied, the rewards are tremendous. The cards and gifts from students who feel my courses have changed their lives, and have inspired them to dedicate their lives to social change, in just three short years have filled my office shelves. Midsemester, one can always find me fretting that the second civil war has erupted in my classroom, and struggling to come up with effective interventions, on both individual and group levels. But just as I assure the students, I attempt to assure myself that by the end it will all be worth it. If we all "calmed down," our collective learning about oppression would likely never take place.

References

Ani, Marimba. (1994). *Yurugu: An African-centered critique of European cultural thought and behavior*. Trenton, NJ: Africa World Press.

Feagin, Joe R. (2000). *Racist America: Roots, current realities, and future reparations*. New York: Routledge.

hooks, bell. (1994). *Teaching to transgress: Education as the practice of freedom*. New York: Routledge.

hooks, bell. (1995). *Killing rage: Ending racism*. New York: Henry Holt.

Kivel, Paul. (1995). *Uprooting racism: How white people can work for racial justice*. Philadelphia: New Society Publishers.

O'Brien, Eileen. (2001). *Whites confront racism: Antiracists and their paths to action*. Boulder, CO: Rowman and Littlefield.

Tatum, Beverly Daniel. (1992). Talking about Race, Learning about Racism: The Application of Racial Identity Development Theory in the Classroom. *Review, 62*, 1–24.

4

Oreos and Bananas:
Conversations on Whiteness

Elena Featherston and Jean Ishibashi

We acknowledge our differences, as African American and Asian American community educators. We identify as women of color who have engaged in public and private discourse around the subjects of colorism and cross-racial hostility and alliances. We participate and identify as parents, grandparents, cross-cultural community educators, and scholars/writers. We hope to address the manifestations of whiteness in those roles. The notion of white as superior and the standard for what is "normal," and the ways in which education as a cultural/political institution and its satellites—individual schools and classrooms—fulfill the meaning of that notion is such a manifestation

*   *   *   *

ISH: "Whiteness" conjures up the "Banana" metaphor for Asians who are stereotyped as yellow on the outside and white on the inside. This issue of colorism and its meaning in my life as a student, worker, and parent has changed over the years. This change in meaning accompanied identity transformation throughout my life as an activist educator, community and labor organizer, and parent of a multiracial child.

My first awareness of the notion of whiteness was while I identified as a community educator and activist. I worked with an organization, the American Friends Service Committee (AFSC), affiliated with the Quakers, or The Religious Society of Friends, who I now believe in part hired me because they had internalized stereotypes of Asian Americans as a "model minority." However, after almost a decade of working with them, I realized that I had internalized a "model majority" stereotype of them as the "best white people" as well. I had wanted to work with AFSC because they were reputed to be committed to: (1) "speaking truth to power," (2) respecting the "uniqueness" of every person, and (3) nonviolence, all stereotypes that were busted for me during the course of my tenure with them. The pedestal on which I had placed them originally was shattered after a decade of joint work. I realized I had committed the same crime/violation of their humanity that they had committed of mine; albeit, the ramifications were decidedly different. Believing they could do no wrong, I was constantly in culture shock as daily incidents of their privilege and dysconsciousness manifested themselves (King 1991). As one of their birthright daughters explained, "[They] came to this country to do good, and they did very well." The lesson I learned from this experience was that my internalized notions/stereotypes of "the best white people" disrespected their human frailties and, therefore, their humanity. I realized that having to live up to some stereotypical image of the "good" and "nonviolent" person has resulted in some of the higher incidents of domestic violence in the country (Brutz 1986). So what is whiteness?

ELENA: Alice Walker says something similar, but with a slightly different emphasis in the film *Visions of the Spirit* (Featherston 1989). She says that whiteness is a burden to white people, who can "look like anything, but they are 'perfect' because they are white." Imagine internalizing the concept of your own perfection, your intrinsic "rightness," and having to struggle daily with the reality of your human imperfections. Living your life knowing that you don't measure up to the myth of whiteness revered by the culture. Imagine the energy it takes not to know how much of your presumed "perfection" is dependent upon how one measures up against the *im*perfections of those deemed "less than." Everyone begins to define himself or herself in relationship to what they are. Color, being the easiest of the many markers of difference to discern, is imbued with assumptions of distinct power, privilege, and lack thereof. These assumptions, values, and beliefs are translated into the policies and procedures of our social institutions, like education, as fundamental truths. Color becomes our primary marker and begins to define us all in very subtle ways. This includes "white" people and definitions of whiteness itself.

ISH: I feel that the two color markers of a banana as "physical visibles" (Robinson 2000), yellow and white, have been imbued with meanings by mainstream and dominant paradigms that supersede cross-cultural meanings of energy and spirit. White and yellow have significance that resists dominant notions of white as "pure" and yellow as "cowardly or jaundiced." And as we are conducting this dialogue about colors and their meanings in written and standard English without the intonations and rhythms of our cross-cultural ancestries and cultures (sometimes referred to as "broken, pidgin, and non-fluent" English), we have already acknowledged a "normalcy"—the assumed and implicit superiority of English, part of the whiteness paradigm, which I had been trained to believe.

ELENA: I don't know that as a subjugated person in resistance that I acknowledge English as superior. My mother tongue(s) stolen generations before my birth was replaced through violence with this language of dominance. Sadly, I know it best.

My challenge is to find and maintain an authentic voice that expresses the multiple-layered reality of my experience with whiteness both in the larger culture certainly, but also personally and at the micro-level in classrooms—as student, as educator, as parent, as interloper. Classrooms are after all only one of many sites of struggle—places where whiteness (white supremacy) manifests in socially sanctioned ways that many consider not just normal and superior, but moral.

The trickiest piece for me is to acknowledge and address my own internalized whiteness (that sits side by side with my internalized oppression) as a by-product of the *mis*education and cultural "terrorism" embedded in the Institution of Education. My desire to speak plainly and simply about the ways coercive training masquerading as education sustains oppression is in direct conflict with notions I've absorbed about how academic exchanges take place. The crippling need to language the most straightforward concepts in unnecessarily obtuse ways in order to substantiate one's prerogative to have an opinion. White cultural norms value intellect over emotion and the formally educated over the informally educated. Ideas must be calmly declared polysyllabically with veiled references to noteworthy scholars (preferably white) who have plowed the now infertile ground before you. Independent thought is deemed without value, critique rooted in cultural experience is suspect if it fails to validate the notional "norm."[1] My internalized whiteness reflects this value and must often be consciously interrupted. I must separate my traditional ways from my learned Eurocentric (white) and conventional ones.

ISH: Yes, the value of "intellect over emotions" permeates educational pedagogy in formal institutions of learning. Emotions and feelings are not recognized in the classroom and, therefore, are devalued and repressed.

When I was once asked what I was feeling, I could not respond because I had internalized this "white" (including patriarchical) concept of intelligence as devoid of any emotional knowledge, including stereotypes of Asians as stoic and inscrutable. When we recognize our own emotional knowledge, we can begin to respect the emotional knowledge that students bring to the educational context. We may need help in recognizing different forms of emotional knowledge. Therein lies the beauty of diverse students, parents, and community members as cross-cultural teachers who may offer alternatives to values constructed in an unconscious "whiteness" paradigm.

ELENA: Indeed. People who are targeted by oppression as "less than" and "othered" in American culture because of their group memberships (race, gender, age, class, first language, sexual/affectional orientation, etc.) and those people who are not targeted (privileged) and are presumed to be "better than" have an interesting relationship to feelings. There is a correlation between groups that are seen as having, acknowledging, and honoring feelings and the dominant cultural assumption of inferiority. It harks back to Plato's dualistic assertion that humans were either thinking *or* feeling beings as he assigned superiority to those who "controlled" their feelings by thinking. For instance, if we use gender as the oppression variable, women are presumed to be in touch with their feelings. Women feel, men think. Women are deemed to be inferior—weaker, hysterical, at the mercy of our hormones, and so on. Men, the thinkers—strong, intellectual, big picture kinda folk—are superior. Play with the pattern using race or class as the variable and see how well it works. People of color "feel, are emotional"; white people are thinkers. The middle class is educated and thinks, the working class is less well educated and presumed not to think as well, making them by definition more emotional. This inability to embrace humans as thinking *and* feeling beings, this splitting off of ourselves is one of the many ways we are prepared from childhood to accept and perpetuate oppression.

ISH: Yes. The whole idea of scientific objectivism critiqued by Marimba Ani in her groundbreaking work, *Yurugu* (1994), subordinated women's culture such as midwifery and witchcraft during a period of intense "power over" patriarchical forces rather than "power with" dynamics. Included in this hierarchical paradigm is the subordination of people of color as heathens and savages. And superior and inferior, the dualistic thinking of what is good and what is bad (discussed by Reverend Daniel Buford in his People's Institute workshops) based on color, reified the normalcy of "whiteness" (Berger & Luchman 1967).

ELENA: Educators, no matter how well trained or how "culturally appropriate" their texts and collaterals, must reflect on the ways whiteness informs their classroom practices. Teachers who are not truly self-reflective, teachers who fail to challenge their own cultural notions, assumptions, and biases will recreate oppressive models; this is not necessarily intentional. It is the inexorable influence of white supremacy in an inherently racist culture, and it can be extremely subtle. Modern expressions of all oppression including whiteness are often unintentional. In order to justify a nation built on the land of one people of color (indigenous peoples, people denied their land base our cut off from it by interlopers with tribal designations too numerous to name) with the labor of other peoples of color (African, Asian, Latino/Chicano) the value of whiteness and its core belief systems must be normalized in every imaginable way and we (citizen, educator, student) must be carefully taught *not* to recognize them.

The implicit and explicit message to people of color in most educational settings is that few of us can excel while white students are expected to do well. And should a white student fail to meet that expectation his/her whiteness is not presumed to be a contributing factor in the failure. This message is insidious and, often subtle. In the fourth grade my teacher accused me of plagiarism and gave me an F+ on a report. The fact that I had no idea what plagiarism meant was to her incontrovertible "proof" that I could not have written my paper. A chilling and confusing assessment of my abilities. I could not understand what was happening. My paper was better than many of those that hung on the walls—an envied place of honor in a competitive learning model. It took many years to decipher what had occurred. My error was exceeding her expectations, challenging her assumptions about who I was, revealing a competence that she had not thought I could possess. Her worldview was shaken by my home values and the knowledge that was my environment was not supposed to support me in her classroom. I had to have done *something* wrong because she was an informed and "perfect" expert on people who looked like me. Was it her *intention* to be racist? Perhaps not, and that did little to mitigate the racist impact of her behavior.

ISH: My daughter faced the same tracking in the 1990s. Examining this reproduction of subordination as "whiteness" four decades later helps name the hierarchical relationship (white supremacy) and liberates us from the internalized attitude of "that's just the way things are."

Whiteness at a high school that is predominantly Asian as a parent of a multiracial child was revealing. My daughter is Mexican and Japanese American. Her Asian science teacher singled her out as someone who would "get pregnant and drop out of school." Her white counselor told us that she would not be able to get into any four-year university because "she's so attractive, and that she must have many boyfriends." My daughter did not get pregnant and drop out. My daughter applied to four University of California campuses and was admitted to each of them. My daughter told me that she had the reputation of contesting the teachers at the high school and felt that she didn't get dates because other students, particularly male students, were either afraid of her or thought that she was weird. What was operating here in regards to whiteness? The collusion among primarily Asian and white students, faculty, and families of the school on the basis of who was a good student was based again on the internalization of white and Asian "model minority" and "model majority" stereotypes. Those who didn't fit those stereotypes had obstacles placed on their path, as did my daughter.

ELENA: A colleague shared the story of a young man who started his high school career at the same school your daughter attended. Teachers and students alike harassed him. His greatest sin was being black and *very* bright. His situation was further complicated by an unwillingness to be silent in the face of his oppression. He was hounded out of school, and moved through a number of others before leaving the school district. He, too, was a victim of whiteness, though his tormentors were Asian and Asian American. I often wonder what role colorism played in his experience. What part of the treatment he received could be traced to his being dark and not lighter complexioned?

My multiracial daughter and granddaughters are afforded light skin and class privilege in school environments. Teachers often respond to children of color based on their class, ethnic origins, or skin color juxtaposed to/against their own. Educators rarely directly address the role of classism and colorism in the classroom setting and their connection to notions of "whiteness." My daughter and grandchildren, favored by teachers and the school hierarchy, often have problems with their darker-complexioned black peers. The teacher's treatment of them (according them some of the courtesy white students receive) is seen as *unfairly* preferential because darker students are so insidiously and subtly "othered."

My eldest granddaughter acknowledges that she is routinely judged less harshly than her darker classmates, and she recognizes the ways her instructors unconsciously push her to "choose sides," to collude with "the rightness of whiteness."

She can also recognize and name whiteness as overvalued when she is *not* heard if she speaks in slang or black Folk English—the former is the language of her peers, the latter the language of most of her black ancestors for centuries in the United States. She has noted teachers either ignoring her entirely or tending to more rigorously critique her answers if she *chooses* to express herself using either of these communication styles, or native tongues. If she code-switches and speaks so-called standard English she is recognized, taken seriously, and praised for the thoughtfulness of her answers. What is the message about whiteness inherent in the way teachers listen? How do choices by teachers validate and normalize the linguistic oppression of people for whom English is either not the expression of choice, not the home language, or is a second language? What value is transmitted when students are taught that *standard* English—often the language of oppressors—has greater value than home languages that are more evocative, precise, and meaningful to them? It says standard English is superior and it says to students that they must choose to split off from some aspect of their authentic self-expression to be acceptable to their instructors.

ISH: I recall how I received many comments regarding how well I speak English. The assumption being that I'm supposed to speak "broken English" as a "foreigner," a stereotype of Asian Americans in this country. The whiteness operating here is: in order to be normal, good, right (on top of the food chain), you must speak standard English. Another whiteness value is also operating here: normal people only speak standard English. Therefore, to be able to code-switch acknowledges a cultural literacy that in this economic transnational context means cultural capital, an ability to "penetrate" various settings, contexts, cultures, countries for your benefit. This is recognized as a power to "get over" in different contexts. That begs the question: When do we code-switch for solidarity? Does this act benefit an immediate short-term vision or the long-term vision for seven generations?

In the exit interviews of Japanese Americans leaving the concentration camps, questions regarding with whom we'd associate or what language we'd speak when we left, my family internalized the "right" answers, which were: we would not associate with other Japanese and would not speak the Japanese language. (Weglyn 1978) The short-term gain was to "get outta prison."

This form of social control and its extreme, cultural genocide, particularly among Native Americans, is another form of whiteness. The English Only campaigns, extolling the virtues of sameness and color-blindness based in the mainstream paradigm of whiteness as normal, is one of the latest attempts to reproduce a set of hierarchical values that have privileged some at the expense of others.

ELENA: I like the idea of code switching for solidarity, it places us inside a circle of relatedness that both empowers and educates (in the truest sense of the word) those willing to participate *with* others to impart information, epistemologies, and ways of being as valued coinage of culture, as meaningful knowledge. It is an opposing site of interaction and relationship to the get outta jail, outta poverty, outta being othered that you named. One makes us stronger and aware of who we are and how we are different yet related to others; the other insists that there is something intrinsically wrong with "how you be" in the world that must change. The sustaining mantras of oppression are "scarcity," "not enough," and "not good enough."

This idea of interrogating whiteness in the classroom is so important because we all need to understand how it operates at the personal, interpersonal, institutional, and cultural levels. Standard English is, even for many of us born in the United States, a language of conquest and dominion. When we say *standard,* if we mean standard as in "everyday," "common," "typical," "accepted," "normal," "average," "usual," "ordinary," how might that support and affirm the notion of conquest, competition, and comparison as normal and necessary precisely *because* in a culture where English is standard it is presumed that there is "not enough"? Not enough resources, not enough time, not enough information, not enough attention, not enough respect, not enough anything. And, if those of us who accept and live inside "not enough" want to get more we must conform our thinking and being to the basic premise of conquest and control by standardizing speech and through it thought patterns. There are things that can be said in Black Folk English, in Spanish, in Japanese, in Wolof, in Dineh that *cannot* be said in standard English; expressions of our unique humanities, multiple, layered, and complex are possible. We can talk back to power from a place of authenticity that exists outside the notion of whiteness. What does it mean to think in and speak languages that exist outside the dominion of English? How does what is standard about English define what can and cannot be said because of the assumptions, beliefs, and values inherent in the language that frame our dialogue? Speaking back to power often means having or acquiring the ability to twist the standards of English usage to say something the language was designed to silence. It is through strengthening a student's ability to see and think from different perspectives that educators can open the conversation about how we interact at the institutional and cultural levels around difference.

ISH: In most teacher education "training" courses we are not taught to think about differences and the inherent power relations involved with what is not considered "normal," or we're taught to distort differences by "assimilating" into a "melting pot" theory of what is a normal "American": white, male, straight, rich, Christian, nuclear family structure, standard English-speaking, and able. We are taught to describe, compare, and compete with one another to attain this value/ideal of "whiteness." Our standardized tests reflect these values. Our curricula reproduce these perspectives.

ELENA: Most students with membership in target groups learn that their experience is not recognized as important;[2] education takes place in environments where the politics of ageism, heterosexism, classism, and so on are essential components of the pedagogy. Teachers teach and deny that their teaching is political.

Despite this knowledge my internalized whiteness led me to trust that the educational system could work for my child if she were removed from the public school system. Public school we were told, and I was willing to believe, is the site of educational mediocrity, the location of inadequacy. I accepted the notion that equity was available in expensive spaces and chose an expensive Montessori high school for her. Surely, the best schools money could buy would work to meet the needs of my child. A lovely fantasy.

In truth she struggled with the jibes of students who wanted to exoticize her or to make her understand her place. Whiteness manifested itself in assessments of both race and class in this elite little setting. Her downfall was the result of my failure to adequately equip her for the "real" world. Just entering her teens, she didn't understand the serious social stigma attached to homosexuality in her school setting and the larger culture. She made the mistake of asking a fellow student if he was gay. For her it was an informational question; our extended family circle included numbers of gay and lesbian friends and colleagues. For her it was not a big deal.

The boy she unintentionally *targeted* understood the consequences of being different in a culture that controls, modifies, or destroys difference; he responded by switching the discussion and shifting attention from sexuality to race. Making her the target. Despite her intention the impact of her behavior was to make him and ultimately herself vulnerable to social attack.

The Montessori teachers were unprepared to use the incident as text for teaching about interlocking oppression. In fact, they made matters worse. Students, "punished" when caught in overt acts of racial harassment, become covert, subtle, and cruel. It was difficult for the white, upper-middle-class headmistress to address the intersections of classism, heterosexism, and racism. She was incapable of meaningful dialogue even after I named them; the question of homophobia she never acknowledged having heard. She refused to address it even inadequately; she took it out of existence as if it had never been said.

Even when parents and/or students are smart enough to challenge whiteness, there is an unnamed conspiracy to silence them. Students actually get detentions for asking the "wrong" questions. One high school teacher unable to answer several questions asked during the course of a discussion of *Things Fall Apart* demanded that a student not question her any more. The child's raised hand was ignored throughout the remainder of the discussion. When placed into study groups the student raised her questions with peers. The teacher overhearing the exchange gave her a detention.

To her credit the teacher called to share her perspective with the child's parent. Interestingly, the parent, also an educator, was able to help tease out the real motives driving the choice to impose a detention. Some of the factors that surfaced were: (1) the teacher not feeling that she had control (a value of whiteness) of her classroom, (2) as her difficulty answering students' questions escalated and students grew restive, she became punitive to regain control because she was frustrated (becoming emotional is not valued), (3) the inquisitive child singled out for punish was an unfortunate casualty of the teacher's discomfort with "not knowing" how to address questions outside her experience and her refusal to relinquish "control" and work with what was coming up in the room. Not included in the teacher's explanation of the problem was any reference to an ill-informed comment she made about African life and culture, as she endeavored to *teach Things Fall Apart*. A comment that several students claimed prompted the pandemonium (emotional expression, which needed to be controlled) in the first place.

She exhibited an inability to be self-reflective about her own whiteness and the cultural biases inherent in her conscious, dysconscious, and unconscious self-definition.

ISH: As teachers we are not taught to value "inquiry" or thinking "outside the box." As a result of a myriad of factors including the "warehousing" of students, the "one-size-fits-all" pedagogy, and curriculum including testing that devalues difference, teachers rarely make a space in their practice to encourage curiosity and inquiry constructed by cross-cultural perspectives and difference. The only questions that are understood, recognized, and valued are constructed from standards of whiteness we have all internalized. As teachers and parents we reproduce the value of "control over" our students and children, another modeling of hierarchical relationships. Please don't question authority figures, especially when the authorities don't understand questions constructed from alternative paradigms of different values. How can we model alternatives to unconscious or internalized standards of "whiteness" for our students and children? Again, I believe learning from our students, their families, and communities will help us recognize those values and perspectives that we have repressed because we were taught to internalize "whiteness" as the standard bearer of what is "good" in our worlds.

ELENA: Reminds me of a ninth grade teacher in a class I observed. Students were assigned a thirty-minute free-write from which the teacher randomly selected pieces for an "anonymous" reading. Two of the four selections read aloud by the teacher were subjected to a substantial and obvious verbal edit designed to make them conform to some idea of what was acceptable. Students *heard* what was happening and greeted each oral edit with groans and laughter. They were cautioned to modify their behavior. The teacher didn't challenge her own, or see the students' response as a red flag or opening for learning—hers and theirs. Young people, who are not eager about the prospect of written assignment to begin with, probably don't enjoy having an unfinished work subjected to a public read and rewrite. Interestingly, prior to reading their work, the teacher instructed students to write descriptive adjectives about each piece that *had* to be positive.

What were students to learn from this exercise? There was no hint as to how students might use the assignment to increase their proficiency as writers and interpreters of text. Nor were they offered any about the value of peer critique. Learning that their authentic expression was not only inappropriate but subject to the whim of an authority figure was disempowering.

ISH: As teachers we don't realize that we are teaching our students to respond in writing to their bosses and supervisors (Bowles & Gintis 1997). Just think what transformations would take place in attitudes and motivation if we taught students that their writing can transform unjust and unhealthy working relationships, that our/their words have power?

ELENA: Now you speak to the larger question of silencing the student-citizen's authentic voice. Where is the place for negative criticism in our society and how do teachers pass the skill of constructive critique to their students? It is possible to use seemingly inappropriate material as text for teaching. How do we honor the existing voices and home knowledge of students as they are moved toward an understanding of the dominant cultural norm? Not to be overwhelmed by it (assimilate), but to have the ability to hold both realities, a critical necessity when speaking back to power (acculturate). This transition from one way of languaging to another should not occur without students understanding the process and actively participating in the shift. I am suggesting a process that serves to make students bi- or trilingual, not one meant to silence their first languages. How do we create spaces for growth, change, and new understanding? The answers to these questions are central to challenging whiteness. It is also important to remember that the teacher has as much to learn and unlearn as the students—perhaps more.

Whiteness is a principal obstruction to the mutual transmission of knowledge inside and outside classroom settings. Embedded in the idea of white supremacy is the notion that the power to define rests with/within white culture. All the unwritten rules, presumed truths, and definitions of beauty in the culture and the classroom exalt whiteness. This means that the values of whiteness are prized above others. For instance, competition is valued above cooperation, individual above community. Information about other cultures is often taught as an add-on, not as part of the central framework. The result often means treating complexities that make students and teacher alike uncomfortable with great superficiality. Well-intentioned teachers often mishandle the topics of social justice and racial-cultural difference in ways that create guilt in white students and anger in students of color. The result is often a very predictable backlash.

ISH: Recently, when talking with Virginia R. Harris, quilter, writer, and scholar, I mentioned how I was attempting to introduce the idea of a volume of works edited by Joyce Harjo et al., called *Reinventing the Enemy's Language,* demonstrating how language can be used to benefit all our communities rich in diverse values and alternatives to linearity, commodification/objectification, consumerism, and scarcity. Her response was a quote from Audre Lorde: "[You] can't take down the master's house with the master's tools." She exclaimed that most of us, especially our students, don't even know there is a "master's house," so how are we going to transform our world? Studying "whiteness" as a set of values and ethics that has disrespected people by objectifying and dehumanizing most of the world will go a long way in transforming our relationships, especially in our classrooms.

So what are the alternatives to the restrictive boundaries and lines of "whiteness?" How do I re-cognize my own internalization of "whiteness" and corresponding stereotypes? I tend to reproduce the values and thinking that subordinate rather than embrace difference. When I do this, I disrespect the humanity in others and, therefore, myself.

As a reentry student I experienced culture shock, which eventually became a culture shuffle. After I had raised a family and worked for thirty years, I decided to return to school to take advantage of the exciting inclusive and diverse curriculum that had been hard won by communities whose epistemologies had been subordinated, marginalized, distorted, and/or omitted. I uncovered that, although social and cultural studies in education existed in name, the lens was, with one exception, Eurocentric/white. Again, the ideals of a good education were coded into the values and ethics of the stereotype of the "good" model white person/worker. Little thought or space was given to different values, and if different values outside the mainstream paradigm were studied, they were seen as exotic or unreasonable, impractical, and unrigorous. To my dismay, even Ethnic Studies or Multicultural Studies were shaped by "white" values. What the community had fought for had been "coopted" or "assimilated." For example, Ethnic Studies and Multicultural Education became "melting pots" fueled by the white value of "colorblindness" rather than the embrace of difference. So Ethnic Studies and Multicultural Education attempted to offer an alternative to "whiteness" and reproduced the same values we (communities) wanted to transform—with some notable exceptions, including the work of the late Edward Said.

ELENA: This is especially disheartening if one thinks of critical multicul-turalism as recognizing differences (age, ability, class, color, gender, home language, place of origin, sexual orientation, etc.) with an eye to acknowl-edging, understanding, and utilizing them (Batts 1998) in a pluralistic soci-ety where no culture is dominant. Scholars, educators, and students of color must work to identify internalized whiteness and internalized op-pression to enable us to do vigorous interventions on society's efforts to coopt our ways of being, to assimilate, and thus neutralize the transforma-tive power of our stories, our voices, our realities and to annihilate our spirits.

ISH: How does my ideology affect my pedagogy? How does my under-standing of or concept of whiteness influence how and what I teach? I ad-dress both these questions by applying what I call the four Rs: Re-search, Re-cognize, Re-spect and Re-tell. I hyphenate these concepts and words because I acknowledge the cross-cultural dynamics present in our everyday relations, i.e., different paradigms, points of view, positions, frameworks, and ideologies. I have not walked in another's shoes nor path. By hyphen-ating I re-spect my unique, cross-cultural, and rich identity construction. How I am in and relate with the world make me who I am, cross-culturally.

In turn I try to model this cross-cultural re-spect with others: my col-leagues, students, community, and family members. Being able to see, feel, think, touch, smell, and hear those epistemological differences in my life is a challenge for me. To uncover "whiteness" in my life and its global im-pact, I ask myself and my students to conduct re-search by studying our own oral histories, herstories, and ourstories. I ask us to look at different perspectives, values, epistemologies, and paradigms within our own stories. This means that as a teacher facilitator I provide resources such as audio-visual/multimedia aids as well as community resource people who offer alternative cross-cultural values and frameworks. In addition, I frame the oral his/herstory process as a participatory action research project where academic research hierarchies embedded in "whiteness" are dismantled and transformed.

By naming multiple frameworks, dominant and alternative, in a pro-ject that is mutually beneficial to all the participants, not just the re-searcher per se, the value of either/or is transformed to both/and. I ask that students look for and name the controlling forces of the mainstream and dominant frameworks that are based on hierarchies and dualities of what and who is good/bad, superior/inferior, and significant/insignificant.

For many students these influential values have not been named or questioned. They are just considered the norm, the standard by which we assess our acceptability in the larger world and/or who we are or desire to be (assimilation). Participatory action research engaged in oral discourse and tradition requires that we interrogate the social constructions of race, gender, class, family structure, age, generation, abilities, language, religion/spirituality; we re-cognize who is on the bottom and who has culture capital, power, and privilege. I follow up this naming with guest presenters who provide cross-cultural alternative values, perspectives, and frameworks. For example, cultural values of shared power and partnerships constructed by embracing and re-specting differences are re-searched and re-cognized as an alternative to hierarchies based on assumptions of color and "power-over" isms.

We re-cognize that in the acquisition of cultural capital some of these groupings are more readily accessed than others, language, for example. Changing one's race, skin color, or physical visibles may be the least accessible in the process of assimilating or melting into the white concept of "colorblindness." In order to gain culture capital in a whiteness framework (of transnational global imperialism: capitalism, competition, consumerism, and colonialism) accessing language and, thereby, class is easier than trying to change one's skin color, eye shape, or length and shape of one's body. However, in the context of today's surgical reality shows, color, in the form of genetic engineering may be possible. Hair dyes, light-colored contact lenses, whitening creams, hair straighteners may be precursors to more permanent genetic alterations.

ELENA: Group membership is fixed, fluid, or mutable. Race and gender, barring surgical interventions, are more or less fixed and visible. Socioeconomic status, for instance, is fluid; one can obviously change class status through education or acquiring wealth. Mutable categories are those that change depending on the person(s) with whom one interacts. Those things physical, visible, and fixed are the hardest with which to have an experiential relatedness outside of our own reality. We often only get this experience of possibility and connectedness through story and empathy.

If students are taught to recognize and name frameworks and to recognize and name differences, they are being engaged in education as an act of freedom. Most teachers are not educating students to live as liberated, informed citizens in a "free world" or democratic nation state. They are instead *training* future consumers, worker bees, and guileless *mis*information junkies. Students are not being equipped to exercise critical decision-making skills. They are victims of a conspiracy; critical information is being withheld from them. Tools for evaluating and reevaluating authority, defining and challenging power and privilege are not being transmitted. How can students learn to explore whiteness without making one another wrong? How do white students learn to look at racism as part of an oppressive power-over framework that diminishes *all* people, not just people of color? How can students of color learn the power of investigating and owning the locations of privilege that may exist in their lives, e.g., being male, heterosexual, middle-class, English speaking, or able-bodied? Students desperately need to understand the political significance of difference in their lives and in the lives of others. Instead, in being educated students are trained to take tests and to fulfill job functions considered necessary by business conglomerates and multinational corporations. Educators who endeavor to teach from a critical, multicultural, liberatory framework are usually isolated, terrorized, and/or terminated.

Institutions of learning all too often function as middle managers training students to punch a time clock, "make a buck," "get ahead," and remain passive. There is less and less academic authentic engagement that challenges the nature of whiteness as it manifests in the larger culture because teachers are unable to recognize and acknowledge how it permeates their pedagogy and their classrooms. Despite the endless high-stake tests that purport to measure academic achievement, training posing as education is a poor substitute for engaged intelligence and authenticity. It deserves a corporate logo, perhaps "McLearning." It is a difficult pattern to interrupt because the teachers are educated in precisely the same ways. How do you remain responsive to new questions and new patterns within the Institution of Education designed to silence counter narratives to whiteness?

ISH: Using language, naming one's reality/identity(ies) as an example, I ask students to re-search each other's stories in class by listening or hearing and re-telling them, re-cognizing and re-specting difference, or stepping outside the box of normative values. By having the storyteller correct the listener's re-telling of the story the listener is privileged by learning how their own frameworks/paradigms/perspectives influenced their seeing, hearing, feeling, thinking, of another's story. Forming pairs/dyads of difference based, at first, on physical visibles reflects how sighted people first make normative assumptions. Instead of embarrassment at not re-telling another's story correctly, students throughout the semester begin to acknowledge that each comes from a unique perspective constructed by the intersection of the mainstream categories in an ideology that promotes and values the social construction of whiteness as a norm.

Recognizing how our re-telling was constructed and continues to be reshaped by colonialism (neo), capitalism (transglobal), competitiveness, and consumerism is critical to our wholeness as human beings. It can be liberating. Naming those constructions allows us to acknowledge or recognize alternatives to the accepted societal norms. By dancing with named values and knowledge constructions we expand and/or deepen the possibilities to reshape our relationships with the world and our own identities. The "unsaid" or what was not allowed to be said, what was so deeply embedded that it was considered the norm and left unsaid, no longer has "power over" us to limit our capacity to know and act on that knowledge. For example, by understanding why many Americans and their ancestors changed their names or had their names changed (which often comes up in this activity) students begin to see why their ancestral cross-cultural and multicultural differences were marginalized or made invisible. Students recognize that they all have culture(s), which is not the case at the beginning of this process. And they re-cognize that those ancestral cultures may not fit the whiteness paradigm with which they may identify. Oreos, bananas, snowballs, and more metaphors become apparent and the transformation of those identities and their meanings possible.

ELENA: How does this serve as a tool to interrupt interlocking oppression beyond race, color, and ethnicity, which are only the basic building blocks of cultural whiteness? The house itself has many rooms with many closed doors. Teachers who by definition are privileged nontargets in the classroom must begin to understand the ways that they engage in recreating whiteness as a value in their classrooms. Of course, Education as a societal institution is neither designed or intended to allow teachers to interrogate whiteness, power, privilege, and difference in ways that initiate and/or nurture change processes. Society's institutions sustain and maintain the status quo; institutions transmit the values, beliefs, and assumptions of the culture, that is their purpose. Recognizing this, how do you keep the doors you have opened from being slammed shut?

ISH: As a teacher educator I use oral history as a pedagogical instrument to uncover the socioeconomic-political and cultural mainstream paradigm of "whiteness" in our own stories. This re-search and re-cognition from one's own ancestral, family, community, and individual memories does not allow us to keep the doors shut. In fact, this process often "raises the roof" on some of our most deeply held assumptions. Students who are aspiring teachers may learn to re-spect their own diverse and multiple identities and at the same time re-spect those of their students. The larger context in which they see their roles as teachers is made clearer as the doors and windows are opened to what had been excluded from their awareness Light is shed on the legacy of "white" values, norms and standards of acceptance, culture capital, hierarchical relationships, and the possibility of alternative ways of being in the world from their re-searched ancestral knowledge. In most current education classes, as teacher educators, we are not required to examine how the mainstream and dominant paradigms constructed our values. Without this re-search, teaching basic skills such as "reading, 'riting, and 'rithmatic" alone as currently promoted can reinforce the "hidden curricula" (Hollins 1996) of mainstream values and perspectives in our classrooms. Certainly repressive regimes have historically forced us to bury knowledge that does not support those in official power. However, ancestral knowledge provides ways to resist and create liberatory spaces in our lives, even in the most brutal and violent contexts. What other practices can keep the doors from being slammed shut?

ELENA: Good teachers, *educators,* teach students the language of power by embracing home knowledge and language, by honoring lived experience and oppositional perspectives, by not assuming that students are empty vessels waiting to be filled. Good teachers recognize, acknowledge, and name their own fears and biases. In order for students to challenge oppression they too must understand their own cultural roots and place in the world. From this vantage point students can learn to utilize the Eurocentric analytical tools, language, and ways of knowing that allow them to speak back to power powerfully and be heard. It becomes code switching, a skill that comes easier to people who have lived with multiple perspectives and realities. Many "mainstream" teachers lack this experience.

Great educators help all students find the connections between different variables of oppression. This means men have the option to challenge sexism. Workers, the poor, and owning class alike can speak back to classism; people of color can name and reexamine ableism; women can interrogate heterosexism; whites can challenge racism, and we can all question the role of linguistic bigotry. If we hold that "ism" implies systems, just as it does when discussing economic *systems*—capital*ism*, commun*ism* (Wise 2002), then understanding how systems of oppression work is a critical component of a real education. Space must be created for students to make the shift from individuals opposed to being oppressed to citizens opposed to oppression, and this must be done without asking that fragments of the students' authentic selves be amputated or left at home.

This real learning is by its very nature a revolutionary act. Students are not asked to choose sides, to reject original ways, to disrespect aspects of their identities. They are invited to embrace an appreciation for other ways of knowing/being and to weigh it against their own. That is to say, appreciation for their own cultures and the cultures of others are seeds for change.

Conclusion

Whiteness must be recognized and acknowledged as more than color. Whiteness is an interlocking pattern of beliefs, values, feelings, and assumptions; policies, procedures, and laws; behaviors and unwritten rules used to define and underpin a worldview. It is embedded in historic systems of oppression that sustain wealth, power, and privilege.

One of the ways to address the reality of multiple, interlocking oppression is to help students develop a clear understanding of their own stories and a set of definitions, a framework for communication and organizing. Oral history is an essential element in developing an analysis to effectively address all oppressions at the interpersonal and institutional levels of interaction. As they unravel the tapestry woven by whiteness, students acquire a sociological, historical, psychological, and emotional understanding of oppression. Soul wounds (Bratt 2001) caused by learned stereotypes, internalized oppression, and patterns of thought/behavior are called out. Oral history, telling personal stories, helps students understand their place in history and helps them build alliances across categories of difference.

Naming, giving students a vocabulary to express personal experiences and feelings, is the first step in honoring difference, and it creates a space for transformation. Cognoscente (cognizant) of their behavior and internalized, socially constructed beliefs, students can consciously choose other options. Oral histories and herstories uncover relationships to/with ourselves and to/with others; it allows students to recognize that they are a multicultural people.

Notes

1. From notion: 1. a concept or idea; an opinion; a vague view or understanding; 2. an inclination or intention. Notional: adj. hypothetical, imaginary (*Oxford English Dictionary*, Oxford, England and New York: Oxford University Press, 2000)

2. Oppression occurs historically and over time by targeting some groups and people as "less than" and other groups and people as "better than." This occurs such that *statistically* those targeted have less chance for success than those who are not targeted by oppression. That is to say oppression is the statistical difference in access to "life chances" experienced by groups who are targets of oppression. Oppression variables, while interconnected, vary; they can be: gender, religion, age, sexual/affectional orientation, physical or mental ability, socioeconomic class, immigrant status, race, and/or language. Adapted from VISIONS, Boston, MA.

References

Ani, M. (1994). *Yurugu: An African centered critique of European cultural thought and behavior.* New Jersey: Africa World Press.

Batts, V. (1998). *Modern racism: New melodies for the same old tunes.* Cambridge, MA: Episcopal Divinity School.

Berger, P. & Luchman, T. (1967) *The social construction of reality: A treatise in the sociology of knowledge.* New York: Anchor Books.

Bowles, S., & Gintis, H. (1976). *Schooling in capitalist America: Educational reform and the contradictions of economic life.* New York: Basic Books.

Bratt, P. (2001). Filmmaker. In conversation.

Brutz, J. (1986). Religious commitment, peace activism, and marital violence in Quaker families. *Journal of Marriage and the Family, 40*(3), 491–502.

Featherston, E. (Dir.). (1989). *Alice Walker: Visions of the Spirit.* Available from Women Make Movies, New York.

Harris, V. (2002). Storyquilter, writer, lecturer in conversation with Jean Ishibashi. Santa Rosa, CA.

Hollins, E. R. (1996). *Culture in school learning: Revealing the deep meaning.* Mahwah, New Jersey: Lawrence Erlbaum Associates.

hooks, b. (1994). *Teaching to transgress: Education as the practice of freedom.* New York: Routledge.

King, J. E. (1991). Dysconcious racism: Ideology, identity and the miseducation of teachers. *Journal of Negro Education, 60*(2), 9–27.

Lorde, A. (1984). *Sister Outsider: Essays and speeches.* Freedom, CA: Crossing Press.

Robinson, B. (2000). Folklorist. Lecture. San Francisco State University.

Weglyn, M. (1978). *Years of infamy: The untold story of America's concentration camps.* New York: Morrow Quill Paperbacks.

Wise, T. (2002). Writer, antiracist activist; in conversation at La Pena Cultural Center, Berkeley, CA.

PART II

Rethinking Self, Rethinking Whiteness

5

Making Whiteness Visible in the Classroom

Laurie B. Lippin

When Judy Helfand first told me about the call for chapters in her book with coeditor Virginia Lea addressing educators on race and whiteness issues in the classroom, I was immediately excited. Their proposed text was long overdue. There are precious few texts available to educate about classroom experiences of white teachers (my personal favorites, Howard's, *We Can't Teach What We Don't Know*, and Tatum's, *Why Are All the Black Kids Sitting Together in the Cafeteria?*). I had been teaching a popular diversity class, Ethnicity in American Communities, at the University of California, Davis, for many years and was encouraged to share my learning experiences and growth process as a white academic.

Although my experience has been teaching on the college level, I know that the earlier we can incorporate teaching about whiteness, the better. As my initially horrified and angry white students are prone to complain after studying a noncleansed history of the United States, "Why didn't we learn this in high school?" If we have any hope of turning out a new generation that is not "whiteness-challenged," we need to share our lessons learned to provision others for their own journeys of discovery.

As I sat down to write this piece, I was motivated by my own bumpy journey from unconscious racism and ignorance to a place where I can only now begin to see how thoroughly I have been impacted by my whiteness. Frankenberg (1993) is quite correct—only by taking a recursive approach can white people fully appreciate the all-reaching impact of whiteness as our "standpoint," a location from which all is viewed. As a white educator, this journey of discovery has been and continues to be, the most challenging, and humbling, and the most rewarding of my professional career. Because of the profound but often hidden (to us) influence whiteness has on our teaching, I urge other white educators to interrogate their whiteness, to make it visible to themselves and in their classrooms. Without it, we cannot do the work of antiracism education in the interests of achieving social justice. Antiracism work *always* begins with us.

My commitment to antiracist education profits from an interdisciplinary background. As an applied behavioral scientist, I like practical theories that work in the field, in this case the classroom, and that inform our outside lives. As a training consultant, I want a methodology that includes experiential activities to engage learners in here-and-now realizations and a laboratory setting for practicing new skills. As an adult educator, I want a transformative learning experience for my students; and I want to learn along with them. I have found my students to be extremely responsive and welcoming of this eclectic approach. For those seeking new ideas for their classrooms, I have included a section describing the educational design for the ten-week undergraduate class, Ethnicity in American Communities.

The Dangers of White Invisibility

I have been teaching Ethnicity in American Communities for more than ten years; and what surprises me the most is how *long* it took me to address whiteness. I was teaching during the closing decade of the twentieth century and Judith Katz's *White Awareness: Handbook for Antiracism Training* had been published back in 1978! I was a mature white woman with an MS in Social Work and a PhD in Adult Education, a senior training consultant with an expertise in experiential education, as well as teaching faculty at a major university, a follower of Freire's theories of liberatory education (*Horton & Freire* 1990) and Kegan's (1997) theories of consciousness. The truth is, I was not fully practicing what I was teaching. In the words of Kegan, my whiteness was so "subject" to me, that I couldn't see it. The identity politics I encouraged in my students did not apply to me.

Education is never politically neutral (Shor & Freire 1987). As a matter of fact, the most potentially subversive act is to teach. Everything from the classroom protocol to seating arrangement and pedagogical style can reinforce or challenge traditional power structures. For the most part, it has reinforced the status quo, white and male elitism, and hierarchical structures. The university is one of the last white, male, imperialistic aristocracies, complete with a monarchy and a royal court of characters in charge of the business of perpetuating themselves.

One of the popular myths of education is that teachers can teach in an unbiased way. All teachers carry bias; the best we can do is to own that bias and invite challenge and discourse with our students. There is greater danger that lies in unacknowledged and unexamined points of view. What we do not bring to consciousness has even greater power to influence us. Without recognition we remain in unwitting collusion with our own unconscious, unexamined perspectives. We must include our own class, race, and ethnicity membership in our understanding of bias and, for white teachers, the power dynamics that go with that membership (hooks 1994).

As classroom teachers we need to realize how dangerous we are. Our consciousness or lack of it becomes a model for inquiring minds looking for something to emulate. Arrogance, being right, authoritative command of information, and racial unconsciousness can be passed onto our impressionable students. Power dynamics that firmly establish faculty authority undermine the basic concept of antiracist classrooms as well as trust and open dialogue. Without conscious intent, white teachers who have not interrogated their own identity issues perpetuate blindness to the impact of who we are on what and how we teach. Gary Howard, in *We Can't Teach What We Don't Know*, does an excellent job of describing three dynamics that power white supremacist thinking and that we must examine in ourselves: the assumption of rightness, the luxury of ignorance, and the legacy of privilege (1999, pp. 50–62). As members of the dominant group, we white teachers who haven't worked to counteract these powerful processes, suffer their infiltration into our teaching style.

Without interrogation and alternative pedagogy, the white European model that infuses higher education dominates in every aspect of teaching. This is becoming more apparent to movements of students across the country. It needs to be as apparent and recognized in the classroom. For example, while I was at a Midwest college campus for a presentation on whiteness, synchronistically, I noticed a posted flier aimed at students of color, calling for an organizing meeting to demand changes in the curriculum by boldly asking the single question: "**ARE YOU SATISFIED WITH YOUR *EURO*CATION FROM *EURO*VERSITY?**" Similarly, in late November 2001, at UC Davis, an anonymous flier appeared on bulletin boards in classroom buildings. It read:

THANKSGIVING
This Thanksgiving I wanted to thank you for:

- ❖ "Discovering" us
- ❖ Stealing our land
- ❖ Raping our sisters
- ❖ Killing us in the name of God
- ❖ Sharing with us your diseases
- ❖ Writing OUR history
- ❖ Taking us from our traditions
- ❖ Teaching us to be like you

And most importantly . . . celebrating this!

To be involved in antiracist education is to be willing to critically examine every aspect of our institutions: from teaching the accepted curriculum to the accepted process of its delivery, from the demographic compositions of administrative and teaching faculty at so-called multicultural schools to their policies and procedures. It's about caring as much about the retention statistics for students of color as for the recruitment numbers. It is not just in the classroom that students are taught. They are taught by example, by the models they see around them, by the identification of who is in charge, by the language we use, and by the subtleties we don't identify. *The Racial Crisis in American Higher Education* has noted that the success of a university in attracting students of color and fostering their development has "much to do with how those students perceive the institutional climate for racial and ethnic diversity and their awareness of institutional efforts to create responsive learning environments" (Smith, Altach, & Lomotey 2002, p. 21).

Antiracist education is about examining relationships to provide more egalitarian relationships, be they personal or community and more equitable access institutionally. It challenges what has been normative and thus seeks to challenge white supremacist consciousness (European American Collaborative Challenging Whiteness 2002). In the classroom, it is about our relationships with our students, and their relationships with each other. Engaged pedagogy requires egalitarian relationships that recognize we all come to the subject of diversity as learners (hooks 1994). Many students each year tell me that what was most valuable for them was listening to the panels of their fellow students representing different ethnicities sharing their perspectives and their stories. When I disclose personal information related to my own journey, I am joining the discourse.

It is problematic, however, that other than subject experts in the field, there are no professors whose Ph.D. credentials include any education or training in antiracism or race consciousness. Nor are there requirements for mastering a college level, effective pedagogical style. A doctorate degree, by virtue of rigorous research and the meeting of dissertation requirements, credentials one as a content expert and earns that individual the right to teach in the classroom. In no other industry that I know are untrained professionals given such responsibility. Although students are the end use "customers" in higher education, they have historically been passive with regard to establishing or demanding quality in the education product they purchase.

Because this is a self-perpetuating system, there is a related tendency of top universities in this country to increase classroom size to numbers that defy anything but lecture style teaching and power point presentations. With an emphasis on rational, objective pedagogy, favored in the dominant ideology, teachers deliver a banking style of education (Shor & Freire 1987) and bankrupt other realms of the mind such as emotional intelligence (Goleman 1995). What is also virtually eliminated is any possibility of relationships between teachers and students, sadly reported in this communication from a recently graduated student:

> Most of college has been the complete opposite of the connection I felt with my teachers in high school. I have adapted but in no way would I choose the learning experience I've had at UC Davis. My major classes are still held in the huge lecture halls with small classes having sixty people. Not a single professor knows my name and I will likely graduate in June as anonymous as when I started. My thirst for learning has been squelched even though I do enjoy the subject matter of my classes. I am a human development major and one would think some personal interaction could enter into my classes, but alas this is far from the truth. My hope is that I can make it into grad school where the class sizes will be smaller and teachers will know my name.

In spite of the unfavorable conditions cited above, there are plenty of educators who care about the classroom, who develop their abilities to be effective, and who are outstanding teachers, appreciated and loved by their students. However, I fear they are not the majority if I am to believe the comments of my students. There is much we can learn to elevate the classroom experiences we have; but those of us who offer training workshops on campus know how difficult it is to get faculty to attend professional development events. If teaching is not valued, if it is not supported by administration, if our classroom performances are not evaluated in any real, functional sense, there is little institutional incentive to improve our craft. The importance of addressing the art of teaching and the positioning of race and ethnicity in all of our classrooms falls to us as practitioners.

Identifying Whiteness/Not Identifying Whiteness

Teachers who do identify and position whiteness in the university classroom are actually doing something quite radical. As white teachers, we begin deconstructing whiteness when we stand before our students in recognition of our own racial identity, the underlying privileges and paradigms it carries, and the lenses that affect our teaching. To name the invisible color, the water we swim in, is an act of bold exposure. To identify oneself in this way in any class we teach is to join the discourse on racism that has been too long the responsibility primarily of people of color. When I describe myself as a white person in a class that is *not* about racism, I can see the look of surprise on my white students' faces; while students of color smile knowingly and thank me, in private, for naming the white elephant in the room.

With this one small act, I learned how important it is for us to see ourselves as we are seen by our students of color and to make visible what is invisible to other whites but glaring to nonwhites. The personal act of self-identification is a political one, but with different consequences than when identifying with a nondominant group. When I speak about being a Jew, I give recognition to that group. If I come out as a lesbian, I make it safer for those nonheterosexual students to self-identify. But when you speak about yourself as a white, middle-class person, a dominant category whose influence is the underlying fabric of our North American reality, you invoke a questioning of the unquestioned. The self-revelation must carry with it an invitation to our students to challenge what has been normative. This invitation goes beyond the classroom experience, in its import to challenge what is normative in society. It is no longer "the truth," it's a white culture way of looking at things. We unprivilege Howard's previously mentioned "assumption of rightness" (1999).

In the earliest stages of my journey, I can identify with what Lugones (1990) terms "infantilization of judgement" [*sic*]. As only one in a series of incompetencies that Lugones challenges in white women, infantile judgment is "a dulling of the ability to read critically, and with maturity of judgment, those texts and situations in which race and ethnicity are salient" (p. 53). As a white person, one can see race and ethnicity as salient in others, and still not notice one's own. I had been involved in a lifelong journey of self-actualization, of expanding my own consciousness and knowledge, and involvement in social justice issues. I saw myself as an activist in my twenties and thirties (complete with a "civil rights Mississippi summer"), defining myself more accurately as a liberal by midlife. I examined the intersection of race and personality type in my professional work, presenting and publishing on this in the 1990s (Lippin 1995, 1999). I was so smart and still so dumb, having muted myself into a "disengaged position in the inquiry" (Lugones 1990, p. 52). In the beginning of my awakening around whiteness, I traveled first through the more comfortable terrain of identifying as a "good white person." And I did a disservice to those who, by inference, were identified as the "bad white persons." I didn't know what I still didn't know. Such was the resistance to seeing myself as an agent in a corrupt and unacceptable system. The cognitive dissonance was not allowed.

A final piece in the puzzle reveals that as knowledgeable as I was in the area of diversity, I had not dealt with my own identity as a Jewish woman. My rearview mirror analysis now tells me that I was unable to do my whiteness work until I had dealt with my internalized Jewish anti-Semitism. As I write the word anti-Semitism, I am cognizant of the fact that there has been recent challenge to its use when referring solely to anti-Jewish hostilities. In reality, although *Merriam Webster's Collegiate Dictionary* (1994) defines the word *Semite* as "a member of any of a number of peoples of ancient southwestern Asia including the Akkadians, Phoenicians, Hebrews, and Arabs," it only defines anti-Semitism in terms of anti-Jewish sentiment. An online search reveals the same definition: "hostility toward or discrimination against Jews as a religious, ethnic, or racial group." Could this be one more "white" appropriation? Have we disenfranchised our Arab cousins? And, is it less confronting to one's own sensibilities to say anti-Semite than anti-Jew? Is it, in fact, a more comfortable euphemism?

The Awakening of a White Teacher

It has been pointed out that whites do not like to identify themselves as racial beings (Howard 1999). That condition is further complicated if you carry a white Jewish identity. Jews are more ethnically diverse than is commonly understood (Ashkenazi, from Eastern Europe, Sephardi, from Spain and Portugal, and Mizrahi, from Northern Africa and the Middle East, as well as Felasha, from Ethiopia). The construction of my own white identity was background to my Eastern European, Ashkenazi Jewish identity, which took a prominent foreground growing up as I did in a

Jewish ghetto in Boston. The diversity that figured for me in my all-white school system was religious, and I remember my childhood confusion and pain from accusations that "I" had killed Christ. Because Jews are targets for anti-Semitism, I identified with other targeted groups and was in denial about special privilege, position, and treatment associated with whiteness.

This identification with the oppressed is all the more interesting because, being raised Jewish, I had embedded in me the Old Testament concept of Jews as a chosen people. However, this chosen-ness did not operate as superiority to gentiles but, rather, rendered status in the eyes of God. Indeed, suffering seemed to come with the territory of the chosen with its history of Jewish oppression in every country Jews have lived. But even as the Jewish identity was focal and I carried a pride and love for my heritage, I struggled with wanting to look like what was attractive to white America. As with many first-generation females born in the United States, the internalized oppression shows up as feelings of unattractiveness and inferiority. "In contrast (to the American ideal), the negative stereotypical image of the Jewish women has darker skin, curly dark hair, a large nose, rounded contours, a loud voice, a Long Island accent, and too much gold jewelry" (Siegel 1987, p. 41). Worse still, the latest prejudicial term, JAP (Jewish American Princess), is doubly racist and anti-Semitic (Beck 1984). The Jewish woman struggles to find her own acceptable image.

Like many other insecure females of ethnic or other differences, I succumbed. In my junior year of college I had a plastic surgeon shorten my nose. To my immigrant mother, trying to assimilate herself and her daughters so that we'd not be "greenhorns" (Zinn 1995), this must have seemed a drastic step but not so strange as to have been forbidden. For her generation, issues of safety, of freedom from persecution, resulted in Jews going into hiding in other ways.

It did not seem contradictory to me, still, that I identified with people of color, more specifically black people, whose ancestors came from Africa. Formative years on the East Coast, participation in civil rights activism, and a historic kinship rendered me in closest harmony with African Americans. This identification caused problems as I began my journey of unraveling my racist conditioning. A favorite activity of diversity training workshops is to separate people of color and whites. I remember one particularly emotional encounter at a training of trainers for dismantling oppression I attended. Another Jewish woman and I felt strongly that the Jewish experience was being overlooked by the requested absorption into the white group, and staged an educational teach-in. Although this did have a learning impact on the training staff, it did not save us from joining the white group eventually. Such was my resistance to seeing myself as others saw me and treated me, as a white person. If I didn't see the whiteness, I didn't identify the privilege, either.

My awakening journey follows a classic progression of stages that is similar to that of many white people (for example, see Helms 1993; Tatum 1997). The significance of white racial identity is a complex, difficult, and far-reaching subject. My own personal unawareness of my own racial identity, combined with guilt and shame as I increasingly understood the realities of racism, persisted even as I engaged in civil rights activities in the 1960s. While still a social work student at Columbia University, I volunteered for a 1965 summer program with the Child Development Group of Mississippi. This was the summer following the discovery of the murders of the three civil rights workers, Schwerner, Chaney, and Goodman. Schwerner had been a social work student at Columbia. I became a preschool teacher by day, and by night and weekends a member of the Mississippi Freedom Democratic Party. I participated in desegregation actions and voter registration drives. This was a project that gave me powerful personal experiences but no tools to examine the thoughts, feelings, and behavior of a typical northern liberal on a mission to "help" those folks in the South get over segregation. How could whiteness go unexamined in this situation?

Certainly my whiteness came up. It came up on a beach outing in Biloxi, Mississippi, where I had taken the children of my African American host family. After we placed our blanket on the beach, all whites around us moved. The white server at an ice cream stand refused service to the teenage son I'd ignorantly sent ahead to purchase our cones. When I went to place the order and offered up the money myself, she slammed the window shut, saying, " . . . and we don't serve no white trash neither!" My white card was no trump here. And my blatant behaviors revealed my northern white girl ignorance of the Jim Crow rules of coexistence, rather than a bold move for integration.

My whiteness came up at home in the evenings, when we would watch TV together and the three-year-old would crawl into my lap and run her hands up and down the soft hair on my arms. It was more apparent when I noticed that all the faces on the TV we were watching were white. It came up in Jackson, Mississippi, when we were in a training phase. We were "Black and White together—we shall not be moved," and other romantic and appealing notions to a basically unenlightened twenty-two-year-old white, Jewish woman. It came up when I was greeted by every person while walking in the black section of town, and shunned in the white section of town. It quickly established what were safety and danger zones for me. I was certainly conscious of being a white person there, but I was one of the "good" ones in a world that got divided between "good whites" and "bad whites." This attitude got in my way later.

The summer following my return from Mississippi, the racial tension in the Roxbury section of my hometown of Boston exploded in violence. My righteous northerner's mentality was busted wide open along with it. In Boston, as in many other places, black sections of town were poor, overcrowded, visibly disadvantaged in every respect. It was while driving through that part of town that my mother would habitually reach past me in the car to push down the door buttons. Nevertheless, this was in code and I didn't get the message that this fear was a legacy of a northern version of racism. Our "righteous mentality" probably dates back to civil war days when slavery was part of the conflict. Northerners were able to claim a moral victory and declare their superiority over the South because they had never endorsed slavery. Northern whites continued to live their privileged lives, oblivious to the social, economic, and political disadvantage that their covert racism imposed on their black neighbors. It was the proverbial powder keg that ignited in the 1960s.

In the 1970s, I was engaged in the work of becoming a human relations training professional. Although incredibly profound in so many areas of self-discovery, the laboratory training I was involved in at that time was dominated by white folks. The few black folks in the training world were treated as honorary whites, and we rarely gave whiteness and racism proper attention. The truth is, I didn't notice. A different experience is told by Judith Katz in the preface to her marvelous training resource, *White Awareness: Handbook for Anti-Racism Training* (1978). Judith also was part of the human potential movement and profoundly affected by her interactions with people of color. She was motivated to begin facilitating "white-on-white" groups as early as 1972 as a way to address racism in white people.

In my East Coast life, my domestic diversity world was being narrowly defined by race (black and white), religion (Jew and non-Jew), and sexual orientation (gay and straight). In fact, my social world included few persons of other racial/ethnicity groups or social classes. Nor did it include bisexual, transgender, or transsexual people. Once again, I didn't notice. My move to California in 1989 brought with it an expanded definition of diversity and a whole new sense of Mexican- and Asian-influenced U.S. history. Not until California, in the 1990s, did I really find a challenge to my collusion with what keeps racism in place. There I was able to find a community committed to pushing the boundaries on a variety of borders that included racism, classism, and heterosexism. Many community-based organizations sprung up in this period to address inequities and oppression and my reeducation began anew.

One such organization, Women's Alliance, was an educational organization whose mission was to support women's empowerment as a foundation for personal and planetary healing (Rosenwasser 1992). Women came together for weeklong residential "camps" to deal initially with leadership and spirituality issues. Angered by the inequities present at one of these camps, women of color took the lead in challenging us to deal with racism and classism. Ultimately Women's Alliance abdicated and a new, more multiculturally constituted organization, Mujeres Unidas, birthed itself to pursue this mission. Pushed by encounters with radical women of color who in their anger and frustration with us exhorted, "You white women need to do your own work," humbled by my own stumbling in this vigorous multicultural setting, I became part of a small white women's group that met regularly for three years.

Unimaginatively, or boldly, we called ourselves, the White Women's Group. It certainly raised eyebrows when mentioned by name. Our objectives included educating ourselves, through reading and attending events, becoming more conscious of our whiteness in our interactions, and using each other instead of people of color to challenge our white supremacist thinking. In our own safe place we could air our confusions, our own pain, and our problematic behavior. In that safety, I don't recall our ever pushing each other past our limits, identifying perhaps a hiding quality also inherent in this safety.

The scars of doing personal work on racist conditioning included our painful recognition that while we professed equality and egalitarian values we still spewed the messages we had been taught that sat waiting in our unconscious. Sometimes these messages found their voice in a moment that felt like danger. Sometimes they narrated a subtext under our experiences or ran a slide show of unwanted images when we approached a new situation. I learned how my whiteness manifested controlling behavior and responded to fear with stereotypes. I learned that in my disintegration/reintegration stage I was prone to both romanticization and intellectualization. I remember when I bridled intellectually against the term "white supremacist," confronting my own need to "make nice" rather than see the ugliness behind white racism reflected in myself.

At the end of this time I entered into a working partnership with Judy Helfand, who had been a member of the White Women's group. Judy was seeking a cotrainer to deliver "Understanding Whiteness" workshops in the local community that she had initiated with another woman. Together we began designing and delivering six-week experiential programs that addressed whiteness, white privilege, and the accompanying issues of fear, guilt, and shame. It was an essential part of this series that participants made a commitment to action as its conclusion. It also was an important aspect of this program that it took place over a period of six weeks, with intercession assignments designed to bring the work into participants' personal and professional lives.[1]

Facilitating work with other white people can facilitate one's own continued learning, if you are open to it. Inspired and motivated, I moved another step on the journey and something clicked into place inside. I was finally ready to begin to integrate several of the activities we used in our community workshops into the ethnicity class I taught at the university. Up until that point, except for the classic article on white privilege (McIntosh 1988), whiteness had not been discussed in my class on race and ethnicity. My curriculum moved from ignoring whiteness to including white students in the invitation to explore their own racial identity. *Understanding Whiteness/Unraveling Racism* not only allowed for a more a thorough examination of whiteness than had previously been offered in my curriculum, but it also legitimized work with the main components of emotional intelligence—self-awareness, personal decision making, managing feelings, empathy, communications, self disclosure, self-acceptance, and personal responsibility (Goleman 1995, p. 303).

In the most recent phase of my journey, I am finding a larger forum at my own campus for bringing whiteness issues to consciousness. Workshops on understanding the role of whiteness have been offered for students through a Leadership Development Series, and to employees through Staff Development. A book signing resulted in a diverse group who discussed the formation of small groups on campus to continue raising their consciousness on the impact of whiteness.

Another expanded audience attends our workshops and institutes at national multicultural conferences focused on education. There we find participants, both people of color and white folks, eager to share their truths, their experiences around whiteness. It is moving and encouraging being a part of a dialogue that addresses the importance of whiteness taking its place in an understanding of racism.

From my own experience I cannot urge strongly enough that white educators teaching a curriculum on race and ethnicity find safe places to do their own work on their identity issues that so impact that teaching. The final section of this chapter deals specifically with the course, Ethnicity in American Communities.

Case in Point: Whiteness in the Classroom

The most challenging aspect of teaching Ethnicity in American Communities (CRD2) for a white teacher is to be able to support and be credible to both the white students and the students of color. Student perceptions of past teachers were that those of color had "sided" with the students of color and left the white students feeling blamed, while white teachers had not been trusted by the students of color. In the early years, I probably erred on the part of supporting the students of color, but managed to keep my white students positively engaged without their getting stuck in the feeling that a racist society was their fault. Ultimately, it is the creation each time anew of an inclusive, responsible, learning community in which all of us, students and teachers together, provide the necessary support and challenge to deal with this difficult subject.

The nature of the class content and process, and a short ten-week quarter, make it essential to build trust immediately. From day one, when students first get their sense of what a course will be about, I engage them in dialogue about the nature of racism in their lives. I let them know that the course is *for* them and *about* them and that I am a learner with them. If I have two TAs who are also white (a majority of the time), I ask them "what is wrong with this picture?" I present the assumptions about oppression work that remind us that none of us are to blame for an oppressive system that is pervasive, but that we need to separate blame from responsibility. And I establish ground rules that include confidentiality, respect, personalizing knowledge, and values for risk-taking and emotional expression. It is necessary to return repeatedly to the fact that the course is not about pointing fingers, that they had not invented racism but, instead, they had inherited a legacy of systemic and institutional racism that affected each one of us on a personal level. Although it goes against the bureaucratic administrative set up for computer-based enrollment, I close the class on the first night, because of the careful attention given to trust building, so that no one is able to add the class who hasn't attended the first session.

Over the first six years I have taught it, CRD2 has grown from 50 students to 132, despite my protestations that the large class size would seriously affect the participatory and experiential style I had become known for and which had proven quite successful and popular. No longer can we be scheduled in a classroom with movable seats. We now meet in a lecture hall, all face front to the pit in which I stand. No longer can we face inward, where each person's voice addresses the group. I have to guard against falling into the sole authority role the position accords and the students get whiplash while attending to peer participation. However, it is an exciting class to teach, and the students continue to testify similarly about their learning experiences.

Davis has a population that is more than 50 percent students of color, as does the enrollment for CRD2. Many students refer their friends to the course. The particular diversity distribution of UC Davis includes approximately 35–40 percent Asian Americans, 15 percent Latino/Chicano, 7–10 percent African American, and 40–45 percent white students, and the enrollment of CRD2 is representative of that diversity.

In a ten-week quarter I have some difficult choices to make with regard to content and process. I favor texts that students would not ordinarily encounter. One text always gives a corrected review of American History from the point of view of the people of color who have been ignored, tokenized, exceptionalized, lied about, or otherwise misremembered. I began, years ago, with Zinn's *A People's History of the United States* (1995) and later moved to Ron Takaki's *A Different Mirror* (1993). I find that either text does the job nicely, and has profound impact on the students.

A mainstay in the class all these years is Anzaldua's *Making Face Making Soul: Haciendo Caras* (1990), which offers students an opportunity to read poems and short personal stories by radical women of color. Not only does this provide a right-brain (intuitive, holistic, subjective) experience for the students, but it also gives us permission to include our feelings and often raw emotions.

From assigned readings in *Making Face, Making Soul,* each week, two or three different students volunteer to choose a poem to read aloud at the front of the class and tell why they picked it. It is not for discussion. The urgency of first person, emotionally charged poetry provides the "voices not heard" backdrop for our weekly encounters with the fallout of racism, sexism, homophobia, and classism. In this simple act, students are allowed to cross boundaries and identify with other's experiences. It is poignant and powerful to hear a Chicano male read a poem written by an Asian sister, a white student giving voice to the anger and pain of another's marginality.

Often students went beyond this assignment and asked to share other authors' works or to read their own poetry. A brilliant and moving example of the latter occurred this fall during a class in which we were discussing the annoying (to students of color) question "where are you from."

Unbeknown to me at the time, a performance poet was a student in the class and had written a piece directed at that very same issue. Another student asked my permission for him to share it with us. He did so, from memory, with all the passion and animation of the spoken-word artist. An abbreviated form of the poem is reprinted below:

no id
what am i?
can somebody please tell me what i am?
am i asian or man or a combination?
i glare in the mirror and picture a figure of vibrancy beyond comprehension
and by extension
just a guy with a lot to say
which is irrelevant
since whatever i utter will just be followed by the question
WOW! CAN YOU SAY THAT IN CHINESE TOO???
as much as i struggle to reveal my true self to you
unfortunately all attempts to model the image of myself as a man up til now
have been tainted with the stereotypes i've been brandished with
so don't act so confused when i ask
what am i?
because society has lied to me and blinded me
to the point where the 9-digit label it cursed upon me
once convinced me that i actually had
social security
and i was convinced that since i was
spawned from american soil
nourished by american resources and
taught in american institutions
that american racism would never bear its ugly head
to bring down
what it brought up
because i was convinced that
that made no sense
and i was convinced that everyone knew that
that made no sense
but see, I've learned since then
i learned since then that i wasn't just another kid with the loose teeth
but instead i'm a crude geek that's unique

i've learned that
though i have a defined skin tone
in this world it seems it's my skin tone that defines me

but most of all
i've learned to be angry because of that
sadly i have this fury instilled within the very depths of my being

that I even have to prove myself to you
to get beyond your illusions of dropkicks and chopsticks
to make my true self seen with even a hint of logic
and you need to realize that though
my eyes are slanted and half-closed
i see your prejudice crystal clear

so now
even though I'm aware of what you mean when you ask
WHAT AM I?
I choose not to feed your prying curiosity
so
what am i?
i'm the epitome of the very reason
you find it necessary to water down my rich culture in your
melting pot
so don't get mad at me because i choose to be that crazy
yellow-skinned nightmare amidst your amerikan dream.
after all
i'm just trying to answer your question
and i'm having a hell of a time doing it
Adriel Luis, aka subSCRYBE (2002)

The reaction in the room was thunderous as the students and I cheered Adriel's performance. I am reminded repeatedly in a classroom on diversity, of the differing ways we are wise, talented, and beautiful.

A third book provides accessible essays on the reality of how the social identities of race, class, and gender operate as an interlocking web to define our experiences. I recently moved from using Anderson's and Collins's anthology, *Race, Class, and Gender*, (2001), to *Names We Call Home: Autobiography on Racial Identity*, by Thomson and Tyagi (1996).

Of the texts above, only *Names We Call Home* addresses whiteness. By 1999 I was beginning to incorporate activities for the students to address white privilege. But in 2001, when *Understanding Whiteness/Unraveling Racism: Tools for the Journey*, was used for the first time in the classroom, it felt like a culmination of both my professional and my personal work. The workbook format, the personal nature of "taking a journey," and the quality of heart and soul it sought to invoke, make it a perfect addition to CRD2. As we state in the opening section of the book:

> Participating in understanding whiteness and unraveling racism is a journey—an arduous, difficult journey with many obstacles, especially for white people. There is no cheering from the sidelines, often the opposite. Seldom is anyone going to pat you on the back for doing it. Your friends and family may question you or be threatened by what you are saying or doing. Why do it then? We must stop par-

ticipating in the perpetuation of an inequitable system that is destroying this country, wounding the next generation of leaders, taking the heart out of many of us, and affecting our very souls. (Helfand & Lippin 2001, p. 6)

Students taking CRD2 encounter a personal element that makes it unlike most of their other academic content-based classes. The course is about them, their thoughts *and* emotions, and the worlds they live in. The course is about becoming more conscious of the legacy of racism they had inherited, and accessing knowledge and skills to work toward social justice. For white students, it's to feel the personal impact of a racist society on their lives. Each quarter, each year, the course is different based on the makeup of the students. I am touched and motivated by their reasons for taking the class, and what they hope to get out of it. Their comments include:

"Because we heard it was a good class to talk about our feelings about racism"

"My roommate (white) told me (white) I should take it because I was a racist"

"To be friends of people of different ethnicities than my own"

"Opportunity to interact with other races"

"To learn as much as possible about ethnic groups different from mine through interaction"

"To be able to feel comfortable about my identity and be accepted by others"

"Since I have never experienced living in such an ethnic/racially diverse location, I would like to learn more about these ethnic groups. I want to overcome the fear that I have when I find myself in between a large group of diverse ethnic backgrounds"

"I mainly want to learn more about my ethnicity and the ethnicity of everyone else in the class. I want to learn to be more open to other people and to be able to share the great things of our ethnicities with each other"

"To make a difference in American communities and to influence others"

These comments fit course objectives that include raising awareness and encouraging new antiracist behaviors. And they also affirm the students' own interests in establishing relationships across the race and ethnic boundaries that seemed to define the college community. Tatum's excellent book is titled from this common phenomenon (*Why Are All the Black Kids Sitting Together in the Cafeteria?* 1997).

The course includes exposures to the raw hurts of the "isms" through media, through personal narratives, field requirements, and through experiential activities. In a class of 132 students, there is a great range of experience and maturity. Class assignments are designed to give them exposure to diversity experience and an opportunity to examine their reactions. It is the intent of the course to make the theoretical real in their lives, and to allow for critical analysis of preconceived ideas.

Many students, both white and students of color, come numb or in denial and don't want to believe that racism exists today on such a prominent level. After seeing "True Colors," an NBC *Primetime Live* twenty-minute video about unequal treatment of a black man and a white man, in a number of retail situations, both white students and students of color report being shocked. Their eyes are opened to a racism they had experienced and didn't think about, experienced and carried feelings they didn't know were normal, or didn't experience at all. As one student wrote later, *"I've always known that racism exists in our society in various forms, but sometimes I need something to remind me just how harsh it really is."* But that harshness takes on an even more urgent reality when, after such a showing, fellow students offer up their own testimonials to similar treatment.

Other effective classroom interventions have included: showing and discussing *The Color of Fear* (film by Lee Mun Wah), a dismantling oppression experiential activity that deals with visible inequities and the isolation of oppression, and use of student panels in each of the last four weeks of class in which students tell their own stories. This last activity is probably the most popular with the students, who sit in rapt attention, moved by these personal and often emotional first-person accounts of growing up in U.S. society in different racial and ethnic social identities.

CRD2 is taught as a three-hour participatory lecture with a one-hour TA-led discussion section. TAs participate in a one-hour prep session prior to the class, in which they also examine their own reactions to the class material. Because of the profound experience that TAs may go through, I have added a written component to their work with me. Weekly, they submit a journal entry on both their personal relationship to the material and how their sections are proceeding.

I have noticed a predictable pattern of growth for white students taking CRD2 during the ten-week class. In the very beginning, I let the white students know they will be confronting difficult areas of our history, that the course is a beginning of a journey, and something about my own journey. As they move from ignorance and naiveté, to an angry enlightenment, I continue to support their open expressions. Anger gives way to the underlying shame and guilt. Sometimes when white students complain that they felt "targeted" in the classroom, a student of color might respond, pointing out that it was but a small taste of how it has felt to them be targeted every day of their lives. This interaction alone can produce a shift in consciousness.

But there are difficult moments with students that you don't handle well and leave you wondering why you're there. In my Fall 2002 teaching experience with this course, I was getting more "push back" than usual from a few articulate white students. They complained of feeling "othered," resented that I posed different questions to their white group than to the groups of students of color, and even objected to the lack of capitalization of "white" in my text. They felt they were being "white" by default. Why did everyone have an ethnicity, and they were "white." They weren't getting enough information about positive white role models.

Ordinarily fairly nimble at providing a facilitative discussion that would bring in other viewpoints, I found myself taking on a dialogue role with the students. I never inquired as to other students' experiences. I didn't even ask what these students might have said, had they been asked the same question as the students of color, that is, "What do you never want to hear, see, or have happen to your people again?" I alternated between defensive responses and pulling rank. It was the process of this exchange as well as the content and the effect on the rest of the class that I was to contemplate and reexamine for many weeks after. Other white students I hadn't heard from communicated with me by email to share opposite views. One white woman shared how this affected her:

> When students speak out in class about feeling like they are oppressed and are being "othered" in this course, I feel very angry at them for being blind to what I believe is the truth about United States' society. I feel that these words act simply as another defense mechanism, and again make people of color the ones who are at fault for society's problems. I feel very guilty about this anger—I wish that I could be more understanding of their emotions, and I very much admire those who have done such a good job of understanding. However, I also feel that the exercises that we have gone through, and particularly, watching the video "The Color of Fear," have sparked the flame in many white people that will eventually help them to see their positions in society more clearly. I hope that this makes sense to you. . . . I am grappling with many emotions concerning these issues right now, and I need a lot of time to process all of the information! I have been very impressed with the course so far—I think that I have learned more valuable information in this class so far this quarter than I have in any of my other classes throughout my four years at UC Davis.

Voicing conflicting and confusing emotions is essential if students are to keep moving through them. And most of them do. Rather than identifying with the racist system, white students need to begin the process of identifying with other white people who have fought for social justice throughout history.

Miraculously, it would seem sometimes, most of the white students find their way to becoming conscious white persons committed to antiracist behavior, to becoming allies of students of color, and to engaging in activities on campus that further multicultural goals. As the following remarks demonstrate, students do develop. Knowing this has inspired me, filled me with compassion, and strengthened my resolve to continue working with white people.

> I remember picking up the Whiteness book when I first started the class. I read the first couple pages and was totally offended. I was sure that this class was going to tell me that I was the devil because I had white skin, and that I have tortured people of different ethnicities. But in all actuality I felt very at home in the class, my [negative] expectations were very quickly shot down and I came to accept the class as a learning experience.

> For me this was a difficult experience, but I have made a few personal breakthroughs due to this class. I had a lot of trouble accepting first the idea of white privilege, and then the idea of un-conscious racism. . . . I never really had the feeling that anything was being blamed or that fingers were pointed at me, but I always felt bad for experiences that I didn't even cause.

> No question this class was a milestone in my life. It opened my eyes to the racist acts that occur every day without the knowledge of them even occurring. This class opened me up to what I had not been seeing my entire life. It was a truly enlightening experience that I hope to pass on to others around me.

> I used to think that it was mostly common knowledge that whites were more privileged than other people, but I am now very surprised at how many white people disagree with that statement. I have been working harder to teach people what I feel they should know about our society. I now understand how little our society actually is aware of when it comes to the topic of racism.

> Through this class I have had my eyes literally opened for me, showing me the truth. . . . This class has opened my mind to new ideas, new ways of thinking, and has allowed me to step out of my white self, and progress to help stop racism instead of causing it myself.

We Have So Much to Gain . . .

White teachers are the teachers of most of the students of color in U.S. schools. It's very difficult to not reinforce systems of dominance in the class in some way. We *are* grading, we *are* writing criteria and determining the syllabus. But the consciousness we can bring that constantly and relentlessly challenges the normativeness of whiteness can make the classroom more inclusive and welcoming for students of color. There is great value in students of color witnessing the work of their fellow white students. I agree with bell hooks (1994), who sees teachers as healers, of developers of conscientization, because we have been given a situation that needs healing and consciousness if it is ever to change.

As the teachers of white students, the essence of our educational work is to actively promote a healthy white identity, confronting the pain of white privilege and white oppression, and bringing white students to a new and responsible awareness. And for that effort, we need to start with ourselves, and find safe places to do our own work. I am hopeful that we can do this work at our universities, together.

What we have to gain is everything. If we are ever to live in a world in which racism does not exist, it will be because white people as well as people of color are working together to replace it with equitable, multiculturally influenced norms, systems, and institutions. That effort will take a quality of heart and mind that will elevate us all. As teachers, we have opportunity to be at the forefront of a new world.

The syllabus for Ethnicity in American Communities contains the following words on its cover page:

> A Senegalese Proverb: In the end, we preserve only what we love. We love what we understand, and we understand what we are taught." Therefore, if we are taught, we can understand. When we understand, we can love, and what we love, we will preserve.

On the final day of class, the students respond in small groups to these three questions:
WHAT DO YOU NOW UNDERSTAND?
- What do you now love?
WHAT WILL YOU NOW PRESERVE?
They close the class by standing to affirm one action they will take to forward their journeys of undoing racism in their lives. What will *you* do?

Note

1. Encouraged by the response to these offerings, and seeking a way to reach a larger audience, Judy and I decided to write the book that would accompany our course. Combining narrative, exercises, and readings, *Understanding Whiteness/Unraveling Racism: Tools for the Journey* was first published in 2001 by Thomson Learning Custom Publishers.

References

Andersen, M. L., & Collins, P. H. (2001). *Race, class and gender.* San Francisco: WadsworthThomson Learning.

Anzaldua, G. (Ed.). (1990). *Making face, making soul: Haciendo caras.* San Francisco: Aunt Lute Foundation.

Beck, E. T. (1984). *Between invisibility and overvisibility: The politics of anti-Semitism in the women's movement and beyond.* (Working paper series, 11). Madison: University of Wisconsin-Madison Women's Studies Research Center.

European American Collaborative Challenging Whiteness (2002). A multiple–group inquiry into whiteness. In L. Yorks & E. Kasl (Eds.), *Collaborative inquiry as a strategy for adult learning,* San Francisco: Jossey-Bass.

Frankenberg, R. (1993). *The social construction of whiteness: White women, race matters.* Minneapolis: University of Minnesota Press.

Goleman, D. (1995). *Emotional intelligence.* New York: Bantam Books

Helfand, J., & Lippin, L. (2001) Understanding whiteness/Unraveling racism: Tools for the journey. Mason, OH: Thomson Learning Custom Publishing.

Helms, J. E. (1993). *Black and white racial identity.* Westport, CT: Praeger.

hooks, b. (1994). *Teaching to transgress: Education as the practice of freedom.* New York: Routledge.

Horton, M., & Freire, P. (1990). *We make the road by walking.* Philadelphia: Temple University Press.

Howard, G. (1999). *We can't teach what we don't know: White teachers, multiracial schools.* New York: Teachers College Press.

Katz, J. H. (1978). *White awareness: Handbook for anti-racism training.* Norman: University of Oklahoma Press.

Kegan, R. (1994). *In over our heads.* Cambridge, MA: Harvard University Press.

Lippin, L., & Poirier, D. (1999) Cultural impact on the expression of type. In *APT XIII, 1999 International Conference Proceedings.* Association for Psychological Type. Glenview, IL: Association for Psychological Type.

Lippin, L. (1995). Personality types of incarcerated women: Implications of race. In R. Moody (Ed.), *Proceedings of psychological type and culture—east and west: A multicultural research symposium.* Gainesville, FL: Center for Applications of Psychological Type.

Lugones, Maria. (1990). Hablando cara a cara/speaking face to face: An exploration of ethnocentric racism. In G. Anzaldua (ed.), *Making Face, Making Soul: Haciendo Caras.* San Francisco: Aunt Lute Foundation.

luis, a. m. j. (2002). *CUT loose.* Davis, CA: Ill-Literate Press. Available from http://www.ill-literacy.org

McIntosh, P. (1988). *White privilege and male privilege: A personal account of coming to see correspondence through work in women's studies* (working papers series no. 189). Wellesley, MA: Wellesley College, Center for Research on Women.

Merriam-Webster's collegiate dictionary (1994). Springfield, MA: Merriam-Webster.

Rosenwasser, P. (1992). *Visionary voices, women on power.* San Francisco: Aunt Lute Books.

Shor, I., & Freire, P. (1987). *A pedagogy for liberation.* Massachusetts: Bergin & Garvey.

Siegel, R. J. (1987). Antisemitism and sexism in stereotypes of Jewish women. In D. Howard (Ed.), *Dynamics of feminist therapy.* New York: Haworth Press.

Smith, W. A., Altbach, P. G., & Kofi, L. (2002). *The racial crisis in American higher education: Continuing challenges for the 21ˢᵗ century.* Albany: State University of New York Press.

Thompson, B. and Tyagi, S. (1996). *Names we call home: Autobiography on racial identity.* New York: Routledge.

Takaki, R. (1993). *A different mirror.* Boston: Little, Brown, and Company.

Tatum, B. (1997) *Why are all the black kids sitting together in the cafeteria?* New York: Basic Books.

Zinn, H. (1995). *A people's history of the United States.* New York: HarperCollins Publishers.

6

Exploring and Challenging Whiteness and White Racism with White Preservice Teachers

Sherry Marx

In the United States today, white people make up about 86 percent of both the teacher workforce (Lara 1994) and the teacher education student population (Ladson-Billings 1999). At the same time, 72 percent of the teaching population is made up of women (Súarez-Orozco 2000), and it is estimated that 97 percent of the American teacher population speaks English only (Darling-Hammond & Sclan 1996). Thus, it can be said that white women who speak only English represent the dominant face of American teachers. However, the American student population is much more ethnically and linguistically diverse. In the United States today, nearly 50 percent of the school-age population is composed of children of color (Lara 1994) and one child in five is estimated to be the child of an immigrant (NCES 2002). Overall, the number of English language learners (ELLs) in this country is increasing faster than "two and a half times the rate of the general student population" (Claire 1995, p. 189). Teachers today cannot expect to spend their careers teaching only white, English-speaking children.

In response to the changing demographics of the United States, numerous schools of education across the country have implemented courses designed to better prepare preservice teachers to become successful teachers of children who speak a native language other than English and who grow up in cultures, ethnic groups, and races that are unfamiliar to the vast majority of teachers. The study presented here is situated within the realm of improving teacher education through courses addressing the linguistic and cultural diversity of children.

Study Background

The impetus for the study presented in this paper goes back several years to my days as a teaching assistant for such a teacher education course. This course, Second Language Acquisition, focused on theories of language acquisition and required a ten-hour field service component where students tutored ELLs in local public schools. Because of the location of the university, nearly all children tutored were native Spanish speakers of Mexican origin. The goal of the field component was to encourage students to connect theory to practice and to gain important "real world" experience.

With the intention of gaining very general information about the tutoring experience, I conducted an exploratory study and spoke with fourteen volunteers from the class about the children they tutored and the tutoring experience in general (Marx 2000). Nine participants were white women who spoke only English; four were women of Latin American origin who spoke English and Spanish, and one was a man of Latin American origin who also spoke English and Spanish. They ranged in age from twenty to fifty-five. Through open-ended questions (Lincoln & Guba 1989), and by meeting with individuals or small groups, I found that all participants thought of their tutees as "bright" and many claimed to "love" the kids. However, the expectations tutees had for the children differed dramatically depending on the cultural, ethnic, and linguistic background of the tutor. All tutors of Latin American origin believed that their tutees could meet or exceed their own level of success, however they defined it. In contrast, all white participants who tutored Spanish-speaking children believed that the children would drop out of school before graduation.[1] *None* of them felt that the children would reach their own level of success.

The disturbing results of this study led the professor and I to restructure the course. We implemented a reflective tutoring journal, assigned a culminating paper, and incorporated several articles on teacher beliefs into the reading packet. Two years after the initial study, the class was greatly improved and I had taken over as instructor. However, although they were much more subtle, negative thoughts about the children continued to emerge through questions and comments in class.

The Study

This experience was the impetus for once again asking the Second Language Acquisition class for volunteers for a study to explore the tutoring experience and beliefs about ELLs in a more in-depth way. Because white, monolingual, women made up the majority of the class and make up the majority of teachers, I looked to this group for participants. Whites accounted for about seventy-five of the eighty or so Second Language Acquisition students. Moreover, because the white students in the course had consistently asked the questions and offered the comments that revealed low expectations and serious misunderstandings about English language learners, I decided that whiteness would have to be an integral aspect of this study.

Whiteness

"Whiteness" is a very difficult construction to define. Its parameters are so rarely articulated in this country that whiteness is most often understood when it is described as what it is not, rather than what it is (see Fanon 1967; Frankenberg 1993, 1997; Katz & Ivey 1977; Tatum 1999; Terry 1981). In discussing whiteness as race, I have adopted a socially constructed understanding of race that is interwoven with notions of ethnicity and culture, indicating a shared conglomeration of European heritage and immigrant experience. However, power and privilege are defining aspects of this construction, more pronounced than actual biological indicators such as skin color (see also Fine 1997; Giroux 1998; Kincheloe & Steinberg 1998). As Hartigan (1999) explains, whiteness is "a concept that reveals and explains the racial interests of white people, linking them collectively to a position of social dominance" (p. 16). The neutrality that typically characterizes whiteness is evidence of this power (Katz & Ivey 1977; Rodriguez 1998; Terry 1981). In understanding race as a social construction, its links "to relations of power and processes of struggle" are highlighted (Frankenberg 1993, p. 11), as are its connections to time and place. Moreover, it must be acknowledged that its meaning "changes over time" (Frankenberg 1993, p. 11; see also Lopez 1995; Omi & Winant 1994; Rodriguez 1998).

Whiteness, like every racial category, is a complex construction characterized by exceptions, inconsistencies, and frayed edges. Multiple identities and experiences complicate and humanize its articulation. Winant (1997, p. 48), for example, points out that "socioeconomic status, religious affiliation, ideologies of individualism, opportunity, and citizenship, nationalism, etc." all contribute to one's racial identity, thus making all human beings variously situated. One can certainly add gender, sexual orientation, political affiliation, ability, and more to this mix. Race is a complicated entity. Unfortunately, naming race necessarily essentializes race. I realize that I am essentializing when I use the terms "whiteness" and "race." Nevertheless, in order to problematize and interrogate whiteness, I find these terms, with their limitations, to be useful, if imperfect, tools for analysis.

Critical Race Theory

While ignorance can explain many of the thoughts the students in the Second Language Acquisition class expressed, ignorance alone cannot explain their low expectations and their tendencies to view the children through a deficit lens (Valencia 1997). Racism, in contrast, explains these impressions very well. Critical Race Theory (CRT) offers a foundation for this perspective. CRT posits that Americans live in a society in which "race continues to be a significant factor in determining inequity" (Ladson-Billings & Tate 1995, p. 48). Through this framework, racism is described as "endemic in American life" and something that is "deeply ingrained legally, culturally, and even psychologically" (p. 52). Much more than individual acts of hatred, racism is described as a *condition* of American life. It is "a system of advantage based on race" that benefits whites in the United States as it disadvantages people of color (Tatum 1999, p. 7). The inequity is so deeply ingrained that Bell (1992) refers to it as permanent.

ELLs and children of color are typically labeled "at risk of failure" no matter their academic grades, nor the quality of their home lives (Valencia 1997). Children of color and those learning English are frequently described as "difficult" and "challenging" to the "normal" curriculum; frequently, they also are viewed and described through negative stereotypes (Solorzano 1997). This is not hate mongering, nor is it violent. Rather, it is the "passive" (Derman-Sparks & Phillips 1997; Tatum 1999), everyday, "business as usual" (Tatum 1999, p. 11) that serves to reinforce, reproduce, and reiterate racial inequity on a daily basis. The ways that whites benefit from the negative characterization and the subtle but continuous oppression of people of color is described as "white racism" (Scheurich 1993). This is the kind of racism CRT and Critical White Studies address. CRT and Critical White Studies together provide the theoretical foundation on which I base this study.

My Own Whiteness

The issues of whiteness and racism, particularly white racism, are very important to me as a white person and a white educator. As an educator, I have witnessed numerous interactions between white teachers and students of color that seem clearly tainted by racism (see Marx 2001). I have also observed and been a part of schools that offer their students of color and ELLs unequal access to opportunity through segregation, tracking, low expectations, and myriad other factors. Moreover, I have made assumptions and comments that reveal my own whiteness and the racism that influences me. I am ashamed and embarrassed when people of color and whites more astute than myself point them out. Thus, although I am engaged in research that seeks to call attention to whiteness and white racism and to disrupt them, I am nevertheless influenced by these same entities. As Scheurich (1993, p. 9) states, "No matter how much I individually confront the issue of White racism, I cannot escape being White." That is, I cannot exist outside my culture and the limitations it necessitates. Consequently, all the while I was examining whiteness in this study, I was examining it in myself.

Developing the Language of the Study

While I still struggle with whiteness and better understanding my own perspective, because of my own studies and my own interest in the topic, I, necessarily, have a more critical understanding of whiteness and white racism than the participants who volunteered for this study. Realizing this, I knew that we would together have to develop a language to talk about these issues and, in order to do so, I would have to be patient with the participants (see also Derman-Sparks & Phillips 1997). I would also have to develop a trusting, mutually beneficial relationship with each of them (Freire 1970/2000; Spradley 1979). It was also important to me to approach all of our conversations and interactions in a caring way (Noddings 1984, 1994) that would illustrate the care and respect I felt for them. I felt strongly that the only way to better understand the ways that race, racism, and whiteness influenced the tutoring experience was to talk about all of them with participants (Howard & Denning del Rosario 2000; Tatum 1999).

Efforts to Illuminate Whiteness

Although efforts to address whiteness in education are becoming more frequent, the body of literature is still very small and it is supported by few examples of empirical research (Marx 2003b; Marx & Pennington 2003). Much of the research that has been conducted has not been portrayed as successful. In two separate studies, for example, Sleeter (1994) and Berlak (1999) found that their white teacher participants deeply resented a critical focus on whiteness. McIntyre (1997) discovered that her participants were mostly confused by it. Lawrence (1998) was optimistic that her students progressed somewhat toward a better understanding of their white racial identity but disappointed that they did not get farther in one semester.

Two recent studies report more positive results. The first is a curriculum model offered by Derman-Sparks and Phillips (1997) that focuses specifically on antiracism pedagogy. The authors present methodologies that gently, but directly, address the whiteness, racism, and cultural biases of educators. The second study is an example of action research where an African American teacher/researcher, Jennifer Obidah, and a white American teacher/researcher, Karen Teel, worked together to examine and disrupt the ways that whiteness and white racism influenced the white teachers work with African American schoolchildren (Obidah & Teel 2001). Through the study, Teel struggled with admitting and denying her own racism and Obidah struggled with Teel. The end result is a sincere, reflective, collaborative work that greatly improved Teel's ability to work with her students. This small body of literature gave me insights into the challenging and potentially rewarding nature of research that examines and disrupts whiteness in educational settings.

Methodology

A few weeks into the semester, I asked the Second Language Acquisition class for volunteers who would like to talk about race, ethnicity, and tutoring. Nine white women who spoke only English eagerly agreed to participate. They ranged in age from twenty to thirty-five. Three participants identified themselves as white and Jewish. The remaining six described themselves simply as white. Ascribing to the socially constructed nature of race, I allowed participants to determine their own whiteness. If they believed that they were white, they were welcome to join the study.

I met with each participant individually for three to ten hours of open-ended interviews over a fifteen-week period (Lincoln & Guba 1989). I also observed each participant tutoring once (Sleeter 1993). I read the reflective tutoring journals of all students in the class, paying particular attention to the journals of participants (Black, Sileo, & Prater 2000; Collier 1999); and I tutored an English-language-learning child in one of our cooperating schools (Henry 1998). As this study was an interpretive project, I examined the large amount of narrative data collected and looked for themes that seemed, to me, to emerge out of the data set (Wolcott 1994). Like Obidah and Teel (2001) and Derman-Sparks and Phillips (1997), I decided to intervene in the whiteness and white racism that I could delineate in the study, based on my understanding of Critical White Studies and CRT.

Critical Cultural Therapy

The intervention methodology I used is adapted from George and Louise Spindler's work in "cultural therapy" (e.g., Spindler & Spindler 1982, 1994; Spindler 1997, 1999). The goal of cultural therapy is to make visible the usually invisible aspects of one's culture. As Spindler (1999) explains, "The job of the cultural therapist is to discover what the subject does not know and . . . then to help the subject to understand and reflect on these discoveries" (p. 470). The Spindlers' (1987) approach with their most famous participant, a popular white teacher who, nonetheless, marginalized his students of color, was to observe his teaching and then to share insights with him about his tendency to best teach to the children in class who shared his culture. Through numerous weekly observations, frank discussion, and the sharing of data with the participant, the Spindlers sought to make this teacher aware of his ethnocentrism and the ways in which it affected his students. These intensive interactions between the researchers and the teacher greatly improved the way the teacher interacted with his students.

I call the approach I took in this study "critical cultural therapy" because I added a critical, race- and power-oriented focus to the notion of culture (Bell 1992; Ladson-Billings & Tate 1995; Scheurich 1993). In conducting this intervention, my goal was to help participants become aware of the ways in which the whiteness and the white racism that were invisible to them influenced their beliefs about, and their interactions with, the children they tutored. Critical White Studies and CRT enabled me to recognize and name the whiteness and white racism that were revealed through the interviews, observations, and journal entries that comprised study data. In inviting participants into the study, I shared that I would be talking with them about their tutees, their white identities, and their feelings about race. I did not specifically tell them about the intervention aspect of the study until the intervention began. At that point, I explained that my goal, like the goal articulated by Spindler (1999) earlier, was to help them "understand and reflect on" the racism and biases that I could see in their comments.

I conducted critical cultural therapy in two ways. First, after one or two interviews devoted to discussions of race, whiteness, and tutees, I gave all participants copies of their own first and second interview transcripts and asked them to spend a few weeks reading and reflecting on them. I then met with them individually to discuss what they had found in the data. I hypothesized that participants would be able to "see" some of the biases and whiteness that characterizes their words when talking about tutees, even if they could not hear such characteristics during our conversations. Second, I drew attention to the whiteness and white racism that I could recognize as someone more educated in both areas. I drew attention to the spoken words of participants and then, after they interpreted their transcripts, I asked them to look deeper for more examples of racism, biases, and whiteness. This second approach was extremely challenging and taxing. I attempted this part of the study only after participants and I built a caring, trusting, respectful relationship (Freire 1970/2000; Noddings 1984, 1994; Spradley 1979). Without this kind of relationship, I do not believe that this kind of intervention can be effective.

A difficult, yet extremely important, aspect of the intervention methodology was resisting the urge to fall into what McIntyre (1997) calls "White talk." White talk is conversation "that serves to insulate White people from examining their/our individual and collective role(s) in the perpetuation of racism" (p. 45). White talk is seductive. It occurs when one person says, for example, "I think I might be racist," and another person responds, "No, no way. You're not racist. You're just honest/thoughtful/too hard on yourself/etc." White talk occurs when discussion of race and white racism becomes too critical and too personal. A fellow white swoops in to comfort and restore appropriate conversation. Participants and I were all drawn by its lure. However, in opening up conversations about whiteness and white racism, my goal was to disrupt white talk rather than contribute to it. By doing this, I hoped to build a more productive "White discourse on White racism" (Scheurich 1993).

Normalcy of Whiteness and Deficits of Color

Through the interviews, observations, and journals, I found that all participants were influenced by whiteness and white racism in many ways, some of which proved to be detrimental to the children they tutored. Giving evidence to the neutrality typically associated with whiteness, seven participants described whiteness as being part of the "normal," "all-American" experience. The other two participants were unable to describe it at all; whiteness was completely invisible to them. In contrast to the nothingness of whiteness, all participants associated color with deficits; that is, they tended to think of people of color as generally disadvantaged by various aspects of their culture (see Valencia 1997). All participants shared thoughts about the deficient cultures, home lives, families, values, self-esteem, and intelligence of the children they tutored and people of color in general (Marx 2001). In addition, participants made very negative judgments about the children's native languages. Nearly all participants felt sorry for the children and judged them to have bleak futures. As they did this, they constructed themselves as role models and saviors who might be able to offer the children hope (Marx 2003a).

Invisibleness of White Racism

No matter what they said in our conversations, participants maintained their abhorrence of racism. Like most middle-class white Americans, nearly all participants in this study described racism as active, hate-filled acts committed by evil doers such as the Ku Klux Klan or the Aryan Nation (Tatum 1999). Thus, no matter what they said about the children of color they tutored, they could not and would not self-identify as racist. Their passive racism did have tangible effects, however: During an observation, I watched Michelle[2] hug and praise her tutee and then turn around and criticize her to me for being a "street Mexican" and for having "the Mexican kind of talk" (Observation of Michelle). Rachel talked to the teacher she assisted about one child's "apathetic attitude" (Rachel's Journal Entry No. 4) and another child's rude behavior. The first child spoke very little English and likely did not understand her directives, while the second child constantly said, "I could read this if it were in Spanish," a comment that Rachel interpreted as disrespectful. Similarly, Elizabeth characterized Martin, the child she tutored, as "insecure" and "trying to be something he's not" because he read "too quickly" (Interview No. 1 with Elizabeth). She thought he was trying to impress her. Indeed he was. I also tutored Martin and discovered that he was reading first and second grade books despite his fourth grade reading ability. The tutoring director had mistakenly placed him into a low level and never again monitored his progress. Elizabeth and the tutoring director were both trying to hold Martin back rather than help him move forward. As these examples indicate, the deficit, biased mindsets that participants held had direct, tangible consequences for the children.

As I was interviewing, observing, and talking with participants, I found that my own whiteness enabled me to empathize with their perspectives. Our shared whiteness also seemed to help participants feel comfortable talking about matters of race and it seemed to encourage their trust. In these ways, my whiteness was an advantage in this study. However, my whiteness also seemed to give some participants the confidence to express very negative views about the children. Like McIntyre (1997), I got the impression that some participants assumed that I would share their negative thoughts about the schools, the children, and their parents because of my whiteness. As mentioned above, Michelle, for example, characterized her tutees, elementary school children, as "street Mexicans" who were likely "homeless" or in "gangs." As she left our interview one afternoon, she shared her pleasure at being able to talk so "honestly." She had interpreted my patience and probing inquiries as agreement. At this point in the study, I decided that the time had come for active intervention through critical cultural therapy.

The Case of Elizabeth

I liken critical cultural therapy to a dance performed by two individuals, one moving forward and the other reacting, moving back, and then, once again, moving forward, prompting the other individual to react. It takes two, and both partners equally influence the outcome. In this way, all interventions were unique. However, a clear pattern emerged that may benefit other educators interested in antiracist work that draws attention to whiteness and white racism. Thus, I present in detail below the case of one participant, Elizabeth, whose case illustrates themes common to other participants. Just twenty at the time of this study, Elizabeth was a sensitive young woman who greatly loved children, abhorred racism, and thought of herself as "open-minded." She was from a wealthy suburb and enjoyed the diversity of her university town, although, like most participants, she planned to eventually move back to her hometown and teach in a white, suburban school much like those she attended.

Step 1—Opening the Floodgates and Recognizing One's Own Racism in the Torrent

The first step in critical cultural therapy is to encourage an unrestrained catharsis of opinions and beliefs from participants so that their feelings can emerge from the depth of their unspoken, "submerged" (Spindler 1999, p. 469) state. By the time of these discussions, participants and I had gotten to know each other over several weeks and they freely shared their opinions about people of color, ELLs, and their own white identities. As participants talked without restraint about their thoughts and their frustrations with their tutees and other people of color, those who were very sensitive began to hear the racism that tinted their words. Elizabeth, for example, was surprised by how "actively racist" (Tatum 1999) she sounded. Afraid I would get the wrong impression, she paused in her talk to emphasize that "I would be willing to put my personal opinions aside [if] I'm going to be teaching children [of color]. I want to do it the right way." This comment was Elizabeth's attempt to repair her image as a giving, loving person who would certainly benefit the lives of all children, regardless of their race, home language, or ethnicity. Satisfied that I now, "knew what she meant," she sought to move on in the conversation.

Step 2—Calling Attention to Contradictions

In my intervention position, I could not let Elizabeth move forward with this excuse. If I had done so, I would have been engaging in "White talk" (McIntyre, 1997). Consequently, I gently asked Elizabeth if she really thought she could put her personal feelings aside. Without hesitating even a moment, she answered, "Yes," and laughingly commented that, "You might think everything I've said is racist. But, you know, I wouldn't call someone a derogatory name or something." Like most participants—perhaps like most white people—Elizabeth considered her own passive racism (Tatum 1999) to be without effect. However, she had just shared some views that were not too far from a more popular characterization of racism. To draw her attention to this contradiction, I asked her why I might think everything she said was racist. After pausing a moment, she thoughtfully answered that she had described the child she tutored as having a "hard home life" about which he would be too embarrassed to talk. She explained that this was probably a negative, racist expectation on her part because she, herself, would not mind if anyone asked her about her own home life. Moreover, she explained that she had never asked Martin anything about his home life, nor met his parents. Thus, she realized she had no basis for this judgment.

Step 3—Sighting and Then Denying the Tip of the Iceberg

This admission of low expectations momentarily stunned Elizabeth. Describing her surprise at herself she exclaimed, "I sit here and listen to myself and it's freaking me out!" At this moment, Elizabeth had seen the "tip of the iceberg"; that is, she had just caught a glimpse of the ways in which whiteness and white racism influenced her own perceptions. Because Elizabeth was so self-critical and self-reflective, I thought she would be able to admit to white racism at this point. However, when I asked her if she could do this, she protested, absolutely horrified. Passionately, she explained,

No. Absolutely not. Because, I don't . . . when I think of someone being racist—all my life—that means you look at someone and you think that they are not as good as you are because of their heritage—and I don't *consciously* do that. You know, I think *racism* is a bad thing. And that's just not the way I was raised—to look at someone and judge them like that. So I wouldn't say—I would never want to admit that I'm racist, but, now that I'm talking about how I—*totally*—Martin—I associated him with hard times and . . . all that, I see that that is probably racist. You know, and some other things are probably racist, but [sigh] I don't know . . . I guess I am, subconsciously, but I don't mean to be. You know, I don't not like someone because of it. You know what I mean? But it *sucks!* Because it makes you feel bad! A bad person. Like, I shouldn't be teaching kids. You know, I'm going to judge them.

As her comments indicate, Elizabeth was able to "hear" the racism in her own words even as she sought to deny it. She realized that even if her racism was not intentional nor even conscious, it could still have an effect on children. Her low expectations of Martin were proof enough of that.

Step 4—Constructing and Challenging Easy Answers

The realization that she might be influenced by, and perpetuating, racism despite her best intentions frightened Elizabeth. Thus, she conjured a quick solution that might easily counteract her racism. Like many other participants, at this point, she vowed "to really be aware" of her own biases so she could control them. She then explained that, "I don't see myself treating a child in a negative way or judging. I mean, it may be judging, but I would *never* portray it, I don't think. Definitely not on purpose, but . . . ." As part of the intervention, I again called attention to the contradictions. I asked Elizabeth if her negative perceptions about children like Martin could "come through" in some manner, despite her intentions. She took a moment to think about Martin and then admitted that he might get a sense of her distance from him and her low expectations for him.

This admission again stunned her. Elizabeth did not want to hurt a child, purposely or not. So, once more, she sought to skirt the consequences of her white racism, contrasting her own more passive (Tatum 1999), more unintentional racism with the more obvious, intentional racism of other whites, something most other participants did as well. Specifically, she emphasized that,

I think that everyone is worthwhile of an education and everyone's worthwhile of, you know . . . of . . . so I don't think it would come through . . . as much, you know? I mean, I would not *ever* do anything to make a child feel bad about themselves or feel different, you know? And if I do, then . . . huh!

Although Elizabeth kept trying to deny her connection to racism and the harm it could cause children, specifically Martin, she kept a critical ear tuned to her own words. Her final comment, "And if I do, then . . . huh!" expressed the helplessness she felt coming to the conclusion that she might unintentionally injure children. Even though she did not want to be racist, at this moment, she realized that she might be.

Step 5—Drawing Attention to the Bigger Picture

At this point, I sought to draw attention to the connection between the micro event of Elizabeth's passive racism and the macro situation of the challenges children of color and English language learners face in schools all over the United States (Scheurich 1993; Tatum 1999). This perspective momentarily overwhelmed her as it suddenly implicated her in this situation. Thus, she again tried to deflect responsibility. This time, she nervously asked me, "So what you are getting at is that minority teachers should teach minority children, right?" Because I do believe that more teachers of color would greatly benefit the field of education, but that many white teachers can learn to become better teachers for children of color (Ladson-Billings 1994; Melnick & Zeichner 1988), I told her, "Oh no. I'm not saying that."

Curious to know what had generated this question, I asked Elizabeth, "Why are you saying that?" She answered,

> Because, I just feel like that's what we are getting at. Because, I know that whatever I've said that is racist is not my fault. You know? It's a society thing. Like you said, American culture is racist. It's not like I'm a bad person. I *know* I'm not a bad person. I *know* I have a good heart. I think I have a better heart than a lot of people I see. So, what I am is, I guess, being a product of society or American culture.

This was Elizabeth's last-ditch effort to reject the responsibility that was quickly falling on her shoulders. These denials were classic examples of White talk (McIntyre 1997). However, because I did not agree with this perspective verbally or silently, her excuses had no support. Rather, her defenses started to crumble.

Step 6—Recognizing and Accepting Responsibility for White Racism

Although I agreed with Elizabeth that racism is a part of our society, I asked her, "Isn't it still a bad thing. Aren't we still responsible for it?" At these questions, she finally capitulated. Very passionately, and very insightfully, she said,

It's a big deal, but I don't think it's made a big deal because I have *never* even thought about it like this. I don't think people realize—reading all those articles about it—and white people say in class that they know people who are racist. You would think they are racist: They don't like black people, they want segregation, blah, blah, blah. You hear them, but you don't really think about that you have the views inside you whether you put them there or not. But as for me, it's a *very* big issue. I mean it is huge. I mean . . . humongous.

As she finished this statement, Elizabeth started sobbing. As I put my arm around her to comfort her, it seemed to me that she had finally seen the whole picture. Rather than just the "tip of the iceberg," she had glimpsed the hulking, colossal entity that is white racism and she began to take some personal responsibility for it. Her comment that, "It's a big deal, but I don't think it's made a big deal," was extremely insightful. Nothing in her home life, her teacher education, her work with children, or her experience with American culture had prepared her to deal with her own racism. Rather, all these aspects of American life had distanced her from it. As she collected herself, she exclaimed, "I never thought I would be crying over racism!" realizing, of course, that white Americans almost never respond so passionately to racism in the abstract. Recognizing the racism in one's self, that is, white racism, is what triggers this kind of emotion.

Step 7—Moving Past the Impotence of White Guilt

Although she had finally seen the white racism that influenced her life, taken responsibility for it, and shifted her gaze from the deficits of children of color to the biases of white teachers, as her sobs indicated, Elizabeth was left in a very vulnerable position after this conversation. Scholars in the area of race and ethnic identity tell us that learning to view the world in a more critical, more race-sensitive manner is often a challenging, frightening experience (Helms 1990; Howard & Denning del Rosario 2000; Kincheloe & Steinberg 1998; Rodriguez 1998). Rodriguez (1998), for example, writes that coming to terms with racism necessarily provokes feelings of "trauma," "unsettlement," and "bafflement" (p. 34). Citing Baldwin (1963), Karp (1981), and J. Katz (1977), Helms (1990, p. 59) adds that realizing the racism aspect of whiteness provokes "feelings of guilt, depression, helplessness, and anxiety" that exacerbate the negativity associated with white identity. However, there is no benefit to becoming immobilized at this point. Helms (1990) argues that the goal of disrupting whiteness must be the development of an antiracist identity situated within a positive white identity. Kincheloe and Steinberg (1998) add that "unlearning racism" and "encouraging insight into the nature of historical oppression and its contemporary manifestations" are useful results of this kind of critical self-examination (p. 19).

With all this in mind, when Elizabeth crumbled at the end of our second conversation, I sought to help her get back on her feet and move forward. As she collected herself, she asked me, "What do you—what do you think?" I answered that I thought she was going through Helms's (1990) disintegration stage of white racial identity development. I passed Helms's book to Elizabeth and briefly discussed the stages with her. Helms's discussion of white racial identity is systematic and accessible. I thought it would help Elizabeth see that, of course, she was not alone in her feelings. I also thought it might help her keep moving forward in her racial development because it would help her recognize additional stages that Helms and other racial identity model theorists outline. Because this seemed to be such a good idea for Elizabeth, I gave copies of Helms's (1990) chapter 4, "A Model of White Racial Identity Development," to all participants. Most found it a source of comfort and illumination.

After our meeting, Elizabeth shared her new insights into white racism with some close family friends. Engaging in White talk (McIntyre 1997), these friends tried to comfort her by persuading her that she was not racist and encouraging her to stop exploring the subject. Indeed, she told me during our next interview that she had tried to stop thinking about race and racism altogether, a common reaction to which Helms (1990) gives much weight in her book chapter (pp. 58–61). I shared this with Elizabeth and we looked at Helms's model again together. Seeing her own struggles mirrored in Helms's words made a strong impression on her. After more discussion and reflection, she strengthened her resolve to press on in her journey of racial development.

After Elizabeth and I parted that day, she decided to put off her marriage until her fiancé changed his actively racist views about people of color. She also made plans to travel to other countries, something she had not wanted to do before the study. She explained that she wanted to learn more about different cultures and their different perspectives. Elizabeth also became very critical of the standard curriculum she followed during her teaching experiences, noting the dominance of the white perspective. It troubled her that Latino children such as Martin were rarely featured in the reading materials she used. Toward the end of our semester together, she searched several bookstores in our university town for more diverse, child of color–centered materials. At times she called me to discuss her concerns and her findings. I was continually impressed with her insights.

Analysis

Of the nine white women who participated in this study, seven moved to a point similar to Elizabeth's. Most of these seven went through the same steps, sometimes making identical comments along the way. Each of these participants seemed to become critically aware of the ways in which white racism influenced their lives and some of the ways in which their own white racism influenced the children they tutored. Once they finally saw the influences of white racism in their lives, like Elizabeth, they attempted to become actively antiracist, the goal advocated by Helms (1990), Kincheloe and Steinberg (1998), and Tatum (1999).

In our dialogues about white racism and racial identity, it became evident that all participants abhorred the obvious forms of racism that they could distinguish in the words and actions of family members, friends, and other white teachers. They also tended to associate goodness with a lack of this kind of racism, so they tended to think of themselves as very good people in contrast to others (Marx 2003b). Through our conversations, however, their own white racism slowly emerged, and when they finally saw it, most participants were shocked and disappointed with themselves. No participant who progressed this far in the study felt comfortable living with the racism she found in herself: All of them vowed to change. As Claire said, "The part of me that is racist is just going to have to . . . go away in order to be a good teacher" (Interview No. 4 with Claire). Impressively, no participant who progressed to this level regretted beginning the journey. Rather, many expressed how grateful they were for our critical conversations.

Our persistent examinations of whiteness and white racism, and each participant's personal connection to them, actually seemed to have the effect of empowering participants. That is, they developed a "belief in [their] ability/capability to act with effect" (Ashcroft 1987, p. 145). In Freire's (1970/2000) words, they developed *"conscientização,"* that is, they developed a critical consciousness "that is understood to have the power to transform reality" (Taylor 1993, p. 52). By better understanding their cultural and racial positionality, the power that accompanies this positionality, and the biases contained within this positionality, most of the young women in this study set a course for becoming much better teachers for all the children who will someday populate their classrooms.

Future Research

As Elizabeth's case makes clear, maintaining one's determination to become an antiracist white can be a difficult struggle, especially when other whites routinely seek to draw one's attention away from this resolve (Helms 1990). It is this factor that points to the advantages of a teacher education class devoted to the study of whiteness. In a class setting, students would be able to develop much-needed solidarity (Freire 1970/2000). However, the solidarity that empowers those who Freire (1970/2000) called "the oppressed," also can mire members of the dominating white culture (the oppressors) in a cycle of avoidance and comfort, characterized by "White talk" (McIntyre 1997). I suggest that teacher educators undertaking an intervention project similar to that described here in a classroom setting introduce "White talk" early in the curriculum, examine it with students, then name it and reject it whenever it is practiced in class. I also recommend that clear definitions of white racism and whiteness are introduced early in the course, so that everyone shares an understanding of what is being examined (Scheurich 1993; Tatum 1999). Teacher educators also must be certain to develop a safe, trusting environment where students feel comfortable expressing their beliefs with the instructor and with one another (Freire 1970/2000; Noddings 1984, 1994; Spradley 1979). Finally, teacher educators must understand well their own racial positionality and, if white, their own whiteness (Titone 1998). Students will expect instructors to guide them, and instructors must be able to do this (Titone 1998). Falling into white talk or ignoring the limitations of one's own whiteness is setting a foundation for failure. Because of the predominance of whiteness in multiple aspects of school culture, examining and better understanding whiteness benefits all educators.

Conclusions

Through this study, it became apparent that the first step to becoming a truly antiracist white must be admitting one's own white racism. Once the participants in this study sincerely admitted their own racism and understood its consequences, they moved away from denying racism to the much more productive mindset of seeking to do something about it. Through this change in mindset, participants turned their focus inward, toward the ways in which they contributed to disparities in schooling, rather than always outward toward the "deficits" of children, something that I argue is a racist construct (see also Valencia 1997). By turning their focus inward, the white preservice teachers in this study were able to make changes in their beliefs and behaviors with tangible results. All whites can benefit from their example.

As teacher educators, we must be brave enough to initiate dialogues on race and racism such as those presented in this study with our students. Students can handle this kind of discussion. As Tatum (1999) and Howard and Denning del Rosario (2000) suggest, the only way to make any progress with the issues of race and racism is to "talk about" them in constructive ways. The more we talk about them, the more progress we can make toward developing a useful, more neutral language with which to discuss the effects of these entities on ourselves, our students, and the world (Freire 1970/2000). Only then can we truly begin to make changes.

Notes

1. One white female participant tutored a Chinese-speaking child. Unlike all other white participants, this participant felt that her tutee could succeed in life by her own measure of success.
2. All names are pseudonyms that participants chose for themselves.

References

Ashcroft, L. (1987). Defusing "empowerment": The what and the why. *Language Arts, 64,* 142–56.

Baldwin, J. (1963). *The fire next time.* New York: Dell.

Bell, D. (1992). *Faces at the bottom of the well.* New York: Basic Books.

Berlak, A. (1999). Teaching and testimony: Witnessing and bearing witness to racisms in culturally diverse classrooms. *Curriculum Inquiry, 29*(1), 99–127.

Black, R. S., Sileo, T. W., & Prater, M. A. (2000). Learning journals, self-reflection, and university students' changing perceptions. *Action in Teacher Education, 21*(4), 71–89.

Claire, N. (1995). Mainstream classroom teachers and ESL students. *TESOL Quarterly, 29*(1), 189–96.

Collier, S. (1999). Characteristics of reflective thought during the student teaching experience. *Journal of Teacher Education, 50*(3), 173–81.

Darling-Hammond, L., & Sclan, E. M. (1996). Who teaches and why: Dilemmas of building a profession for twenty-first-century schools. In J. Sikula (Ed.), *Handbook of research on teacher education* (2nd ed.). New York: Macmillan.

Derman-Sparks, L., & Phillips, C. B. (1997). *Teaching/learning anti-racism.* New York: Teachers College Press.

Fanon, F. (1967). *Black skin, white masks* (C. L. Markmann, Trans.). New York: Grove Press.

Fine, M. (1997). Witnessing whiteness. In M. Fine, L. Weiss, L. Powell, & L. Wong (Eds.), Off-white: Readings on race, power, and society (pp. 58–65). New York: Routledge.

Frankenberg, R. (1993). *White women, race matters: The social construction of whiteness.* Minneapolis: University of Minnesota Press.

Frankenberg, R. (1997). Local whitenesses, localizing whiteness. In R. Frankenberg (Ed.), *Displacing whiteness* (pp. 1–33). Durham, NC, and London: Duke University Press.

Freire, P. (1970/2000). *Pedagogy of the oppressed* (30th anniversary ed.) (M. B. Ramos, Trans.). New York: Seabury.

Giroux, H. (1998). Youth, memory work, and the racial politics of whiteness. In J. Kincheloe, & S. Steinberg, (Eds.), *White reign* (pp. 123–36). New York: St. Martin's Press.

Hartigan, J., Jr. (1999). *Racial situations: Class predicaments of whiteness in Detroit.* Princeton, NJ: Princeton University Press.

Helms, J. (1990). *Black and white racial identity: Theory, research, and practice.* New York and Westport, CT: London: Greenwood Press.

Henry, A. (1998). *Taking back control: African Canadian women teachers' lives and practices.* Albany: State University of New York Press.

Howard, T. C., & Denning del Rosario, C. (2000). Talking race in teacher education: The need for racial dialogue in teacher education programs. *Action in Teacher Education, 21*(4), 127–37.

Karp, J. B. (1981). The emotional impact and a model racist attitude. In B. P. Bowdser, & R. G. Hunt (Eds.), *Impacts of racism on white Americans* (pp. 87–96). Beverly Hills, CA: Sage.

Katz, J. H. (1977). The effects of a systematic training program on the attitudes and behavior of white people. *International Journal of Intercultural Relations, 1*(1), 77–89.

Katz, J. H., & Ivey, A. E. (1977). White awareness: The frontier of racism awareness training. *Personnel and Guidance Journal, 55*(8), 485–88.

Kincheloe, J., & Steinberg, S. (1998). Addressing the crisis of whiteness: Reconfiguring white identity in a pedagogy of whiteness. In J. Kincheloe, & S. Steinberg (Eds.), *White reign* (pp. 4–29). New York: St. Martin's Press.

Ladson-Billings, G. (1994). *The dream keepers: Successful teachers of African American children.* San Francisco: Jossey-Bass.

Ladson-Billings, G. (1999). Preparing teachers for diverse student populations: A Critical Race Theory perspective. *Review of Research in Education, 24*, 211–47.

Ladson-Billings, G., & Tate, W. (1995). Toward a critical race theory of education. *Teachers College Record, 97*, (1), 47–68.

Lara, J. (1994). Demographic overview: Changes in student enrollment in American schools. In K. Spangenberg-Urbschat, & R. Pritchard (Eds.), *Kids come in all languages: Reading instruction for ESL students* (pp. 9–21). Newark, DE: International Reading Association.

Lawrence, S. (1998). Research, writing, and racial identity: Cross-disciplinary connections for multicultural education. *The Teacher Educator, 34*(1), 41–53.

Lincoln, Y. S., & Guba, E. G. (1989). Ethics: The failure of positivist science. *The Review of Higher Education, 12*, 221–40.

Lopez, H. I. (1995). The social construction of race. In R. Delgado (Ed.), *Critical Race Theory: The cutting edge* (pp. 191–203). Philadelphia: Temple University Press.

Marx, S. (2000). An exploration of pre-service teacher perceptions of second language learners in the mainstream classroom. *Texas Papers in Foreign Language Education, 5*(1), 207–21.

Marx, S. (2001). *Turning a blind eye to racism no more: Naming whiteness and racism with preservice teachers working with English language learners of color.* Ph.D. dissertation. Austin, TX: University of Texas.

Marx, S. (2003a). Entanglements of altruism, whiteness, and deficit thinking: White preservice teachers working with urban Latinos. *Educators for Urban Minorities, 2*(2), 41–46.

Marx, S. (2003b). Reflections on the state of critical white studies. *Qualitative Studies in Education, 16*(1).

Marx, S., & Pennington, J. (2003). Pedagogies of Critical Race Theory: Experimentations with white preservice teachers. *Qualitative Studies in Education, 16*(1), 91–110.

McIntyre, A. (1997). *Making meaning of Whiteness: Exploring racial identity with white teachers*. Albany: State University of New York Press.

Melnick, S., & Zeichner, K. (1998). Teacher education's responsibility to address diversity issues: Enhancing institutional capacity. *Theory into Practice, 37*(2), 88–95.

National Center for Education Statistics. (2002). Schools and staffing survey: 1999–2000. [online]. Available: http://nces.ed.gov/pubs2002/2002313.pdf

Noddings, N. (1984). *Caring, a feminine approach to ethics & moral education*. Berkeley: University of California Press.

Noddings, N. (1994). *The challenge to care in schools: An alternative approach to education*. New York: Teachers College Press.

Obidah, J., & Teel, K. M. (2001). *Because of the kids: Facing racial and cultural differences in schools*. New York: Teachers College Press.

Omi, M., & Winant, H. (1994). *Racial formation in the United States: From the 1960's to the 1990's*. New York and London: Routledge and Kegan Paul.

Rodriguez, N. (1998). Emptying the content of whiteness: Toward an understanding of the relation between whiteness and pedagogy. In J. Kincheloe, & S. Steinberg (Eds.), *White reign* (pp. 31–62). New York: St. Martin's Press.

Scheurich, J. (1993). Toward a white discourse on white racism. *Educational Researcher, 22*(8), 5–10.

Sleeter, C. (1993). How white teachers construct race. In C. McCarthy, & W. Crichlow (Eds.), *Race identity and representation in education* (pp. 157–71). New York and London: Routledge.

Sleeter, C. (1994). A multicultural educator views white racism. *Multicultural Education, 1*(39), 5–8.

Solorzano, D. (1997). Images and words that wound: Critical race theory, racial stereotyping, and teacher education. *Teacher Education Quarterly, 24*(3), 5–19.

Spindler, G. (1997). Cultural sensitization. In G. Spindler (Ed.), *Education and cultural processes: Anthropological approaches* (3rd ed.), (pp. 498–512). Prospect Heights, IL: Waveland Press.

Spindler, G. (1999). Three categories of cultural knowledge useful in doing cultural therapy. *Anthropology & Education Quarterly, 30*(4), 466–472.

Spindler, G., & Spindler, L. (1982). From familiar to strange and back again: Roger Harker and Schoenhausen. In G. Spindler (Ed.), *Doing the ethnography of schooling: Educational anthropology in action* (pp. 20–46). New York: Holt, Rinehart, & Winston.

Spindler, G., & Spindler, L. (1989). Instrumental competence, self-efficacy, linguistic minorities, and cultural therapy: A preliminary attempt at integration. *Anthropology and Education Quarterly, 20*, 36–50.

Spindler, G., & Spindler, L. (Eds.) (1994). *Pathways to cultural awareness: Cultural therapy with teachers and students*. Thousand Oaks, CA: Corwin Press.

Spradley, J. (1979). *The ethnographic interview*. New York: Holt, Rinehart, & Winston.

Súarez-Orozco, C. (2000). Meeting the challenge: Schooling immigrant youth. *NABE News*, *24*(2), 6–35.

Tatum, B. D. (1999). *"Why are all the black kids sitting together in the cafeteria?" and other conversations about race*. New York: Basic Books.

Taylor, P. (1993). *The texts of Paulo Freire*. Buckingham, England and Philadelphia: Open University Press.

Terry, R. W. (1981). The negative impact on white values. In B. P. Bowser & R. G. Hunt (Eds.), *Impacts of racism on white Americans* (pp. 119–51). Beverly Hills, CA: Sage Publications.

Titone, C. (1998). Educating the white teacher as ally. In J. Kincheloe & S. Steinberg (Eds.), *White reign* (pp. 159–75). New York: St. Martin's Press.

Valencia, R. R. (Ed.). (1997). *The evolution of deficit thinking: Educational thought and practice*. London: Falmer Press.

Winant, H. (1997). Behind blue eyes: Whiteness and contemporary U.S. racial politics. In M. Fine, L. Wiess, L. C. Powell, & L. M. Wong (Eds.), *Off white: Readings on race, power, and society* (pp. 50–53). New York: Routledge.

Wolcott, H. F. (1994). *Transforming qualitative data: Description, analysis, and interpretation*. Thousand Oaks, CA: Sage Publications.

7

Deconstructing Whiteness: Discovering the Water

Kelly E. Maxwell

"The fish would be the last creature to discover water." This quote by Clyde Kluckhohn in Frederick Erickson's (1986) chapter on qualitative research methods is a metaphor that continues to resonate with me. Erickson is making reference to qualitative research as a vehicle for understanding the meaning in a particular situation. But it is also an appropriate metaphor for whiteness.

A colleague of mine, a longtime educator and professor once referenced this metaphor in relation to her students. She said that the goal of her classes is for "[students to] begin to see what this water looks like, they're the fish. You don't know that you're in this particular water, and I make them examine the water that they're in." The water is whiteness. It is all around yet is illusive. It is only when my colleague begins challenging her students to think about "the water" that they are pulled out of it and given the opportunity to look at it differently. While acknowledging that some will be confused, some will actively resist, and others will embrace this new challenge, this has become my classroom task as well.

However, it has taken time for me to get to this place. When I was twenty years old, I was "in the water." Like many of my white students, I could not have described what it means to be white. I probably would have said that it is like being an American (overlooking that many Americans are people of color). I might have said that being white is like being of Scottish heritage as my ancestors were (overlooking that many white people have an ethnic heritage different from mine). In any case, it would have been very difficult to describe what it means to be white.

This is the illusive construction of race, specifically whiteness. Physical or biological variations between people are small, but the meaning that we make about those variations is significant. People ascribe meaning to seemingly unchanging characteristics. Yet it is people with power and their historical and political circumstances that have created racial categories, not the biology that produces these minute differences.

Michael Omi and Howard Winant, in their book *Racial Formation in the United States* (1994), discuss the ways in which political struggle led to the categorization of people by racial characteristics. Ronald Takaki (1993) and Howard Zinn (1995) also discuss the linking of political or economic conditions to the manufacture of racial categories over time. Whiteness was constructed as the norm and nonwhite peoples were compared unfavorably. Ironically, these racial categories were far from static. Peoples of color have been classified as white, then nonwhite, and white again based on changing representations that benefited the interests of white people (Takaki 1993).

It is quite possible then, that one who is white will not notice the "water" of whiteness. Why? Whiteness in this society is the norm. It is the standard by which others are measured. Because of this, white folk do not have to think about being white.

Peter McLaren (1991) writes that "being white is an entitlement, not to preferred racial attributes, but to a raceless subjectivity. That is, being white becomes the invisible norm for how the dominant culture measures its own civility" (p. 244). White people, then, do not have to see themselves as white but rather as without a race. They may see the race of someone else as a way to make comparisons with their own lives but never have to recognize their own racial group. Many authors have agreed with McLaren's interpretation of whiteness as standard. By naming that whiteness, as a social construction, exists, they attempt to subvert the very normalcy of its properties (see, for example, Clark & O'Donnell 1999; Frankenberg 1993; Helms 1992; Katz 1978; Kivel 2002).

Discovering the Water in My Own Life

Although it would be a while before I would read any of the literature about whiteness, there were a few experiences in my early twenties that "took me out of the water" and catalyzed my process toward understanding and describing it. I liken my own experience to an awakening. There are a number of definitions of awakening and some of them are appropriate here. One definition is "the act of awakening from sleep" (Random House Webster's Dictionary, 1995). That fits. Maybe rousing from a coma would be more appropriate. I could never see what was in front of me until I woke up. I was roused from my slumber, my unconsciousness, my inactivity, my apathy. Another definition is "the revival of interest or attention." Because I was in this deep coma or unconscious state, there was no revival of interest. In fact, there was no realization that interest even *should* exist. A third definition is probably most accurate: "a recognition, realization, or coming into awareness of something." This is the process that I hope to engage in my students.

For me, this realization was very slow. After all, for the first twenty or so years of my existence, I had never even thought about this conception of whiteness. Once I did, there was a struggle to understand myself and my family and to reconcile the messages I had received over a lifetime.

Probably the most significant event in understanding my whiteness was coming out. Sometime during my senior year of college I identified my sexual orientation as lesbian. It might seem irrelevant to mention but it was actually one of the greatest gifts in helping me understand my whiteness. I began to look at advantage/disadvantage through a different lens. As a lesbian, I was part of a target group that experiences discrimination. I actively sought out other gay people because I wanted to be in a community of others who understood me. I was part of a culture that had specifics unto itself. Somewhere along the line, it just clicked for me. I saw myself in one social identity as the recipient of discrimination and then, as a white person, the recipient of privilege. I equated my white self to the heterosexual community. How often do heterosexuals think about their sexuality? It certainly pervades every ounce of life, from the high school prom, to college date parties, to marriage, to the benefits of being able to be in a heterosexually partnered relationship. It is so ubiquitous that it is difficult to see. It is the water. Peggy McIntosh (1988) writes about white privilege in this society. She compared it to sexism and men's "unwillingness to grant that they are over-privileged." The concept translates easily to whiteness. It was not until she examined sexism from her point of view as a woman—the disadvantaged position—that she began thinking about the advantages of being white.

This shifting of focus allowed me to see my whiteness in a different way. There are several current television commercials using technology where the image on the screen freezes but the camera swings around to view the frozen image from a different angle. This is how viewing my whiteness was for me. I stepped outside of the picture and walked around the other side to view it differently. I saw something completely new. Peggy McIntosh (1989) calls it "an invisible weightless knapsack of special provisions, maps, passports, codebooks, visas, clothes, tools, and blank checks" (p. 10). The "it" in this case is privilege. White privilege. It was not until I saw this thing called whiteness from a different angle that I could see the "knapsack" that was attached to my back. Then I could begin to understand why I had never noticed whiteness before. I could see that being white was always morally neutral, the normative way of being, the ideal. People were compared to me instead of the other way around.

This new view opened up unique aspects to being white. I actively sought to understand these white privileges that McIntosh revealed. Furthermore, I spent time looking back over my lifetime at the subtle messages I had received about skin color. For example, there was a boy in my kindergarten class whose last name was Jackson. He was black. Because I associated his name with his skin color, it was not until years later, probably as late as seventh or eighth grade, that I realized that our seventh president, Andrew Jackson, was not black. Without knowing it, I was keenly aware of my classmate's color, so much so that I made assumptions about people who I thought were like him in other ways, too. This strikes me as so appallingly ironic now, knowing Andrew Jackson's legacy of white supremacy and his particularly shameful treatment of various groups of color, particularly Native Americans (Takaki 1993).

Growing up, I received mixed messages about people from other races. I once asked a teacher why my friend, who was black, was a different color than me. With the best of intentions she swallowed hard and in a low voice, quickly stated that color does not matter; my friend was just like me. My teacher was certainly well meaning, but she reinforced for me that the color of someone's skin that was different from mine was something to avoid talking about. I learned to pretend not to see it whenever it was there. Just as able-bodied people are taught not to stare at people with disabilities and yet are keenly aware of the disability, I learned that color was indeed significant but that I was not supposed to notice it.

Yet rarely did I have to pretend not to notice. Because I grew up in a rural town in Ohio, there were very few people of color living there or going to my school. The newspapers showed white candidates being elected to local political offices, my textbooks showed white people in history, the television showed white people living lives similar to mine. But I did not see their whiteness. I was not cognizant that all these people were white; they were simply people. I observed that the criminals on television were by and large portrayed as black. But I never questioned either phenomenon. Despite learning in school that I should not see the color in others' skin, I constantly saw it. I knew it was different from me. Some of the messages suggested that somehow, in an unspoken, silent sort of way, I was better. My teacher told me so. Not explicitly, of course, but by implying that my friend was "as good as" me, she taught me just the opposite. She compared my friend to me. I was the standard. Without ever talking about "whiteness," I received messages about myself as a white person.

So today I see my whiteness when I look in the mirror. I can see it and know that is not the neutral skin tone that I grew up *not* thinking about. It has meaning, which confers privileges upon me. But I have also chosen to acknowledge the privilege that comes with it and have committed myself to antiracism tenets. I notice my whiteness and that of others because I constantly think about racism. Yet still, I have a choice. It is a decision I have chosen willingly on a path toward an antiracist life. This is part of privilege—the choice. And it is necessary that my students understand this.

Although I did not have a teacher of color until the twelfth grade, no teacher ever mentioned her or his whiteness. I keep thinking that if we had talked about whiteness and I had been exposed to the concept of white privilege earlier, it would not have taken me into my twenties to begin thinking about the significance of white skin. Because I am not a K–12 educator but one who teaches at a university, I hope that I can expose students, both white and of color, to the concept of white antiracism and ally building.

For me, it happened through a series of crystallizing events. I had been living as a horse pulling a buggy. Horses wear blinders to protect them from being startled by movement out of the corner of their eyes. They do not get the full view of the road or it might scare them into running uncontrollably. My blinders protected me from seeing the full picture as well. Once they were removed, it was difficult to reconcile what I saw with what I had always believed. I was not out of control, but I was scared. There was an apparent dichotomy between what I knew about whiteness as "good" or at least morally neutral and the new words that I learned, such as self-serving, racist, and supremacist. These are certainly not perceived as good or neutral descriptors. How can whites be both? We are implicitly and sometimes explicitly told throughout our lives that we are "good" because we are the standard to which everyone else is compared. At the same time, we are also "evil" because we created a system where we are, in fact, the normative position. In my white students, I see a struggle for understanding and reconciliation of these dichotomous messages. Once the blinders come off, it is a difficult journey. It can be very painful. Some students actively resist while others work through the pain toward a positive, antiracist white identity. It is part of the process that Janet Helms outlines in her white racial identity model.

Helms (1990) suggests that by examining one's own whiteness and the constructs of privilege that are tied to it, one comes to have a positive understanding of white identity and a consciousness about oneself in the world. Having this consciousness then may allow oneself the ability to step into the worldview of others in a way that empathizes with and respects another's perspective. This theory parallels identity models developed for people of color (Cross 1971; Helms 1984). However, one major difference is that the developmental issue for whites is about the abandonment of entitlement rather than overcoming internalized racism (Helms 1995).

If I can begin to get students, particularly white students, to think about the social construction of race and its meaning in society, I can begin to pull them out of "the water" as I was pulled at that same age. Undoubtedly, a single course will not change a lifetime of messages about whiteness and racism, but it can be a catalyst for continued exploration and change.

But I wondered how to construct a classroom experience that would move students along the identity development process. I never had a course in college that emphasized the social construction of race, let alone whiteness. So, I often questioned whether having a salient target identity was necessary to understand one's privileged identities? I have found, however, that significant events occur in all kinds of spaces. Like me, target identities may play a role for some, but events or people are equally as significant for others. Becky Thompson's (2001) recent book *A Promise and a Way of Life: White Antiracist Activism* helped me to understand the uniqueness of each person's experience in understanding whiteness. At first, this was troubling. How can I structure a classroom experience that will create a significant experience? Then I remembered the fish in water metaphor. My role is to make that water visible. I have seen students change in a semester, and I believe that what we do in the classroom is vital to the understanding that race, specifically whiteness, is a social construction.

Process Issues in the Classroom

Currently, I teach with the Program on Intergroup Relations at the University of Michigan. We are a social justice education program. As such, we assume there is structural inequality and seek to make students aware of institutional forces, oppression, privilege, and power so that students can make decisions about working for social change. This produces a clear imperative to consider whiteness in the classroom.

So in my classroom, with this subject matter, it is fairly clear that race is there. However, it is actually present in every classroom. What I mean is that our society is so race-conscious that the topic cannot help but be infused. We can choose to acknowledge it or ignore it but it is still there. For a long time, as someone who is white, I could not or maybe refused to see this. "If I am not thinking about race, then how is it there? I am trying to treat everyone the same (i.e., like little white me) so what's the big deal? *They* (People of Color) keep bringing it up and I do not understand it."

What I realized is that racism, white privilege, and institutional inequality exist. Therefore, when talking about it outright in the classroom or considering its broader impact on the course, race is relevant. As such, there are two important "process" considerations that are relevant for any classroom, regardless of course topic. These are: the impact of the teacher's identity on the course and the classroom teaching style. My identity as a white, lesbian, Christian-identified woman from an upper-middle-class background shapes the worldview I bring to any classroom. For example, I recently developed a new course called Foundations of Intergroup Relations. I carefully considered the goals and objectives of the course and chose texts consistent with the goals. It was not until I was getting ready to order the books that I realized that I had chosen three texts by white men. I did have a coursepack that included perspectives by white women and women and men of color, but my primary texts were all written by white, heterosexual men. Needless to say, I dropped one book, changed the other text, and added articles to the coursepack to reflect a wider perspective. That is not to say that the texts I had originally chosen were bad. On the contrary, I still find those books to be valuable. But they all spoke to me and my experience. They reflected my identity perspective as a white antiracist person. My whiteness got in the way.

So before I can engage students in a process, I must be critically aware of the impact of my own identity on the classroom. Without knowledge about my own worldview and a commitment to challenge my own biases, I could, in fact, reinforce viewpoints that are intolerant and insensitive in the courses I teach. Therefore it is vital for me to remain present with my own learning about identity and white privilege. Jennifer Holladay of the Southern Poverty Law Center calls this doing one's "white homework." Speaking at a conference on white privilege (2002, April) she named a number of important homework steps. Three of them are particularly significant to me and are the pieces of white homework I frequently engage.

First is to read. I did not live through much of the civil rights movement in this country. I sometimes complain about my students' lack of historical memory, but I am also too young to remember some of the major events that shaped intergroup relations in the United States. I read to learn about those significant events that I did not experience directly. I also read to keep current with what authors of color have said and are saying about the imperative issues in antiracism. Furthermore, I read about allies and activism by white antiracist educators and authors.

Another important homework assignment is to talk with others. One way I do this is through a community group called Race Matters. It is unconnected with the university and allows me to listen, learn, and challenge others and myself around racial issues in the lesbian, gay, bisexual, and transgender community. The group is composed of people of color and white people in the LGBT community. This is only one avenue I utilize for talking with others. It is a means of engaging the theoretical knowledge I gain from reading and writing.

The third homework piece for me is about examining whether my behavior matches my values. Am I truly living my life in an antiracist way? If not, how did I get off track and how do I get back on? This scrutiny occurs through personal reflection as well as through dialogue with colleagues and friends who are white and of color.

Obviously through these examples of white homework, it is clear that thinking about whiteness is intentional. For me, opposing the standard construction of whiteness has to begin with myself and has to continue deliberately. It is very easy to forget about doing my homework. Sometimes I want to take a day off. I am busy and other issues are pressing. Yet, my friends and colleagues of color do not have the luxury of taking the day off from the impact of white privilege on their lives. If I ask my students to notice whiteness and its effect, I must be willing to steadfastly do it myself.

Another "process" consideration is teaching style. More and more research has indicated that student-centered teaching is positive. The research on student learning highlights a twenty-five-year trend related to student performance in the classroom. Today, students are understood to engage in "surface" and "deep" approaches to processing material (Entwistle 1998; Marton & Säljö 1997). These learning perspectives lead to primarily two modes of classroom teaching emphasis: teacher-centered and student-centered. Typically, a teacher-centered classroom is one where "knowledge and methods/techniques [are] transmitted from a knower to the learner" (Terenzini 1999, p. 36). This has been and continues to be the primary method of university classroom teaching. The faculty member is perceived as the "sage on the stage" providing information for students to absorb (Terenzini 1999).

A student-centered approach is markedly different. It is an environment "designed to take advantage of the multiple opportunities we have to shape or influence student learning" (Terenzini 1999, p. 38). Also called learner-centered, it introduces students to other people who can provide a greater breadth or depth of learning about a subject matter. Nevitt Sanford (1967) identified the primary process of learning as confronting something different from what one has experienced in that past. His theory relates to challenging and supporting students in that learning process. For him, the purpose of student-centered learning is to provide the challenge by engaging students in "the Different" while at the same time providing them an outlet for response and support (Terenzini 1999).

So, not only is a student-centered approach a positive one for "deep" student learning, this mode of instruction also helps students to engage in new knowledge in ways that support meaning making. Learner-centered approaches position students to engage with other students, the teacher, and the course material to grapple with difficult issues like socialization and the construction of knowledge.

In addition, the traditional method of learning from a teacher-centered approach stems from ubiquitous conceptions about whiteness. Cultural values such as individualism, rationalism, objectivity, and competition have been identified as typical white cultural norms (Helms 1992). These have produced classroom practice often emphasizing what Paulo Freire (1970/1998) calls the "banking method" of teaching, in which the teacher is the primary transmitter of knowledge while students are simply receivers. This method leads to teacher-centered practice, which supports traditional notions of white culture. Ironically, this practice was not even working well for white students. So I make an effort to utilize cooperative learning techniques involving small groups, dyad pairs, group discussion, and student-centered knowledge. For me, this has been a good way to circumvent traditional notions of whiteness as well as support students with various learning styles and social identities.

Revealing the Water

In addition to the process issues that impact the classroom, I utilize three strategies to interrupt the social construction of whiteness in the classroom. By naming its presence, by talking about white privilege, specifically how I as a white person have benefited from being white, and by acknowledging the institutional system of racism that continues to benefit white people, I attempt to get students to feel more comfortable thinking and talking about whiteness. To return to the metaphor, I expose them to the water that is surrounding them.

The issue of naming is very important. I recognize that to name my whiteness is surprising and uncomfortable for white students and odd and sometimes dubious for students of color. As I mentioned, never in my formal education process up through my undergraduate years, did any of my white teachers talk about being white. Indeed, the concept seems new to my students as well.

It is my understanding that the process of naming comes from second-wave feminism. It was not until the 1970s that women began to collectively name and talk about their life experiences. This occurred in consciousness-raising groups in which, often for the first time, women could talk about difficult issues and have a safe place to recognize that they were not alone. Naming is the process of getting out in the open what everyone knows is there but no one is talking about. It is often the elephant in the room. We can choose to ignore it or we can address it. However, it is clear that when we ignore it, the elephant does not go away. It continues to sit there in the room and it eventually has agency in the very place where it is trying to be overlooked.

It is similar with whiteness but not identical. As previously established, whiteness is socially constructed and therefore has meaning that we, as a society, create. The difference, however, is that white people who have not been exposed to talking about whiteness do not necessarily sense this "elephant." They speak about race when it "becomes an issue," a coded term that means when people of color talk about race. There is an assumption that conceptions of race or racism do not exist unless we are talking about people of color issues.

For example, I was watching a morning talk show recently and they showed a clip of the television show, *Survivor*. Following the clip, the host interviewed an African American man who had just recently been voted off of the show. The interviewer said, "You made race an issue. Why?" Yet the clip from the show clearly revealed that the white folk were talking about race long before the African American man named it. They used coded language but it was clearly based on race. For example, this man did not "want to be part of the team." He was "threatening" to them because of his athletic ability to win any immunity challenge. They never called it race; indeed, it is possible that they truly did not recognize their comments as racialized, yet race was clearly central and wrapped up in the entire conversation.

As this one situation exemplifies, race can be present in the most ordinary examples, even when it appears to white people to be a racially neutral subject. The elephant is there. In a class on intergroup relations, where discussions about diversity, oppression, and privilege are central, the discussion of whiteness has to be specified. It is even more critical for me to name this issue early and create a space for the "elephant" to be revealed and discussed. I generally do this by telling my story—my story of coming out as white. It sounds kind of strange and indeed, students have told me, it is. I do not think my experience in school was radically different from most of theirs. They, too, have probably had few white teachers talk about their whiteness.

By naming my whiteness, my white students generally become very uncomfortable. As in my previous examples in this chapter, white people learn early it is not polite to talk about whiteness. In fact, it is taboo. We have been taught that to notice whiteness and to talk about it is synonymous with active racists like skinheads or Ku Klux Klan members. I cannot think of a time when any adult every told this to me outright, but I learned it as well as anyone. The Klan's message was one of supremacy and to associate oneself with them was bad. As long as we were not actively participating in racial bigotry, then we were not racist. But begin to talk about whiteness and people get nervous.

Students of color, I have noticed, respond differently. I think they, too, are surprised when I begin talking about whiteness, likely for the same reasons as my white students. It just is not something that white people do. To do so certainly gets attention and diminishes the colorblind thinking where the mention of race, mine or anyone else's, is taboo. The students are also skeptical. Rightly so. I have talked with a number of students of color who have told me that white teachers who engage in talking about race have invariably hurt them over time. The reason has to do with trust. The teacher builds up a level of trust with these students and then lets them down with an unintended racist remark or a limit to their understanding of racial issues.

Clearly that will happen with me, too. Good intentions cannot make up for racism when it occurs. I try to let students know that I am engaged in a learning process about my whiteness and about white racism in general. I am explicit with them that I am going to make mistakes and when I do, I am committed to working through them. Understanding that I am not infallible and that I take responsibility for my own learning leads to diminished skepticism over time. This typically occurs after a series of challenges. These are tests to see if they can trust the ally in me. I support their healthy skepticism. I do not take offense; in fact I would be worried were it not there.

The next way I engage directly in the classroom is by talking about white privilege. Beverly Daniel Tatum (1999) calls racism a system of advantage based on race. To utilize this definition is to really make white people feel uncomfortable. Because we learned that we were not culpable in racism if we were not actively engaged in supremacist organizations, it is discomforting to believe that we, as white people, have played a role in racism.

White privilege comes in the form of economic, educational, and psychological privilege. It is often difficult to recognize economic or education advantages until they are challenged. For example, white workers take for granted their privilege until economic changes lead to job loss. It is at that time when many laborers blame people of color for "taking" their jobs. Similarly, white students who feel entitled to be admitted into college blame affirmative action and students of color for "taking" their spot when denied admission to college. Psychological privilege stems from the "whiteness as standard" argument. Always knowing that one's racial position is the norm is an advantage that whites experience in U.S. society. Having the option to think about one's race or not is also a psychological privilege that only white people experience in this U.S. context (Frankenberg 1993; McIntosh 1989).

So I begin to talk about my own experiences with privilege. Some examples are based on white privilege while others are based on social class. I mention some of the examples that have been presented in this chapter and try to model taking responsibility for my learning around racism. I also try to demonstrate how these privileges (which I did not initially recognize as advantages) unconsciously taught me to feel entitled to be treated in a particular way. For example, I never worried about being followed in a store because I looked threatening or like a thief. I never connected that innocence to my whiteness. But when I recognized that people of color were often profiled as potential shoplifters and treated accordingly, I denied that it had anything to do with me. Instead, I blamed those people of color who actually *had* been shoplifters and therefore gave innocent people a bad rap. According to my logic at the time, it was unfortunate but okay to lump an entire category of people together based on the color of their skin. But because white people are viewed as individuals and not a racial group, any white shoplifters were seen as perpetrating crimes as individuals, which had nothing to do with me. This individualized approach is a privilege that white people enjoy. Additionally, it was not until much later that I recognized that images, stories, and writings about people of color actually gave me messages about my whiteness, as well.

A further discussion strategy in acknowledging the social construction of whiteness involves an emphasis on institutional racism. That is, the "policies of the dominant race/ethnic/gender institutions and the behavior of individuals who control these institutions and implement policies that are intended to have a differential and/or harmful effect on minority race/ethnic/gender groups" (Pincus 2000, p. 31). This coincides with white privilege. To understand social institutions like the educational system, the legal system, media organizations, or religious establishments is to understand that white people benefit even when white people in general are not acting out in hatred toward people of color. This goes back to Tatum's (1999) definition of racism as a system of advantage based on race. To me, understanding white privilege hinges upon understanding institutional racism. Similarly, grasping the process of socialization (from various institutional forces) helps to realize the social construction of whiteness.

I believe that the discussion of institutional racism is critical. It can help white students get beyond their guilt and can help students of color recognize that individual white people have been socialized by powerful institutions. White students are often resistant to hearing about white racism because few have ever consciously (in their minds) engaged in openly, outwardly racist actions. So they do not want to be lumped into the racist category. Tatum (1999) explains the question from white people: Are all whites racist? She suggests that what whites are really asking is "Are you saying all whites are bad people?" (p. 307). Because racism is linked to being a bad person, it is a terrible affront to be considered racist, especially when one does not conceive of ever having acted in a racist fashion. So when white students can recognize that they are not personally to blame for racism but that they have been taught a racist ideology through social institutions, they too can be a part of a creating change in the world. However, the other message they must receive is that even though they may not be personally culpable, they do benefit from a system that privileges white people. Therefore, they also have a responsibility to act on this new knowledge.

For students of color, my experience has been that they are already keenly aware of both white privilege and institutional racism. At the same time, through discussions in the classroom, I try to move them beyond personal blame of "all whites are bad people" to instead critique those institutions that continue racist knowledge construction. At the same time, students of color must hear from me and probably more significantly, from their white student colleagues, the commitment to unlearn racism.

In the Program on Intergroup Relations generally, and in my courses specifically, I conclude the semester with a segment on building alliances across groups. To me, however, this is the weakest part of any of our or my courses. White students are just beginning to see their whiteness. Many are in various stages of identity development, which may include resistance to the issues or blaming people of color for their own oppression. I have found that white students, after a single semester are typically not ready to be antiracist allies. They often talk about stopping racist jokes among their friends and family or continuing their reading about other groups. But fundamental lifestyle change has not entered their minds.

This is often a frustrating time of semester for me. I want change. I want to know that I was successful in subverting whiteness in the classroom. At the same time, I return to my "fish in the water" metaphor. I exposed the water. The students, as fish, can now look at it a little more closely. They can compare it to the air and critique it. This is the change I must look for in a thirteen-week course. Indeed, understanding whiteness is a lifelong process. It certainly took me much longer than a semester to decide I wanted to engage in that process. I recognize that most of my white students are no different.

Summary

I have been white since the day I was born. I know that sounds like a ridiculous statement. To look at me at any point in my life, one would know that I am white. As a child my hair was blond as snow. Today my hair is darker but my skin is still fair. My features are similar to my Scottish and Anglo-Saxon ancestors. No one would mistake me for anything but white. But for so long, I never saw my whiteness. It was masked by a privilege that made my skin color the standard. But by being "pulled out of the water," I began to notice my color and recognize the benefits it gave me. Some will deny those benefits, hold fast to longtime beliefs, and sink back into the comfortable surroundings of the water. I would rather make the decision to abandon racist practices. The consciousness of my whiteness is finally with me. Today, some people call me hypersensitive. Perhaps that is so, but it is only recently that I have begun to acknowledge the significance of being white. My awakening will never be complete nor will that of my students.

I try to model antiracist practice in the classroom and in my life. I engage in my own "white homework." In the classroom, I name whiteness, white privilege, and institutional racism as issues. I attempt to include authentic voices of color through textbooks and discussion. I utilize a student-centered teaching method that allows students to ask difficult questions and engage experiential exercises to see new ways of being in the world. Is this enough? For some students, I know I plant a seed. They leave the class angry and frustrated that I have turned their world upside down. For others, I see a spark. I observe students of color who gain a measure of hope that there really are white folk trying to live an antiracist existence (certainly without perfection) and white students who want to continue their learning. Maybe they will take another course from the Program on Intergroup Relations, engage in social activism, or continue on a path toward antiracism. These are the students I hang on to. They give me the spirit to continue. Their enthusiasm and struggle electrify the learning process. They have discovered "the water" and are challenged to stir it up, make it known, and create a fresh understanding of who they can be.

References

Clark, C., & O'Donnell, J. (Eds.). (1999). *Becoming and unbecoming white: Owning and disowning a racial identity*. Westport, CT: Bergin & Garvey.

Cross, W. E., Jr. (1971). The Negro-to-Black conversion experience. *Black World* (July), 13–27.

Entwistle, N. (1998). Improving teaching through research on student learning. In James J. F. Forest (Ed.), *University teaching: International perspectives* (pp. 73–112). New York: Garland Publishing.

Erickson, F. (1986). Qualitative methods in research on teaching. In M. Wittrock (Ed.), *Handbook of research on teaching* (3rd ed., pp. 119–61). New York: Macmillan.

Frankenberg, R. (1993). *White women, race matters: The social construction of whiteness*. Minneapolis: University of Minnesota Press.

Freire, P. (1970/1998). *Pedagogy of the oppressed* (rev. ed.). (M. Bergman Ramos, Trans.). New York: Continuum.

Helms, J. E. (1984). Toward a theoretical explanation of the effects of race on counseling: A black and white model. *The Counseling Psychologist, 12*(4), 153–64.

Helms, J. E. (Ed.). (1990). *Black and white racial identity: Theory, research, and practice*. New York: Greenwood Press.

Helms, J. E. (1992). *A race is a nice thing to have: A guide to being a white person or understanding the white persons in your life*. Topeka, KS: Content Communications.

Helms, J. E. (1995). An update of Helms's white and people of color racial identity models. In J. G. Ponterotto, J. M. Casas, L. A. Suzuki, & C. M. Alexander (Eds.), *Handbook of multicultural counseling*, (pp. 181–98). Thousand Oaks, CA: Sage.

Holladay, J. (2002, April). Keynote speech. Presented at the 3rd Annual Conference on White Privilege, Pella, Iowa.

Katz, J. H. (1978). *White awareness: Handbook for anti-racism training.* Norman: University of Oklahoma Press.

Kivel, P. (2002). *Uprooting racism: How white people can work for racial justice* (rev. ed.). Philadelphia: New Society Publishers.

Marton, F., & Säljö, R. (1997). Approaches to learning. In F. Marton, D. Hounsell, & N. Entwistle (Eds.), *The experience of learning: Implications for teaching and studying in higher education* (2nd ed., pp. 39–58). Edinburgh, Scotland: Scottish Academic Press.

McIntosh, P. (1988). *White privilege and male privilege: A personal account of coming to see correspondences through work in women's studies.* Working paper no. 189. Wellesley, MA: Center for Research on Women.

McIntosh, P. (1989). White Privilege: Unpacking the invisible knapsack. *Peace and Freedom,* (July/August), 10–12.

McLaren, P. (1991). Decentering culture: Postmodernism, resistance, and critical pedagogy. In N. B. Wyner (Ed.), *Current perspectives on the culture of schools* (pp. 232–57). Boston: Brookline.

Omi, M., & Winant, H. (1994). *Racial formation in the United States: From the 1960s to the 1990s* (2nd ed.). New York: Routledge.

Pincus, F. L. (2000). Discrimination comes in many forms: Individual, institutional, and structural. In M. Adams, W. J. Blumenfeld, R. Castañeda, H. W. Hackman, M. L. Peters, & X. Zúñiga (Eds.), *Readings for diversity and social justice* (pp. 31–35). New York: Routledge.

Random House Webster's College Dictionary (1995). New York: Random House.

Sanford, N. (1967). *Where colleges fail: A study of the student as a person.* San Francisco: Jossey-Bass.

Takaki, R. (1993). *A different mirror: A history of multicultural America.* New York: Little, Brown, and Company.

Tatum, B. D. (1999). Defining racism: "Can we talk?" In A. Kesselman, L. D. McNair, & N. Schniedewind (Eds.), *Women images and realities: A multicultural anthology* (pp. 303–8). Mountain View, CA: Mayfield Publishing.

Terenzini, P. T. (1999). Research and practice in undergraduate education: And never the twain shall meet? *Higher Education, 38,* 33–48.

Thompson, B. (2001). *A promise and a way of life: White antiracist activism.* Minneapolis: University of Minnesota Press.

Zinn, H. (1995). *A people's history of the United States: 1492–Present* (rev. ed.). New York: HarperPerennial.

PART III

Ways of Knowing

8

Teaching within the Circle: Methods for an American Indian Teaching and Learning Style, a Tribal Paradigm

Rosemary Christensen

As was the routine for many Indian children of my age group, I attended a school designed by the state and the federal government, aided and abetted by charitable organizations for my village (reservation). It reflected the values, customs, and religious milieu of the white man's world. This form of schooling was not chosen by my parents but was imposed and enforced through government policy that provided funds to missionary groups and others (Fuchs & Havighurst 1973). I come from an orally based society, one functioning through and framed by Elder epistemology. Another name for this form of instruction, still practiced today among Indians, is oral tradition.

The schooling structure imposed on my grandfathers, grandmothers, parents, and siblings continues and is the current form in use. In college and graduate school, I wondered why instruction was presented in the particular way it was—and still is. I still wonder, because the data is unequivocal in stating that minority children have and continue to have trouble in school. The measure most often cited as an indicator of this trouble is called the *achievement gap*. Theories of why the gap continues, after decades of funding for increasing achievement through many programs, place blame on poverty, peer pressure, student turnover, parenting, teacher quality, teacher expectations, television, and test bias (Viadero 1999, p. 30).

However, the complex factors involved in the achievement gap issue are not understood in their entirety. Researcher Grissmer and colleagues (2000) at RAND,[1] the California-based think tank, indicate that money makes a difference, yet maintain that the gap is there and will continue to grow. Another RAND study highlights the contribution culture makes toward learning (Vernez, Krop, & Rydell 1999). In an effort to address the achievement gap, the Carnegie middle school project asks schools to "shift from departmentalized, impersonalized, content-driven classrooms to child-centered, interdisciplinary learning communities, rich with opportunities for students to learn collectively and experientially through deep engagement in thematic, problem-based curricula." (Oakes, Quartz, Ryan, & Lipton 2000, p. 27). As these studies suggest, it may be the time to try radical new ideas, methods, and concepts. I suggest a teaching method based in traditional ideas from Indian society.

Oral Tradition: An Indian Way of Learning

Indian society vocalizes belief in and continues to practice oral tradition. The values and principles given through eons of Elder teachings are pervasive throughout the holistic world of the Indian. Elder knowledge passed through oral tradition is important and even structural in the holistic world of the Indian. Elders advance traditional teachings from generation to generation through conversational word of mouth, stories, ceremonies (participation learning), and other teachings. The teachings may vary from Tribe to Tribe, which constitutes cultural difference among Tribes; yet the Tribes commonly reflect heritage from a holistic world (see, for example, Cajete 1994; Brown 1982/1988 [chapter on Time and Process]; Deloria 1999 [chapter on Philosophy]).

Growing up in the Indian-dominant village of my mother meant I saw and spoke to Elders on a daily basis, absorbing their form of instruction. At the same time, with other Indian children I attended the mission school on my reserve, taught by white nuns. High school was spent off the reservation, with non-Indian children dominant, and with white teachers and other white (non-Indian) adults dominant. In some cases, during graduate school days, I was fortunate enough to work with other Indians, and sometimes we had an opportunity to teach a class or two. It was then that I knew, for sure, that we could amend and or extend the ways of teaching to reflect better the Indian way of learning, knowing, and enlightenment. For thirty-two years, I have tried and continue to try out various methods of teaching college students that might reflect the world I know: the Tribal world.

Tribal people learning the "white man" or dominant "Western" system, try to fit it within tribal traditions, culture, and ways of behaving that reflect and mean normalcy, saneness, and rightness. Ross (1996) describes native understanding on how to share information, or educate others, by noting that it should be shared in ways that allow listeners or readers to take whatever meaning they may find, based on their own background and experience (p. x). Schein (1985) explains that a breakdown of communication may occur when two culturally different people interact because the assumptions behind the same English words may vary. Researchers, teachers, and others glean meaning out of interactions based on their own cultural norms. Leas (1982) defines norms as rules that allow groups to function smoothly. People are not always aware how these unwritten rules shape behavior. Leas also indicates that norms not only dictate behavior but also impose sanctions for unacceptable behavior (p. 88). When culturally different people meet and interact according to their specific group norms, misunderstanding will follow. In the case of schooling, children taught by a teacher reflecting and acting within a cultural norm different from the child may not succeed in that classroom. Research shows that children may do better if the teacher is aware of and practices some of the culturally related activities the child is used to from home and community (see, for example, Demmert & Towner 2003). I am not advocating that teachers must learn and teach in methods conducive or favorable to each child's culture, as that may be impossible; but I am suggesting that we try out methods, in addition to our current methods, that include techniques that resonate with other cultures.

This chapter examines, explores, and explains teaching methods, techniques, and behaviors learned through experience during approximately twenty or so years. The techniques and varying procedures within the methodology change from time to time, as I learn more from observing Elder teachers, discussing my activities with them, and talking with peer-age colleagues. Professors William Demmert (Tlingit/Lakota, Alaska) at Bellingham, Western Washington University, and Linda Oxendine (Lumbee, Pembroke) at the University of North Carolina, Pembroke (UNCP), for example, use a similar teaching form. I teach American Indian Studies in a state university. I believe the methods (or variations of) described in this chapter, which are based on an understanding and knowledge of oral tradition as learned through experience growing up in a dominant Indian society and reinforced in later years by close association with teaching Elders, are appropriate for grade school, high school, and community school as well.

The method of teaching described here is based on American Indian values, psychology, and philosophy as understood, reflected, and articulated by one American Indian professional educator. It is these intellectual constructs that form the basis for Circle Teaching, not the actual teaching methods and techniques. Circle Teaching is a pedagogy that has methods and techniques in the same way other more familiar pedagogies used in educational institutions have their methods and techniques. The techniques I developed depend on the experience, knowledge, and schooling of its practitioner as is the case for any teacher. I have used Indian and non-Indian sources to document and flesh out articulation of Circle Teaching. The most important resource, however, is and remains Elders, those from my childhood village, and others met throughout my life, whom I work with and continue to engage in dialogue as I teach at university.

Implementing Oral Tradition in the Classroom

At first, I was just trying to imitate old people who taught me in my home village. Their way of telling me information made me feel comfortable and smart. Then, I got interested in why they passed on information in the way they did. Now I am a serious practitioner of the art of teaching, trying methods that reflect the values, moral and ethical code, customs, rules, beliefs, and practices passed on by our old people. This frame of reference is Elder epistemology.

From time to time, scholars discuss epistemology. Recently, indigenous knowledge was the subject of a series of exchanges on the Internet.[2] Peter Hanohano (1999) discussed Elder knowledge in his article on native epistemology. He speaks to a holistic model fusing culture and education (p. 207). Alaskan Native organizations in February 2000 adopted "guidelines for respecting cultural knowledge," which can be viewed at their Web site (http://www.ankn.uaf.edu/standards/CulturalDoc.html). The document reinforces the idea that Elder knowledge is important. We know, as scholars articulate (Gill 1999), that "all knowing takes place within a cultural and political context, as well as necessarily being achieved by concrete persons who bring with them certain values, aspirations, and commitments . . . these factors actually contribute to what knowledge means . . ." (p. 242).

Most people who have attended school in the United States can describe a common teaching method in which the teacher stands, behind a barrier usually, in front of the students who are sitting in rows. Students are given information, usually from written sources, with use of tools such as the blackboard, the overhead projector, and videos. The teacher gives exams or tests featuring questions, required essays, or written answers. The teacher is in charge. Within this teaching method, students who are naturally competitive will have a better chance of getting noticed by the teacher. The teacher often asks questions regarding factual knowledge or comprehension. Students study for tests by memorizing chunks of materials. The teacher may augment testing with essays graded on a variety of things including the quality of the writing and presentation. Written references are highly valued. As long as the student gives back to the teacher something close to what the teacher lectured about or emphasized during the class, the student will receive a good grade.

The teaching method just described is familiar to the dominant society and is reinforced in daily life, through the way knowledge is communicated in mass media, in childrearing, and in economic practices. It is commonly used in colleges and universities for training teachers (although no longer the only method). It is the method used by the white teachers that taught Indians on my home reserve/village. But it is not the only method of teaching, nor does it fit every value orientation in the world. Dominant American society is dominant in numbers and in its value structure; it appears to value aggressive behavior in the search for knowledge. People with different ways of seeing and using knowledge teach their children in a vastly different way. Within American Indian society, learners are treated as participants in learning by experience, with the teacher, who, by virtue of possessing additional experience, is obligated to help those younger. Care is taken to provide information that will allow the learner to experience the learning, in his own way, at his own pace, and in as much comfort as is possible to provide, given the circumstances and taking into account others involved. The older one ensures that the younger one gets credit for his ideas and is treated in the special manner one would use with young people. The old one apologizes if the young one feels bad about anything that might be said and be construed to be demeaning to the learner. The young one is evaluated from where he began, and then where he moved from that beginning, with the teacher recognizing how his own limitations influence his ability to appraise and teach the student. Young people bring something very special to any learning situation. They have great, renewable stores of energy, possess untapped reservoirs of creativity, and have new ways of solving problems. Plus young people are beautiful. Each learner brings something special to any learning mix. An effort is made to build a learning environment comfortable for using individual skills in an exchanging, reciprocal way between the teacher and the learner.

The teaching process emphasizes individual skills within a protective grouping that encourages individual skills to mesh with other individuals' skills toward something that might not be possible alone; yet each individual is important. The importance of the individual is reinforced through the group in learning to respect each other, learning behaviors meant to not interfere one with another, and building communication skills burnishing such behaviors. Creating such a learning environment may involve seeking out an old one, giving a special, little gift, and asking if we can learn together. If the old one accepts, learning proceeds, with the Elder teacher providing small but important clues toward learning progress. The old one uses subtlety within a simple-seeming complexity to show his understanding of the learner's excellent learning aptitude.

The Teacher's Role

A teacher's primary function in Circle Teaching is as a coach, a limited expert on a portion of what is learned, a tutor when needed, an oral and written library source, and a poser of subtle, diffident learning comments at the right time and the right place to the right person for the right reason. Good teachers reinforce learners at the appropriate time and do not expect them to exhibit learning in all its forms. Our Elder teachers expected us to learn at our natural pace, proceeding carefully but firmly through the circles of learning and knowledge, just as the Hero proceeded through a burning circle in the Germanic legend to claim the Valkyrie.

The teacher is not a being above the learner, more valued than, or better than the learner. The learner and the teacher strive to reach levels of respect, relationship, and reciprocity that must exist among living things to maintain a healthy balance. *Respect* means to be considerate of each living thing, every day using a process that ensures that life needs are met in an honorable way. *Relationship* means being connected one to another through unbroken, eternal ties that commence from birth to death and that present constant obligations of responsibility and honor. *Reciprocity* means action one to another on the base of mutual respect and giving in return. One cares more for a relative than oneself, thus whatever is done to, for, or with the living relative is done in that context.

The Teaching Circle

Form and its relationship to function is taken for granted in most schooling situations. Within an American Indian style of learning and teaching, the circle of teaching, an ancient Tribal usage, is form and function. Of these, functioning within the circle, always in existence among living things, is paramount, regardless of the form. For example, in educational institutions, tables may be bolted to the floor, or it is cumbersome for students to move chairs at the beginning of a class and then move them back at the end of a class. The rooms are configured for rows, with the writing-board, overhead machine, computer, television monitor, and other teacher-used technologies in the front of the room. Although it may be difficult to sit in a circle, it is more important to approximate the function of a circle regardless of the physical form. Using a circle in the classroom means students will see each other's faces instead of each other's backs. They will be able to see gestures and facial movement, learn and use names, and with the simple movement of the teacher joining the circle, participate in learner-teacher reciprocity. Utilizing nametags, when everyone is unknown, means that in a circle, everyone can see the names, and hence the learning of names is made easier. Speaking and hearing is more even in a circle than when trying to hear someone from the back of the room, for example. However, it is harder to hide in a circle, and students accustomed to "hiding" at the back of the room may assume a hostile attitude toward the form. For that reason, the form used becomes a total group choice for students during total group events, and in small group presentations, the smaller group decides the form. Eventually, students freely choose a circle, or semicircle depending on the mode of participation and what goals they have for providing information within the classroom.

The circle of teaching is formed by the concepts or principles of independence or personal sovereignty, respect for Elders, connectedness to all living things, and indirect communications through the screen of Elder traditional knowledge. These value concepts with accompanying behaviors are functions of the circle form. Through participation, a teaching-learning embryo forms from the interaction of teacher and learner; one that will form and reform constantly and perhaps grow out of the rudiment state into another form of life—as all living things do. As in all living things, the form may grow in a negative fashion as well as in a positive one, or elements of both may be present.

An emphasis on *personal sovereignty* is the fundamental difference between the ideals of Indian Tribes and the dominant society. We see freedom expressed through the behaviors of Turtle Island (name given to North America by many natives) natives as an intellectual gift to the spoken values and written creed of the (relatively) young United States (see Weatherford 1991; Barreiro 1992; Johansen 1998). This notion is at variance with what is usually taught in schools, that Americans owe their allegiance and grateful thanks to the Greeks for the intellectual view of freedom celebrated every July Fourth. Roy Harvey Pearce speaks eloquently, albeit painfully to the Tribal ear, on the issue of how, where, and why white America received its ingrained ideas about American Indians (Pearce 1988). Wax and Thomas (1961) speak of the doctrine of noninterference relating simple yet compelling behavioral examples of how noninterference works in Indian society. In one memorable passage, they flatly state that interference is prohibited. In this method, students are provided choice whenever possible. The reason is based on the notion or core value of personal sovereignty. This value is pervasive and visible in Tribal society in North America, or Turtle Island (Wax & Thomas 1961; Wasson 1973; Poupart et al. 2000). Definitely, students are exposed to a cultural context utilizing behaviors based on a core Tribal value.

Age respect is an important Tribal concept. This pervasive native value is considered normal and expected, is natural and practiced as almost instinctual or habitual in one's action and demeanor toward Elders. It is a learned response. Indian manners demand Elder respect regardless of the Elder's outward manifestation relative to clothing, dwelling, position, social situation, or relative wealth of the living being. This particular competency is sometimes difficult for students to understand as they are bombarded daily through media and daily interactions by the lack of age respect in the dominant society. To say someone is "an old woman" or "acting like an old man" is an insult (designed as such) heard daily. Merchants buy their ads on television based on particular age groups and networks base their economic design on certain age groups that determine the standings of its offerings on a daily and weekly basis. Dominant society, as represented in the media, values youth over age, and the hoopla that surrounds the promotion of youth culture ensures that the wisdom and learning provided by the old ones is often a scarce, lightly valued, disregarded, and dismissed commodity.

American Indian society admires and places a high value on age deference not only because we are all intertwined in symbiotic relationships dependent on the value of knowing something life-sustaining that is best learned through experience, but because we value the undeniable worth of lived experience itself. Our Creation stories in many Tribal cultures speak to the youth of humans in the Creation cycle, and by implication value the Elders in the panoply of all living things. It is a value introduced and reinforced through ancient, recurring practice among Tribal people and other living things. However, learners and teachers may be from all age levels, supporting each other in learning through behaviors of age respect, reciprocity, and personal sovereignty.

The circle of relativity (the connectedness of all living things) is seen clearly in the ideals and practices of American Indians. The powerful Lakota intellectual, Black Elk, provides one well-known example in literature as he reminded his editor, John G. Neihardt (1932, p. 164):

> ... there can be no power in a square. You have noticed that everything an I   n-dian does is in a circle, and that is because the Power of the World always works in circles, and everything tries to be round ... Everything ... is done in a circle.

This poetic, beautiful, powerfully intellectual Lakota way of speaking suggests to us what scientists are proving to their satisfaction, that we live on a fragile globe with a hugely important connection to the sun, the moon, the stars, and indeed all living things; therefore, there is an inexorable connection between pervasive nature and humankind's sustainable behaviors.

Tribal goals speak to spiritual, cultural, social, economic, political, and cognitive well-being, intertwining or connecting life's dimensions on the Medicine Wheel of life. Cottom (1989) observed that cultural boundaries may move normally and naturally toward greater particularity or greater generality in our natural daily lives. The notion of the Medicine Wheel and its application to our lives is reflected in our normal behaviors. The ancient Medicine Wheel with four points on a circle represents the sacred four directions: the symbolic black, yellow, red, and white races of humanity. It also represents four worlds: the two-legged, the four-legged, that which grows, and that which forms the earth—or animal, vegetable, mineral, and humankind. It portrays the four cognitive dimensions of action, reflection, interpretation, and understanding or comprehension. These four worlds must balance (see Bopp 1989). Connectedness is wholeness. Cajete (1994) reminds us that the reason for creating a mandala is to "engender a process that recognizes the relatedness of elements in a specific context to a person, place or group" (p. 151).

An Indian perspective is evident, too, in writing, in that Indians write in a manner that reflects the way they hear stories, and the way they hear their Elders talk about themselves and others. Indian writing reflects dialogue heard from other Indians, in a customary tone, with lots of Indian humor. The writer, or storyteller, or communicator does not usually make connection between thoughts or ideas in writing. That is left to the independent listener to fill in as he or she sees fit. The Indian writer may paragraph differently. The sense of time and fillers between the time-space grids will reflect Indian ways, mores, and sense of correctness. Brumble (1988) mentions N. Scott Momaday (1966) as an example of this Indian form. He points out the use of short paragraphs with almost no connectors in the writing. Indian writers emulate the story form, the oral tradition in the writing medium.

Those who want to use the Circle Teaching methods described in this chapter will find it helpful to acquire competency in indirect communication, which interferes with another as little as possible. Indirect communication allows a range of subtlety not always evident in direct communication. For many Indians, indirect efforts used in interaction among living things reflects one's sense and grasp of good manners expected and used by well-brought-up people in a polite society. It means seeking and using other forms of communication other than questioning, which by its very nature is very direct. Indians value and highly appreciate a subtle approach. For example, an elder might say nothing when a younger person disagrees with an expressed point of view. Later, the young one might start to think about the lack of response, and wonder, therefore, how to approach expressing disagreement without interfering with the person's right to his/her view.

An important concept to consider and discuss in regard to communication is the art of *asking questions*. Questioning reflects cultural difference, and yet it is rarely discussed in scholarly research except to advocate honing the skill. Teaching need not rest solely on the technique of asking questions. Tribal people are taught to listen to Elders, not interrupt them as they are speaking, and to make sure a person is finished talking before entering a speaking mode. Silence is greatly valued and utilized by Tribal people. "Elders emphasized listening and not asking WHY . . . listening is considered very important. Questions were not encouraged. Asking questions was considered rude . . ." (Diamond, Cronk, & Von Rosen 1994, p. 9).

Western cultural forms are an overwhelming force. Frequently, Tribal people bow to the dominant force and forgo their natural functioning as Tribal individuals; giving in is less trouble and is commonly reinforced by white society. Abstracting traditional functions and then reapplying the concepts in other contexts as a new way to enact them may therefore be necessary if Indians are to withstand the vast strength of the Western form. The specific cultural function for which we were born and raised and that we pass on to the next generation can continue regardless of the form within which we must live because of outside forces and circumstances beyond our control.

Classroom Techniques

The brief discourse on Tribal value differences with accompanying behaviors is necessary background to an understanding and appreciation of the Circle Teaching described in this chapter, based as it is in a holistic Tribal cultural context. As just described, Circle Teaching uses an American Indian value construct consisting of the core value of personal sovereignty, connectedness, age respect, and indirect communication with the accompanying interactive behaviors of respect, reciprocity, and relationship that emanates from the Elder epistemology or knowledge practiced by Tribal communities as described earlier. Small group work is particularly suited to Circle Teaching as it supports these values, providing quality teacher-student exchanges. Teacher and students work with each other on a basis that allows for individual interaction, with discussion centering on a specific group and or student concern, not always possible where interaction takes place within a larger, total student classroom. Teachers then do not spend time working with a few students in a large group, which may be the normal routine in Academy classrooms where a few students take the time and attention of the teacher, while others may not be engaged in anything.

Circle Teaching emphasizes participation learning and remembering through thought patterns within a group process where the individual's skills are important and each has an opportunity to use his/her skills. Commonly, within classrooms talking and writing by individuals is prized; in Circle Teaching students are reminded that participation is not limited to talking, but that other personal skills are equally important. Peer teaching is emphasized, with listening a focus of group interactions. Students are asked not to take notes, raise their hands, or seek written instructions for daily discourse in the classroom. Instead, they are asked to listen, listen carefully, use mnemonics, seek a pattern of thinking that reflects what goes on during the entire interaction so they might, if need be, visit it in their minds, reconstruct or visualize what happened (Ross 1992, pattern thought), and use reasoning to figure out learning. They listen to each other, talk with each other, and with each other arrive at learning conclusions or summaries they may take with them and keep forever. An important part of the technique is critical thinking with its important elements for learning such as identifying central issues, comparative analysis, identifying assumptions, recognizing bias, noting values, and so on. Providing small-group interaction with the instructor regarding learning evaluation, materials examination, analysis, and an interactive human process that uses time and space dependent on each person's need is also part of the methodology. Students learn how to remember important teachings using techniques that do not depend on taking notes as a re-membering tool. Exams and other ways of evaluating learning are utilized through group process, oral activity, and independent choice.

This method is framed in a wholeness concept. In American Indian Tribal experience, wholeness is experienced in learning and teaching wherein wholeness defines and frames the interrelatedness of all living things. The intactness, a connected or linked circular inclusive worldview with the accompanying logical behaviors that reinforce that concept is the backbone of the method. It is different from the linear world with its ac-companying behaviors that make sense in that world. When possible, the methodology is utilized within forms that make sense to the wholeness concept. Inclusive circular spiral forms are utilized instead of linear, hier-archical, exclusive ways of current teaching models prevalent in modern classrooms. No negative connotation is meant by this comparison; it is provided as an explanation for the difference in techniques and methods in the model.

Teachers are advised to assist and guide students in using techniques described below, as students are accustomed to the "normal" way of doing things in the classroom and take time to get accustomed to different behav-iors. Groups are a focus and the nucleus for learning information, yet the individual is encouraged to use his or her skills in the working process of the group.

Circle Teaching begins the first day of class. Students are asked to sit in a circle. The teacher takes time to listen to students introduce themselves and either say something about what is expected in the class or answer a simple question posed by the teacher. For example, "Tell us your name, where you are from and explain where it is, and tell us one thing you know about Indians in Wisconsin." The teacher also takes a few minutes to speak about him/herself. In this way, students and teacher learn about each other. In the classroom, where students do not know each other and will not spend the entire day with each other, it is a simple thing to ask students to make nametags with names visible and, if the teacher wants to learn the names, to ask the student to put a picture on the back of the tag. In that way the teacher can take the tags and study them at home. In a col-lege classroom, this technique helps students learn each others' names and reminds them, as Socrates noted, "Names are important, a name is an in-strument of teaching, and of distinguishing natures" (as quoted in Sim-mons 2000, p. 432).

The teacher explains the group process during the first day of class, then gives the students time to mill around and visit a little before asking them to go out of the room, come back in again, and select a group of people for a base working group. During this time it is important to ask the students to move around, talk to each other, and look over people as possible group members. Give an adequate time for this, probably ten or fifteen minutes. Numbers in the groups may vary, but it is unwieldy usually to have groups larger than six (although some groups of eight work okay). After a period of time, when students are quite comfortable within their small group, the idea of working within the larger (total group) student set is introduced. Eventually students get quite good at group interaction with each other, but it doesn't come easy. I remind students they will probably work within a group for the rest of their working lives. Learn well how to do it in school.

The main group work consists of presenting class material to the other groups. Students approximate oral tradition by seeking knowledge (the teacher provides suitable materials), learning the teaching, then teaching it to the other students. Each group is responsible for a chapter or chapters from the teacher-assigned or recommended texts or materials. The class as a whole decides which group will do which portion of the materials. These choices reinforce the notion of personal sovereignty in a small way. Students do not need to read and present the books from front to back with Indian-written books, as the subject matter usually reflect a holistic world, with learning/teaching repeated throughout the book. By taking sections of the book in an order of their choosing, students experience a nonlinear way of approaching learning. However, it is up to the entire class to decide in what order to present the materials, and some classes may want to present them in a linear fashion (chapter 1, chapter 2, and so on). However, given choice, students almost always do not choose a linear schedule. Students are allowed, within reason, to decide when they are ready to present, even if the group as a whole has to change the set schedule to accommodate them (usually students ask the large group for permission). In addition, after the small groups make their choices, the groups work together to make final choices affecting the entire class.

Each group presents two or three times during the semester. After the first presentation, groups use question/comments to help the class integrate the material presented. For the second and third presentations, they use an oral remembering circle. Both these methods are described later in this section. Students are responsible for reading all of the course texts but are responsible for studying and presenting only a portion of the text.

Their learning of the texts they don't study is provided by their peers during the other group presentations, questions/learning comments, review circle, and preparation time during oral exam exercises. Students are reminded prior to group presentations that participation (that is required in group process) does not mean that each person must talk. When students are freed to not talk, if that is not their skill, they shine with other skills. They will create fun games, neat exercises, and other learning devices that include the total group in the learning process. As peers understand each other, students tend to use ways that their peers understand when teaching learning materials. Visuals drawn by talented students, ad hoc sculpting forms, and other illustration-type items are made by students to get their points across to their peers, along with writing and acting out skits.

Initially, student groups usually elect to go ahead and divide the materials in portions that they each study alone, and present alone, although ostensibly working in a group. After the first cycle where each group makes a presentation, the teacher provides feedback on how to integrate the materials each learned so that the total little group is responsible and each member knows the material well enough to respond to questions or lead discussion with the total class. Integrating their individual parts into a unified whole is the most difficult for the students, as they are accustomed to learning portions of work and giving it back to the teacher in some way. However, during the second cycle of presentations, when each group presents for the second time, with new material, the students usually do better at integrating the materials for themselves, and they are *always* more creative on how to garner participation from the total group.

I can plan on two complete cycles, where each group presents material it selected with agreement from the entire class, although in some semesters it is possible to do a third cycle. I look at the amount of material listed in the syllabus, usually two or three texts, and I suggest the number of chapters or sections each group ought to strive for. However, I ensure they know that is only a suggestion, and that gives the groups leeway to portion the material the way they decide in the big group discussions. This approach reinforces the personal sovereignty issue.

As mentioned earlier, during the first cycle, the students use questions and learning comments written after the presentation. Learning comments are remarks that in some way explore the teaching point, whether through comparing with something already known, exploring what other words might describe it, questioning the correctness of the teaching for use or application by the learner, or simply associating it with something as simple as what a person may have worn that day, whether it was hot, and so on. This reinforces respect for teaching methods students know and are used to. As students become comfortable and feel safe in the classroom they will respond to questions or learning comments with responses that have real depth and personal emotional insights.

For the second and (if time) third cycles, students participate in a remembering circle. Each student is asked to speak of what he or she remembers from the previous group presentation. I tell students that anything remembered during the time frame is gist for remembering, not just actual material presented. For example, a student may remember what another wore, as happened recently. She said how Joanne dressed like J. Lo and that is what she remembered. Because she did that remembering, others chimed in, and said, oh yeah, but you know what she said, and they remembered the lesson. Thus, students learn to absorb the total situation within which the material is presented, not just the material itself. This helps in learning remembering skills, the elders say. The students that presented the materials do not offer anything but are asked to say at the end how the class did with their presented materials. A person who cannot remember anything is allowed to pass and may have a chance to say something later as his or her memory is stirred by what other students say. Such secondhand remembering is a form of learning too, and reinforces the actual chosen learning. It is always reinforcing to the presenting group to see how much is remembered. From time to time, the teacher brings the class back to a remembering mode to reinforce earlier presentations (and the learning contained within them).

It is important to give students class time to do their small and total group orientation, to discuss how to divide the work, and to tell each other what was learned from individual reading and study. This latter activity needs coaching by the teacher, and I frequently join a group after they have read the material to model how to exchange material so that each small group member knows the entire assigned materials. One might talk, for example, about Black Elk during his formative years, but know nothing about his later years, because they divided up the work. I ask them to exchange their information, so both know the total. Because I know the material, I can demonstrate this with both individuals, and they see then how to integrate the information. Subsequently, as they exchange with other groups during formal presentations (in a group of forty-five students, one will usually have six to eight groups), students will see how to enlarge and present their materials for teaching to other groups. They get very creative in this regard, and soon the instructor realizes that it would be almost impossible, and very labor-intensive to try and reproduce the student activities within the unusual instructor-lecturer popular academy form. Students are more creative and energetic and know what will appeal to their peers, more so than any one teacher, so this form of teaching may reinforce the actual materials being "ingested" at a faster rate and the learning may be retained for a period of time. I usually provide a class period or two for students to work on their presentations, as they have difficulty doing it after class (remember they present as a group), although individual work agreed to within the group can be outside class.

As stressed before, the alignment of form with function is important because students are learning through, and in this method about, the holistic world that is so very different from the linear, categorical world that is ever-present in all of our lives. Students tend normally and naturally to use the form they are accustomed to, such as standing or sitting in lines and rows, standing in front, PowerPoint or overheads (which are really print on a board or screen, very similar to a book), television-type games such as jeopardy (very popular with my students), and so on. I tell students this is okay to begin with, as they must transfer from one form to another, but I suggest they think of other forms that might work for them.

Students are urged to critique the texts, materials, or other knowledge presented so that they are aware that knowledge presented by scholars changes over time according to new knowledge, and because it is a part of evaluating materials according to critical thinking elements. When students are participating in a culturally different form with culturally different materials, it becomes difficult for them to separate their form of knowledge based on their cultural norms from that of a universal form of knowledge. For example, one student asked in all seriousness how could anyone learn if they didn't ask questions. Frequently students appear to think that what they know, feel, and were taught is what all humans should know, feel, and be taught. Providing a different form of teaching and learning assists in working through the cultural knowledge proffered. Undertaking the learning within the form of a group process approximates the ways many Tribal people work and learn together.

Note that Circle Teaching reinforces the importance of attendance in that attendance, or lack of, affects the smooth working of a group. Students learn how important it is for them all to do their share, both in class and for work sessions after class. Attendance also reinforces the relationship built during the group process. Attendance and fair work from each member is a way of showing respect for the group. Therefore, students are involved in relationship building, respect, and reciprocal behavior, again, in a small way.

Exams: Oral and Otherwise

Grades are given on the presentations, and for the midterm and for the final exam. These are group grades. Presentation grades are for the small group, and midterm and final grades are for total group. The teacher gives group grades, usually after a cycle of presentations, offering feedback on what can be improved on for the next cycle of presentations (it is okay to provide for some individual grading throughout the class). Group and individual grades are carefully spelled out in the syllabus (I use a four-point embedded scale explained to students prior to the presentations). Groups are told that if a person in the group is not working to group standards, it is possible for the group to remove the student by talking with the instructor and discussing the best method of doing so. In some cases, it may be appropriate for the instructor to talk to the student instead of the students doing it, but my past experience shows that most times, students want to talk with the nonworking student themselves. In most cases, students resolve the issue, with the wayward student working to par according to group standards.

Students are provided a choice on method, kind, time, and duration of examination on learnings. The teacher provides an exam; either a series of questions or (as I usually do) guiding comments that reflect the desired learning for the class. The teacher also provides a grading guide and the elements of critical thinking to be used in presentations. Two choices (an opportunity to practice personal sovereignty) can be posed, although other choices are possible. Students are asked to determine whether they want to remain in their small groups and write an exam (using all appropriate standards for writing), turning in one paper for each group; or, as a total group choose to do a large-group oral exam. The entire class makes the choice. Other choices are possible given instructor and institution limitations.

In a large group oral exam students prepare a presentation based on several learning comments from the teacher, which suggest areas of learning to focus on. They decide how much time is required to present the oral exam and hand in an outline of their presentation, including responsibilities of each student, in advance. The total group oral exam allows students to organize and provide oral discourse on ideas, knowledge, and concepts provided throughout the class examination of selected teachings with appropriate use of skills individual students may have in the total group. The teacher hears the exam the students have prepared at the time agreed to by each. In this technique/method, the teacher is providing a way for students to learn how to work in a much larger, unknown, perhaps uncomfortable group, but with the help, support, and comfort of the small group. Also, each small group holds concentrated information gleaned from its presentation. Indeed, each group holds specific information that when put together forms a lot of information that is useful for the entire group.

Students tend to fall apart when faced with the actual independent movement of working within a total group without specific, narrowly framed directions from the teacher. I do not succumb to these feelings, but encourage them to work with each other. Classes have difficulties with this technique, but they work with it, mostly because it was their choice. The group is provided with class time to prepare for the oral exams, and it is usually better if the teacher is not in hearing distance while the preparation is under way. The class has the opportunity to work wherever it is most comfortable, which includes, but does not mandate, the classroom. Students usually meet in the classroom at first, to hammer out total group options, questions they may have of each other and what they know, and small group assignments. These latter usually conform to what each small group presented during the semester. It reinforces the learning of each small group, and they appear to value their stance as "experts" on a given topic in the exam. They may then go elsewhere to prepare as planned by the entire group.

Other Class Activities

Students are asked to write a required, although grade-neutral, think piece after reading an assigned article that everyone must read (this is done only once, and gives groups a discussion point in order to learn about each other). In this assignment there is no right or wrong, just thinking through what they read, and thoughtful processing of that information in light of what they know at the time or what they may learn from talking with each other. Assigning think pieces from time to time on various topics allows the students an opportunity to act as an individual, if desired. As usual, a choice is provided: students may write think pieces individually, or in a group, or they may elect to present their ideas orally to the rest of the class. Think pieces that are required but grade-neutral provide an opportunity to show respect for individual thinking on a given topic. If or when their thinking begins to change, they and the teacher can chart it through these think pieces.

The teacher augments student presentations by providing, from time to time, "normal" lectures with overheads, power points, and so on that summarize knowledge presented, focus on a particular portion that is important or missed, or present already presented knowledge in a new way. During these lectures, students are encouraged to take notes if they want, to give them an opportunity to learn some of the material in accustomed ways. In a semester's time, the instructor's use of linear-type lectures occupies approximately two class periods, hardly more than that.

Elder Evaluation of These Methods

I ask Elders to assist me in this form of teaching by requesting they evaluate me. I use class videos and a syllabus that I take to Elders. I give them small monetary as well as traditional gifts for this effort. I then find a mutually arranged time to visit them and get their oral responses. I appreciate whatever brief *written* summary they may be willing to provide me. In a recent Elder evaluation time, I was asked what went on in small groups when students were working or preparing for presentations. I said I didn't know, as I was not in a small group with them. I accepted their suggestion that I ask the groups about this aspect of the methodology. I do this during the grading process. I ask students what they did that was good that I missed when telling them about their grade. I also ask how much time they spend in preparation. Because this is information I do not know, or have not mentioned anyway, I usually will raise the grade, dependent on the additional information. That is because, truly, I have not considered what I am told, or I did not know, and it should impact the grade. I always tell the students this was an evaluation point by Elders that helped me in grading them in a proper and fair fashion.

Finding Comfort in Circle Teaching

Using the Circle Teaching methods and techniques allows a student to work within a protected environment of a small group of equals that provides opportunity to speak and discuss and learn from peers while utilizing choices during learning and teaching. Circle Teaching also encourages creative inclusive activities as each student uses his personal skills in teaching the learning materials. Students also learn several chunks of knowledge in depth through interaction that emphasizes the connectedness and inclusively of all those who live. There is quite a bit of emphasis or repetition of the learning materials in this method for students, based on *their* choice of materials (within that provided by teacher).

As described earlier, first, they read the entire materials; then concentrate on their particular choice; "teach" it to peers; and during remembering time, assess how other students do in remembering stuff they presented. Usually during an oral total-group exam, they take charge of "their" material. By the end of class they reinforce at least four times their "own" material, which by this time they know really well and, as peers, are presented with and "taught" the rest of the selected materials by other students.

Methods that approximate cultural norms may help students who continue to provide the fodder for the achievement gap increases. We do know that many things have been tried, yet the gap continues to be maintained and even increases from time to time. It is fitting to acknowledge these methods/techniques and explanations are but a poor approximation of skills, abilities, and capacities of Elder teachers, and for mistakes present, I apologize to Elder teachers.

Also, it is a risky business to go up against the might, form, and pervasive majesty of the Academy. But it is worth it if, with others of like experience, we promulgate methods and techniques for use in the classroom that in some small ways reflect our brilliant Elder teachers who in the web (of life) time, practice and teach Tribal people, these thousands of years in Turtle Island, North America.

Notes

1. You can order documents from RAND: 1700 Main Street, P.O. Box 2138, Santa Monica, CA 90407–2138. Distribution Services: 310–451–7002.
2. This discussion was begun by Dale.A.Turner@Dartmouth.EDU in Spring, 2000.

References

Barreiro, J. (Ed.). (1992). *Indian roots of American democracy*. Ithaca, NY: Cornell University, Akwe:Kon Press.

Bopp, J. (1989). *The Sacred tree*, 3rd edition. Twin Lakes, WI: Lotus Light Publications.

Brown, J. E. (1982/1988). *The spiritual legacy of the American Indian*. New York: The Crossroad.

Brumble, K. H., III. (1988). *American Indian autobiography*. Berkeley: University of California Press.

Cajete, G. (1994). *Look to the mountain: An ecology of indigenous education*. Skyland, NC: Kivaki Press.

Cottom, D. (1989). *Text and culture: The politics of interpretation*. Minneapolis: University of Minnesota Press.

Deloria, Vine. (1999). *Spirit and Reason: The Vine Deloria Jr. Reader*. Golden, CO: Fulcrum Publishing.

Demmert W. G. & Towner, J. C. (2003). A review of the research literature on the influences of culturally based education on the academic performance of Native American students. Portland, OR: Northwest Regional Educational Laboratory website: www.nwrel.org/Indianed/CBE.PDF

Diamond, B., Cronk, S., & Von Rosen, F. (1994). *Visions of sound: Musical instruments of First Nations communities in Northeastern America*. Chicago: University of Chicago Press.

Fuchs, E., & Havighurst, R. J. (1973). *To live on this earth*. New York: Doubleday.

Grissmer, D., Flanagan, A., Kawata J., & Williamson, S. (2000). *Improving student achievement: What state NAEP scores tell us.* CA: RAND.

Gill, J. H. (1999). Knowledge, power, and freedom: Native American and Western epistemological paradigms. *Philosophy Today,* Winter, p. 424.

Hanohano, P. (1999). The spiritual imperative of Native epistemology: Restoring harmony and balance to education. *Canadian Journal of Native Education, 23*(2), pp. 206–19.

Johansen, B. E. (1998). *Debating democracy: Native American legacy of freedom.* Santa Fe, NM: Clear Light Publishers.

Leas, S. B. (1982). *Leadership and conflict.* Nashville, TN: Abingdon.

Momaday, N. S. (1966). *House made of dawn.* New York: William Morrow.

Neihardt, J. G. (Ed.). (1932). *Black Elk speaks.* New York: William Morrow.

Oakes, J., Quartz, H. H., Ryan, S., & Lipton, M. (2000). *Becoming good American schools: The struggle for civic virtue in school reform.* San Francisco: Jossey-Bass.

Pearce, R. H. (1988). *Savagism and civilization: A study of the Indian and the American mind.* Berkeley: University of California Press.

Poupart, J., Martinez, C., Red Horse, J., & Scharnberg, D. (2000). *To build a bridge: Working with American Indian communities.* St. Paul, MN: American Indian Policy Center.

Ross, R. (1992). *Dancing with a ghost: Exploring Indian reality.* Ontario: Reed Books.

Ross, R. (1996). *Returning to the teachings: Exploring aboriginal justice.* Toronto: Penguin Books.

Schein, E. H. (1985). *Organizational culture and leadership.* San Francisco: Jossey-Bass.

Simmons, Dan. (2000). *Darwin's blade.* New York: HarperCollins.

Viadero, D. (1999). Bridging the gap. Teacher magazine in *Editorial Projects in Education 11,*(8), p.30.

Wax, R., & Thomas, R. (1961). American Indians and white people, *Phylon, 22*(4, Winter), pp. 305–17.

Wasson, W. C. (1973). *Philosophical differences between Europeans and Native Americans as an explanation of the alienation of Native American students for the educational system.* Doctoral diss., University of Oregon, 1973. University Microfilms international, 73–28, 641.

Weatherford, J. (1991). *Native roots: How the Indians enriched America.* New York: Ballantine Books.

Vernez, G., Krop, R., & C.P. Rydell, C. P. (1999). *Closing the educatiion gap: Benefits and costs.* Washington, D.C.: RAND.

9

Naming Race and Racism as a Problem in Schools

Pauline E. Bullen

> . . . there are times when personal experience keeps us from reaching the mou n-taintop and so we let it go because the weight of it is too heavy. And sometimes the mountaintop is difficult to reach with all our resources, factual and confessional, so we are just there collectively grasping, feeling the limitations of knowledge, longing together, yearning for a way to reach that highest point. Even this yearning is a way to know.
>
> (hooks 1994, p. 92)

During the 1999–2000 school year as a consultant in the Equity Department for the Toronto District School Board, I sat through several department meetings chaired by the coordinator of the department who repeatedly referred to Board administrators, government officials, and so on, as "f***ers" in an attempt to underline her feelings of frustration at administrative and government incompetence. As I looked around the table chaired by this young white coordinator of equity studies, I saw a collection of visible minority support staff—Asian, Black, Latin American, as well as gay and lesbian staff. I noted that none of us would have dared to express ourselves in such a manner without the "fear" of having our credentials and expertise criticized and scrutinized, our "professionalism" questioned. I also felt that this action effectively highlighted "difference, privilege, and power" in a white racist society. So-called minority educators are constantly given subtle, and not so subtle, reminders of who "really" is in charge, and often our silence and acceptance reinforces the unequal power relations. The research presented here highlights this acceptance, even as we want to be acknowledged and want to be respected.

Introduction

In this chapter, I will share the responses of five Black educators of various cultural and class backgrounds based on a one-and-a-half hour taped interview with each that involved open-ended questions pertaining to their professional experiences and how these experiences may be linked to the fact of their race or African Canadian heritage. There are differences among the individuals that I have been able to interview for this work, although they share the similarity of race. Differences based on place of birth, age, gender, socioeconomic status, professional positions and status, personal and professional experiences, and perspectives are those that emerged as particularly relevant within this study. My focus however, will be on the differences based on personal and professional experiences and perspectives.

It is my intention to analyze critically various historical and "everyday" events in the lives of the above individuals in order to add to the weight of evidence that there is indeed a gap between the myths and reality of what constitutes race and white supremacy in Canada. I will combine what I expected to emerge from the various educators' accounts and that which I did not expect to emerge, with my readings pertaining to race and racism in education. I will use the accounts from the teachers to describe some of the historical contradictions and contemporary complications that arise in naming race and racial oppression as a "problem" in the schools.

All of the teachers are individuals who have been part of training courses on antiracist education, and they all employ an antiracist philosophy in their practice. They all identify themselves as being "Black" as defined in the 1986 work by Bhaggiyadatta and Brand, in which "Black" is given an initial capital to stress a common heritage, a cultural identity, and personal identity proudly claimed by Black people who assert their African origins (p. iii). They all also accept the definition of "race" as a socially constructed category that lacks any sound scientific validity but gains in social currency because of its utility in distributing unequal power, privilege, and social prestige. They see race as having been used within a culture of white supremacy as an effective tool for determining the distribution of rewards, penalties, and punishments. They note, too, that the concept has been used to "divide and rule" peoples and that central to the concept of race is the importance of understanding how society is racialized through historical and contemporary conditions that give rise to and sustain the production of racial boundaries.

I feel that there is a need in our society to examine the various ways individuals, consciously and unconsciously, reaffirm difference and sustain the racial boundaries. I feel that there is a need to acknowledge that structures and behavior are inseparable, and that institutions and values go hand in hand. I feel it is important to note that how people act and live are shaped, but not determined, by the larger circumstances in which they find themselves (West 1993) and that there is a need for self-examination and self-reflection. There is a need to examine and challenge the "status quo" and the "traditions" that have been passed on for generations —especially those traditions that are blatantly discriminatory. There is a need to be able to recognize the voice of complicity and to recognize that silence can be a form of complicity that allows structures of inequality and discriminatory acts to flourish. There is a need to understand that Black people often function from the belief that because of systemic discrimination and racial oppression they may often have to be overqualified for the various positions they "win." However, it should be understood that this need to "prove oneself" also may be indicative of a fundamental sense of insecurity" that comes from centuries of being labeled inferior (Case 1977, p. 59).

I also bring the perspective that the history of white supremacy needs to be taught in our schools in order to give Black people the opportunity to draw parallels between past situations of slavery, segregation, and racial hatred, with their present-day reality of "being excluded emotionally, culturally, and racially, while being expected to contribute to the success of efforts for which they are given little recognition" (Case 1977, p. 59). It is my contention that individuals need to examine critically the "cohesiveness of racism" (p. 59) because racist practices create, in our schools and in our society, conflict situations that render large groups of people powerless and a small minority powerful. In fact, in 1985, the educator Enid Lee wrote in *Letters to Marcia* of students in the school system who felt that they were made to hate themselves. In 1986, Dionne Brand and Krisantha Bhaggiyadatta wrote in *Rivers have Sources, Trees Have Roots: Speaking of Racism* about the devastating effect of subtle and not so subtle forms of racism in our society—the type that causes you to wear your hair a particular way, change your routes, the clothes you wear, what you expect, and the responses you make. They spoke of the "random and institutional" (Bhaggiyadatta & Brand 1986, p. 3) ways in which racial oppression pervades the lives of Black folk and of racism as always present, always threatening, and part of what they called the "culture of everyday" (p. 8).

I contend that Black folk need to know the history of racism in order to effectively examine how we live out the stereotypes that are applied to our race and to understand that, in the "eyes of the naïve and of the racist we are all born in the same distorted image of whatever stereotype is applied to us" (Case 1977, p. 63). The goal is to develop a greater understanding of the obtrusive and insidious ways in which racism influences our everyday thoughts, beliefs, customs, practices—our culture—to acknowledge racial oppression as our "colonial" legacy and to restructure our "systems" in order to achieve interracial harmony and social justice.

I have been a teacher, counselor, and consultant with the Toronto Board of Education for over a decade. I approach my work from the perspective that I see myself—an outsider working within—forced often to remain "motionless on the outside," while developing the "inside" of a changed consciousness as a "sphere of freedom" (Collins 2000, pp. 99–118). My experiences have become a shared resource. I write about what I think and feel "in the actualities of my everyday/everynight living . . . there is always rethinking of established positions and representations to be done"(D. E. Smith 1999, pp. 16–17).

Many North American investigators have examined power and racial oppression in the educational realm and their impact on the lives of Black people in North America (Winks 1971; Bhaggiyadatta & Brand 1986; Li & Singh 1988; C. James 1990; C. West 1993; E. Lee 1991; Lewis 1992; hooks 1994; Delpit 1995; Dei 1996, 1997). Many of the above have looked specifically at how Black children cope with their education systems. They have examined how these students fare on test scores, how they integrate into the school community, how they experience being "raced" in their school environments, and how they attempt to cope with the devastating effects of discrimination and racial oppression.

Fewer investigators have done any extensive research into the oppression experienced by Black educators within school systems and the manner in which racism impacts on the scholarship, work, and upward mobility of these individuals. Lisa Delpit does so in her 1995 work *Other People's Children;* bell hooks does so in her 1994 work *Teaching to Transgress: Education as the Practice of Freedom;* Linda Carty speaks of the racism encountered by Black women in academia (1991); and Barbara Smith (1990) also speaks of the blatant and subtle ways that white feelings of superiority are communicated during interactions with Black individuals.

Frederick Case (1977) tells us that racism is not an independent force or theory but the most visible form of a given structure of a given society (p. 8). Linda Carty (1994) tells us that, "it is not accidental that some of Canada's lowest immigration quotas have consistently been for peoples of African descent" (p. 199). Carty notes that Black individuals have always been in a relationship of social subordination in dealing with the state. She points out that it is irrelevant whether the relationship is with the government, the judicial system, the education or social welfare systems, or any other state-controlled or state-influenced institution, because the defining feature of the relationship has been Eurocentrism. In fact, in 1850, in an apparent attempt to allay the mounting fears of whites, the Ontario legislature passed a law that resulted in many Black children being prohibited from attending public school. For twenty years before this law, actions of hostile white parents kept Black children out of the public school system.

In his work *The Blacks in Canada,* R. Winks (1997) noted that a process of exclusion of Black children from public schools across Canada had begun two decades before the 1850s because white parents would not allow their children to mix with Black children (p. 365). The Hamilton police at the time also had records of strong prejudice against Black folk and had recorded the fact that white parents would withdraw their children entirely from school if Black children were admitted (p. 367). In 1846 in Amherstburg, Ontario, the provincial superintendent of education, Egerton Ryerson, had received a letter from "Negro" ratepayers from the Amherstburg community, stating that local trustees had declared that rather than send their offspring "to school with niggers, they will cut their children's heads off and throw them into the road side ditch" (p. 368). Winks tells us that Egerton Ryerson considered himself a "friend" of the "Negro" and had therefore "suggested that Negroes be given separate school privileges because of the intensity of the prejudice directed against them in some quarters" (p. 369). Winks writes that Ryerson had expressed the belief that the prejudices and feelings of white people toward Black people were "stronger than law" (p. 369).

In fact, many people had accepted and internalized many of the racist stereotypes of Black people as inferior and ineducable. The attitudes and discourse mirrored those of the colonial "Empire," where white individuals (female and male) located themselves as superior to Blacks, who were socially constructed as the uncivilized, ineducable "other," and examples of this abound as early as the seventeenth century (Carty, 1991). Today, "the politeness of Canadian culture can no longer conceal the racism in its fabric. . . . many racialist incidents once pointed to as typical of the culture south of the border are now acknowledged as very much present in Canada" (Carty 1993, p. 11).

Peter S. Li and Bolaria B. Singh (1988) state that, because of the racially homogeneous and ethnically diversified nature of Canadian society, many people find it hard to consider race an important aspect of Canadian society. The concept of racial oppression, with its roots that are grounded in the daily experiences of people and in the practice of social institutions, is even more difficult for some people to accept, given a lack of awareness of what constitutes race and oppression and what causes racial antagonism. They point out that coercion, the law, and ideological domination have all historically been used by dominant groups in North American society in order to produce and maintain a "color-stratified" society. They reference Karl Marx's work in order to highlight the fact that the "class which has the means of material production at its disposal, has control at the same time over the means of mental production (Li & Singh p. 24). There are numerous "everyday" examples of this in the school system where the voices of the "privileged"—whether white-skinned privilege or economic, class, gender, sexual orientation, or ability—are heard and catered to in terms of programs and service. The less privileged often do not have the "means" (education, time, money, and so on) to give "weight" to their voiced concerns. Consequently, many are silent and/or silenced.

Teacher #1

Teacher #1, a vice principal of a secondary school, was raised in Canada from age one by Caribbean parents. She has studied at three Canadian universities and has partially completed a master's in education. She noted that many people assumed that she got to where she is because she is Black and that she is "not allowed to make mistakes" or be anything other than what is defined by others as "professional." She noted that she has had to work harder because she is Black and accepts that this has been necessary because of the fact of her skin color. In fact she stated that her parents taught her that she had to be twice as good as her white peers and that this has made her more effective as a teacher and administrator. Here we see the irony of indeed having to work "twice as hard to go half as far" and the irony of also having to prove continually that you did work twice as hard to go half as far.

Teacher #1 said, "I became a vice principal in order to get more power so that I could change things," and she saw her ability to influence Black children in particular as largely attributable to the fact of her Blackness. She admitted to spending much of her time being "extra careful to be very professional" because of a lack of trust of her colleagues and in fact stated, "many of them are just waiting for me to make a mistake." bell hooks (1994) writes of this desire to be "very professional" and "extra careful" and says, "if we fear mistakes, doing things wrongly, constantly evaluating ourselves, we will never make the academy a culturally diverse place where scholars and the curricula address every dimension of that difference" (p. 33). What we are doing, bell hooks states, is allowing bourgeois racist attitudes to create a barrier that blocks the possibility of confrontation and conflict and wards off dissent. We do not name the racism and classism that determines that we work two and three times as hard in order to become acceptable carbon copies of the white "majority." hooks says that this "fear of "losing face," of not being thought well of by one's peers undermines all possibility of constructive dialogues that critique relations of domination (p. 179).

This teacher felt that she was able to "fit" into the white majority culture because she grew up in an all-white school environment and had always found herself to be one of a small minority of Black folk within her school and work environs. She said her early lessons in assimilation, have helped her to gain insight into the "majority" culture's way of doing things and that, "Being surrounded by white people and having white friends allowed me to understand white people. I was used to being the only Black person so I was not intimidated or uncomfortable being around them. Throughout most of my teaching career I have been the only Black teacher on staff. Had I not had the experience of being with white people this could have been daunting and intimidating." In fact, hooks (1994), also points out that in order to "avoid feelings of estrangement, students from working-class backgrounds could assimilate into the mainstream, change speech patterns, points of reference, drop any habit that might reveal them to be from a non-materially privileged background" (p. 181).

Winks (1997) wrote that in 1949 "the growing African United Baptist Association of Nova Scotia . . . established an Urban and Rural Life Committee which stressed that 'Negroes had to be shown how important it is to look right and to act right if they wish to be received rightly'" (p. 387). It was acknowledged by one of the reverends who spoke on behalf of the committee that "much discrimination was rooted in problems of social standing or class rather than in race" (p. 387). Like Teacher #1 who saw her education and position as vice principal as a means of acquiring power within our racist and classist society, it was felt in 1949 that problems of race and class could be overcome "only through employment and consequent status. A status that would follow from intensified education at all levels" (Winks 1971, p. 387). Thus we see the oppressed and expressed need to learn the ways of the oppressor in order to live among them and survive in the capitalist, race stratified, society.

Teacher #1 said that she "sees racism and is able to identify it" and that many teachers are reluctant to raise issues involving Black students. She expressed the belief that "Black teachers are used in many schools for containment" and that "because there are so few Black teachers and such a huge demand for them, the status of these teachers is high." She noted that it would appear that "every school wants at least one Black teacher who can be used for "containment" and because that person often proves to be "able and professional" there is a struggle to keep her or him." This teacher noted, too, that there is a limit to how many Black teachers are welcomed in any particular school and that often schools do not want more than one unless the one they have is not considered "good enough." She stated that having several Black teachers in one school may pose a "threat"; however, she does not state a threat to whom. But Teacher #2 sheds light on this in her account of an incident that occurred as she left one of the educational offices one day early in her career. She recounted standing on the steps as a young white woman walked by her with tears running down her face. She stated that she automatically reached out her arms to the woman asking her what was the matter. She said that the woman slapped her hands away and screamed, "Get away from me, get away from me. You filthy immigrants are taking away our jobs and making it impossible for us to be hired".

Teacher #1 noted that her white colleagues were "cautious" around her as they tried "to get a read" on her. She noted a lack of trust that led to attempts at undermining her authority by taking certain issues to the principal rather than first to her as vice principal.

Teacher #2

Teacher #2 was born in the Caribbean and at age ten received a full scholarship to attend high school. She went from high school to a teacher training college because the tuition was free. However, she had to agree to be bonded for six years' service before being able to leave the country. On finally immigrating to Canada she returned to school on a part-time basis and earned a bachelor's degree in education and a master's of science in administration. She is a principal and sees her role as an advocate for students, staff, and the larger community. She notes that within her work environment there are, at times, competing interests. She says one must often strike a "sensible" balance between being an educator, politician, and diplomat while striving to be a person with "strong moral convictions." The professional barriers that she identified were in the form of not being privy to information that gives you "visibility" in the system—information about the "unwritten rules."

Lisa Delpit (1995) says that we are judged on our product regardless of the process that is utilized to achieve it. And that product, she says, "based as it is on the specific codes of a particular culture, is more readily produced when the directives of how to produce it are made explicit" (p. 31). Delpit identifies this withholding of information as a coercive use of power.

bell hooks also speaks of an unwillingness to share information as coercive in that it allows some individuals to function as "all-knowing, silent interrogators." Teacher #2 notes that she has had to be astute as a "leader who invites herself" into various forums in order to take note of the "power committees" and dynamics and examine the current focus. She said that professional jealousy; refusing to cooperate, especially when the classroom door closes; patronizing attitudes; and telephoning the federation and superintendents to complain about her practice are all examples of racist attitudes that have impacted on her teaching and administration. She expressed the view that racism creates stressors that can "destroy you" and said that she is often forced to "look over her shoulders" because of a lack of trust (as mentioned previously by Teacher #1).

Teacher #2 said that her desire to understand the "culture of power" that exists and her desire to "network" may be seen as "sucking up to a racist, classist system." She stated, however, that the system is a homogenous one, where many who are employed within it have known each other for years and have shared youthful experiences. In order to gain the trust of her colleagues, who on the most part have been white, she stated that she has had to develop a conversation that included praise for things that she might have normally seen as "acceptable" practice and part of one's job. She has had to learn to give public praise and to be "effervescent" in giving praise, in order to be perceived as an acceptable leader.

As an administrator, she said she felt many of her decisions were made knowing that there would be opposition based on her race rather than the issue at hand. Being a clever strategist is important, she felt, because often one's timing in bringing forward certain issues becomes essential. She stated that it was important to plan carefully in order to minimize expected opposition. It is important "to form alliances with individuals who hold positions above and below you" she said, in order to survive. She stated that it is important to be aware of the structure and the guidelines for performance within the institution in which you are employed. She said she had been given what she called "a fashion profile" and often has had to face stereotypical comments such as "it seems all Black women like to shop" or "Good God, can't you ever wear the same thing twice so we can know who you are." She says that she has been labeled confrontational because she has responded at times to personal attacks and criticisms. She states that in her position as principal some see her as an effective administrator but dislike her personality as confrontational.

Teacher #2 said that the "majority" group appeared to see equity hiring as reverse racism, and as a consequence "there is always a subtle or not so subtle questioning of whether one has the qualification for the position one holds." Among the "majority" she also noted that there is resistance to having an inclusive curriculum and this is expressed by the claim that it is "too much work." She regarded her role of principal as allowing her the power and autonomy to bring into the school environment individuals who can subscribe to her philosophy; she described herself as an antiracist educator working for social justice.

Teacher #3

Teacher #3 was the only male respondent for this study. Although three Black male teachers/administrators were approached, he was the only one who immediately and positively responded. Teacher #3 is an elementary (grade seven) classroom teacher and librarian who said that he was raised in a very conservative home with his mother, who taught at the elementary school he attended and was his classroom teacher for two years. He was born in the Caribbean and completed his post secondary education in Canada. He linked his teacher training and staff development opportunities in Canada to his becoming less authoritarian in his practice than are the teachers in the country of his birth—even less authoritarian than his mother who was his earliest teacher role model. He said that he has made a "personal commitment to teaching excellence and to being effective professionally." He said his mother was a teacher who "taught with passion and dedication and who always found ways to get a point across to all the varying abilities in her classes." He said his mother's example helped to shape his practice and that his students have often returned to say that it was his "commitment" that encouraged them to strive and succeed.

He noted that although he is aware of many racial assumptions that are made because of his skin color, he has refused to allow such assumptions to prevent him from teaching "to a standard of excellence and of having high expectations of both his peers and his students." He claimed to live out the stereotype of moving to "Colored Peoples Time—CPT" by sometimes arriving late for meetings and noted that there is a North American notion of "punctuality" and "not wasting time" that links the ability to prioritize and organize with being a "professional." He said he feels the term "professional" is used in a way to appear "raceless" and that the definition of a professional is shaped by a culture that does not respect diversity. He described teaching as "most definitely" rooted in antiracist struggle and sees himself as "an agent of change" who does not work to maintain a very conservative curriculum that allows the reproduction of the status quo. He said he challenges the status quo in his position as a teacher librarian who is aware and who lets students know that their worlds are narrow.

As a teacher/librarian, teacher #3 said he attempted to give students a definition of "Canadian" that is inclusive—one that moves them beyond their own neighborhoods; their own cultural "Canadian" groups. He wanted his students, for example, to read Margaret Atwood and Dionne Brand.[1] His is not a politically neutral position, he said, and he believes, like bell hooks (1994), that we have to acknowledge that "the education most of us had received and were giving was not and is never politically neutral" (p. 30). Like bell hooks, teacher #3 said that we have to acknowledge that we are living in a culture of domination and that we should ask ourselves "what public and private rituals do we daily engage in which help maintain the culture of domination and an unfree world" (hooks 1994, p. 27). He said it was apparent that Black teachers were regarded as "necessary" for the success of students in "special needs" schools where dominant groups are Black and "essential in less diverse schools to correct misconceptions and stereotypes and, finally, essential to change." He identified "special needs" schools as "already predominantly Black schools because of demographics, socioeconomics and the experiences of people of color in Canada." He expressed the viewpoint that "all children" would benefit from being schooled in a progressive setting with an antiracist curriculum in place. He said that Black children would benefit not necessarily from all-Black schools but "from the best in the profession." He spoke of the "best in the profession" as those "teachers who do not allow the color of their skin to determine their ability to take children forward."

Teacher #3 said he sees, in Canada, an opportunity to teach of the interconnectedness of peoples—of cultures—and that his is not a philosophy of "I blow out my candle so that yours can glow brighter." In fact, bell hooks (1994) speaks to this when she states, "Some folks think that everyone who supports cultural diversity wants to replace one dictatorship of knowing with another" (p. 32).

Teacher #3 stated that there appeared to be a culture of resistance among Black youth that involved rejecting values such as the high achievement of fellow Black students as "acting white." He noted that it is the Black student who does not "act white" who is included in the "in group" that many of the students aspire to join. However, I am not sure that it is specifically the high achievement of their fellow Black students that is being rejected by Black children. As a teacher and counsellor, I have never met a child who has said, "I want to fail" or "I want to be a failure in life." It appears that Black children in attempting to be successful in a white racist society experience the same frustration and despair as their "parents" when expected to untiringly aspire to be "twice as good, to go half as far" (Lee 1993). Black children want to succeed and they want to succeed on their own terms. They want to see themselves within the school curriculum. They want to be taught by teachers who understand where they are coming from and do not make fun of their culture and sometimes demean them by making fun of the way they speak—making fun of their accents. They want to be taught by teachers who are self-actualized or are striving to be and who want the same or more for "their children," as they would want for themselves. Black children are aware, however, that they are often not seen as "children" but as criminals or potential criminals—deviants, ethnics, marginal or submarginal, immigrants—often in the country of their birth. They know and this knowing fuels their anger and resentment.

Bhaggiyadatta and Brand (1986) also point out that children of color—Black children—grow up quickly: they have to, because the adult figures of authority they encounter all too often do not see their youth, their childhood, they see only their color (p. 52). Black children may at first understand power and oppression only as a source of discomfort, but soon they learn it is more than that. They learn that white society is not as caring or kind toward them (p. 52). Carl James (1990) points out that it would appear that there is a tendency for whites to seek out aspects of individual Blacks that help them to maintain their stereotypes while dealing with the contradiction that relates to an individual's qualities (p. 16). Many of the youth interviewed by James stated that they understood that stereotypes are largely based on perceptions that date back to historical times and that they did not expect whites to "simply observe" that these stereotypes were inappropriate. Some felt that it was their responsibility to "shatter" any negative perceptions of Blacks, held by white individuals, by their own exemplary behavior. They, like many Black professional adults appear to feel that to be "accepted and given a chance to succeed in this society is something that must be earned through special effort" (p. 94).

Beverly Daniel Tatum (1997) says, "People pay attention to those who control their outcomes. In an effort to predict and possibly influence what is going to happen to them, people gather information about those with power" (p. 25). When one grows up in an environment in which one faces the violence of racism on a daily basis, one becomes sensitive to its practice. Black children know, says Tatum, that "when a subordinate demonstrates positive qualities believed to be more characteristic of dominants, the individual is defined by dominants as an anomaly" (p. 24). Black children may reject such "anomalies" as individuals who benefit from this level of acceptance but who do not analyze it and who in fact glory in it. Black children are aware and as they sit at the back of the cafeteria, the bus, or gather together on the steps of the school buildings their discussions are political as they attempt the deconstruct their disturbing realities. We see it in their stance and we hear it in their rap. Contemporary artists NAS (2002) rap about "Black zombies" who are "walking, talking, dead, though we think we living, we just copycat following the system" (2001). They also rap about teachers who downgrade the work of Black children and then have them placed in special education classes, "dumber classes." As they face inequity and injustice, the gaze of Black children is knowing and often oppositional. Perhaps the arrogance of their youth wants the racist to know that they recognize their racist practices. In their rap they ask, "What do we own? Not enough land, not enough homes, not enough banks to give our brother the loan." They say, "We begged, we prayed, petitioned and demonstrated just to make another generation Black zombies".

Many Black children are the children of primarily working-class women who traditionally have not employed passivity as a survival mechanism, yet we often expect them to "turn the other cheek," and they do not. They say, "Why care what they think; why wear what they wear; just be you; use your own intuition; control your own destiny . . . why listen to somebody else telling you you can do it, when you can do it yourself—it's all in you." Yet, lacking education—the language, the voice, the confidence, to challenge white hegemonic relationships, many sink into despair, and as a result our communities sink into disrepair. bell hooks tells us that "fear and anger about appropriation, as well as concern that we not be complicit in reproducing servant-served relationships, have led Black women to withdraw from feminist settings where we must have extensive contact with white women" (hooks 1994, p. 105). Our children withdraw. They withdraw from the curriculum. Some, angry and frustrated, unwittingly cooperate in their own oppression, allowing themselves to be pushed out or drop out. Others who may feel that something is wrong but are unable to name it or confront it are unwittingly "pushed out." Without an education many have no future in our capitalist, racist society.

George Dei (1995) points out that oppositional behaviors such as "acting out," adopting styles of dress that conflict with dominant cultural norms, use of language, and sometimes violence may be interpreted as practices of resistance. Dei says that the intent may be to assert a marginalized perspective and attempt to subvert dominant norms and values (p. 11). Audre Lorde (1995) spoke of a "mythical norm" that is used to define power in America. A norm that says everything white is all right. This "norm" needs to be debunked in order to empower Black children, and it can only be debunked by living examples of "fearlessness" in the face of inequity and injustice by those (including teachers) who parent them and claim to have their best interests at heart. It cannot be done simply through the continuous (although sometimes necessary and valuable) unearthing of dead sheroes and heroes.

Teacher #4

Teacher #4 was a vice-principal at a secondary school and has since become a principal. Born in the Caribbean she has lived most of her life in Canada and has a Master's degree in Educational Philosophy from the Ontario Institute for Studies in Education (OISE). She stated that "nepotism"—people hiring their friends, cousins and children—is one of the greatest barriers to overcome within the educational system. Their intention she said, may be to help a friend or family member; however, the impact is that so-called visible minority people—many Black, are then often left out. The other barriers she identified were a blatant disregard for her expertise and for her as a person. She said that because she has had a good grounding in antiracist education she does not allow the negative things that others may say or do to interfere with, "the essence of who I am."

Teacher #4 noted times where her name may have been placed last on an agenda, rather than perhaps alphabetically, and would "adjust" the situation by inoffensively pointing this out. She said she had observed, for example, a workplace routine of opening the administrator's doors and leaving hers untouched. She saw this however, as a situation that afforded her a good amount of privacy and consequently never felt a need to "adjust" it. She said she noted that at various events held at the school she was never asked to do more than hand out an award or shake hands until she requested an adjustment to her involvement. She said, "There are some things I stand for and I don't allow anything to affect this." She said she feels she knows what she is about and tries to affirm that but "sometimes it takes a lot of work." In fact, Audre Lorde, poses the profound and heart-breaking question, "What other creature in the world besides the Black woman has had to build the knowledge of so much hatred into her survival and keep going?" (Lorde 1984, p. 150).

Teacher #4 stated that many Black educators "become like ghosts in the system after they have stuck their heads out and endured a lot of hardship." She acknowledged however that many do not even become engaged in the struggle. Frederick Case (1977) in fact stated at that time, and it appears to still be true today, that far too many Black teachers are preoccupied with showing how well assimilated they are. He said "economic fear and the desire to be accepted and recognized, drive those cowardly teachers into a position of support of the active racists within the school system" (p. 58).

Teacher #4 said there are several practices that are questionable that she works at changing—some are simple and some complex. She said that in her work with children she has made a personal commitment to always be "a caring adult" who believes in the philosophy of the National Alliance of Black School Educators—an organization founded in the United States that says, "All Children Can Learn." She admitted to having a lot of power as a vice-principal and to exercising and using it to make structural changes "without any apology." For example, in time-tabling staff she had noted that certain educators—primarily Black individuals—rarely got opportunities to teach particular classes—usually senior classes with students perceived to be the brightest. In attempting to change this practice, she has had to negotiate with department heads who, she anticipated would be quite hostile if they were told of her antiracist agenda. She noted that the impact racism has had on her practice is not clear-cut because issues are often multidimensional. She stated however that when you are an administrator "everyone tries to present their issues to you as though they were fair—though the impact may be racist." She has had to be very creative in supplying what could be perceived as reasonable responses to potentially hostile individuals. She expressed an awareness that staff would not necessarily agree with everything she did, but felt that because she tried to "balance out" opportunities for all, she may be perceived as fair. She said, however, that she found it difficult to state how she was truly perceived by her colleagues.

Teacher #4 credited her early upbringing in the Caribbean for the commitment she brings to her profession. She remembered a place called "Lessons Place" in the area where she lived where for a twenty-five-cent contribution to help pay for chalk, her parents could send her for tutoring by student and teacher volunteers. In keeping with the tradition that she had been a part of, she now finds herself to be a strong advocate for "students of color." She said coming to Canada and having had to struggle gave her an appreciation of being and having someone to rely on to "show the way and lessen the hurdles." She expressed her concern, from the vantage point of the vice principal's office, for students who are often overlooked by teaching and guidance personnel, for paid job opportunities and scholarship opportunities in and outside of the school community. She noted that Black children in particular, appeared to often be left off of recommended lists and said she takes on the task of finding names to add to the lists given to her.

Bateson (2000) notes that "subtle indicators of discrimination, deep pessimism in the behavior of adults reflecting the lack of meaningful opportunities later in life, may affect the learning process very early, so that a child may be primed to fail long before starting school" (p. 9). Teacher #4 noted that many Black students do not listen to the announcements and many even when they do, are not confident about filling out applications and are reluctant to ask for assistance. She said many believe they will be excluded from gaining access to jobs or scholarships or that they will fail at the interviews anyway and do not want to try. She noted that even though many teachers realized this fear of failure in some of the students they seldom offered extra support.

Teacher #4 felt that many of the youth are misguided and do not know what will bring them success. Students too often, she said, looked for negative things to emulate and those who did well often tried to hide it from their peers for fear of being accused of "selling out" to an oppressive system with individuals who appeared to want to see them fail. As a consequence she stated her concern that many Black young men appeared to want to "look like gangsters" while young women placed emphasis on their bodies—"wearing tight clothing and showing a lot of cleavage." She expressed her desire to penetrate this youth culture where many young women "focus on the social" as they tried to get the attention of the "bad boys." She stated also that many Black students came from poor and not highly educated families and that educated family members often had not received much of their early education in Canada and were therefore unfamiliar and uncomfortable with the Canadian educational system. She felt that cultural expectations clashed within homes and family reunification issues brought a lot of controversy into many homes. She felt that Black children would "most definitely" benefit from being in all-Black schools, because many were not really grounded in their history and past and that this is often the missing ingredient in their lives.

Lisa Delpit (1995) in fact tells us that "if we plan to survive as a species on this planet we must certainly create multicultural curricula that educate our children to the differing perspectives of our diverse population" (p. 177). Delpit tells us also that, in part, the problems we see exhibited in school by African American children and children of other oppressed minorities can be traced to this lack of a curriculum in which they can find represented the intellectual achievements of people who look like themselves. Were that not the case, these children would not talk about doing well in school as "acting white" (p. 177).

Teacher #5

Teacher #5, a secondary school teacher in a large suburban area, stated that she is West Indian of African heritage. She completed high school and university in the West Indies and a postgraduate degree in Canada. She stated that the professional barriers that she has encountered are linked to stereotypes about the role of women, counterproductive management styles that hinder efficiency, a lack of available resources, and a teachers' union that prefers "featherbedding to productivity." She stated that she was not aware of any racial impact on her teaching since she had not been denied access or treated unfairly in any way. She stated that there have always been "subtle racial overtones" but they had not impacted on her in a negative way. She expressed the belief that some students were openly rude because of her race and sometimes there was a lack of cordiality on the part of administration. However, "none of these prevent me from doing my job, it is their issues, not mine," she said. She did state that she saw herself as very much an agent of change, speaking out loudly in action and words whenever and wherever she saw injustice—"not only racial but other forms of discrimination." She felt that she was perceived by her colleagues as a "professional who adheres to the highest levels of excellence and an outspoken defender of the cause of the dispossessed." She did not feel that she needed to be "allowed" to be an agent of change within her workplace, and did not need permission "to do it everyday in the curriculum that she teaches." She did express the feeling that there are "limits" to what she could do given the resources that are available.

Teacher #5 felt that her cultural background affected her style of teaching, because she shared stories that were told to her as a child. She felt that her cultural background also affected her approach to discipline, and the expectations that she had of the students.

Summary

The above research began with the premise that racism and inequality are "entrenched realities" within Toronto's educational system. What has surfaced as "real" in this study is the pain that racism brings to the lives of its victims—its survivors. The respondents of this study are all victims, and they are all survivors. All of the respondents want to live lives with "dignity and decency," but all of the responses show how each must face the indignity of racial discrimination, in various ways, in their daily lives.

The narratives of the teachers clearly show that they actively apply their professional philosophies, skills, and knowledge in ways designed to make their practices a rich learning experience for their students. They also reveal their efforts to address the various needs of their students—whether these needs come from the students' developmental stages, upbringing, past experiences, or economic or cultural backgrounds. Underlying these efforts is their goal of "racial uplift"—a key concept in their pedagogical worldviews—and a strong desire to enhance the self-esteem of their students. The theme of racial uplift, which has historically been seen within North American Black communities as the responsibility of middle-class Black women who were educators, is a recurring one in all of the narratives by the four female and one male educator interviewed. Indeed, since the early 1800s, community uplift and self-uplift have become intertwined, as those more fortunate assist those in need. These responses assume neither "a black essence that all black people share, nor one black perspective to which all black people should adhere . . . rather, [it] encourages moral assessment of the variety of perspectives held by black people and selects those views based on black dignity and decency that eschew putting any group of people or culture on a pedestal or in the gutter" (West 1993, p. 28).

All of the teachers speak of inclusion. Their voices are voices of inclusion, not exclusion. Their concern is how to confront a culture of domination that "necessarily promotes an addiction to lying and denial" (hooks 1994, p. 29), a culture that insists that "there are no problems here." They are concerned with being forced to face disempowered collective backlash, backtracking, ostracism, and belittlement designed to dissuade paradigm shifts—a moving aside of Eurocentric thinking, according to Enid Lee (1994, p. 19), in order to cope with a society eager to return to an age of narrow nationalism, isolationisms, and xenophobia (hooks 1994, p. 28).

These teachers recognize racial discrimination as a seemingly permanent problem in Toronto schools, and armed with this knowledge they make certain that they learn the policies that allow for antiracist practice that can effect even small changes within their school systems. Their survival strategies are not a part of a postmodern phenomenon, as Black folk have a rich history of resistance to oppression. They know that Black Canadian history is a history inseparable from, although not reducible to victimization. All of these teachers have a support network of like-minded Black educators and friends in the larger community, employed, unemployed, and underemployed, with whom they identify. All also have strong loving familial relationships that help to soothe their often battered souls and are thus not afraid to use "conflict" as a catalyst for new thinking—for helping to facilitate paradigm shifts.

Delpit (1995) tells us that it is important to learn to be a part of the world instead of attempting to learn to dominate it. She says, "Learn to see rather than merely to look, to feel rather than touch, to hear rather than listen. Be still. Be open" (p. 45). My own experiences and the experiences of my Black colleagues cited in this study tell me that some of us feel and hear more than our hearts can bear. It makes us weep and it makes us weak, even as we strive to be strong. Even as Black educators demonstrate a "messianic zeal" to transform young lives and demonstrate their commitment to the concept of "racial uplift," even as they give love, accept love, and ask each other in the vernacular whether you "feel the love," the disease that afflicts our community threatens to choke us and creates in some of us what West (1993) refers to as that "mind/body" split, as we deny the impact of racism in our lives even as we attempt to name it.

I believe that reflection and action will bring about change in our society. I believe that we have reached a time in history where the policies and laws can effectively be used to bring about change as long as we form united fronts with individuals who believe in the struggle against oppression. Black folk are truly not a homogenous, monolithic group of people. We are not all the same and our responses to oppression cannot therefore be the same. Some of us are defiant warriors and others are foot soldiers, but we are all deserving of the respect we seek every day of our lives because, according to Audre Lorde, we were never meant to survive but, "we are powerful because we have survived, and that is what it is all about, survival and growth" (Lorde 1984, p.139).

Note

1. Both Margaret Atwood and Dionne Brand, one born in Ottawa, Ontario, who grew up in Northern Ontario and Quebec, and the other an Afro-Caribbean Canadian born in Trinidad, write from their experiences of women in a patriarchal world. There work is not neutral, and this is evident, for example, in Atwood's works *The Handmaid's Tale* (1983), *The Edible Woman* (1970), and *The Robber Bride* (1974). Brand,

however, in her award-winning book of poetry, *Land to Light On* (1997), and novels, *A Map to the Door of No Return* (2001) and *Bread out of Stone* (1998), writes from her experience of multiple displacements as an African Canadian lesbian who has had to struggle to survive the racism within Canadian society.

References

Bateson, M. C. (2000). *Full circles, overlapping lives (Culture and generation in transition).* New York: Random House.

Bhaggiyadatta, K. S., & Brand, D. (1986). *Rivers have sources, trees have roots: Speaking of racism.* Toronto: Cross Cultural Communication Centre.

Carty, L. (1994). African Canadian women and the State: "Labour only, please." In P. Bristow, D. Brand, et al., *We're rooted here and they can't pull us up: Essays in African Canadian women's history* (pp. 193–230). Toronto: University of Toronto Women's Press Incorporated.

Carty, L. (1991). Black women in academia: A statement from the periphery. In H. Bannerji, L. Carty, et al., *Unsettling relations: The university as a site of feminist struggles* (pp. 13–45). Toronto: Women's Press.

Carty, L. (1999). The discourse of empire and the social construction of gender. In E. Dua & A. Robertson, *Scratching the surface: Canadian anti-racist feminist thought* (pp. 35–47). Toronto: Women's Press.

Case, F. I. (1977). *Racism and national consciousness.* Toronto: Plowshare Press.

Dei, George J. S. (1995). *Drop out or push out? The dynamics of black students: Disengagement from school.* Toronto: OISE, Department of Sociology in Education.

Dei, G. J. S. (1996). *Anti-racism education: Theory & practice.* Halifax, NS: Fernwood.

Dei G. J. S. (1997). Race and the production of identity in the schooling experiences of African-Canadian youth. *Discourse: Studies in the cultural politics of education, 18*(2), pp. 241-7.

Delpit, L. (1995). *Other people's children: Cultural conflict in the classroom* (pp. 21–47). New York: New Press.

Hill Collins, P. (2000). *Black feminist thought: Knowledge, consciousness, and the politics of empowerment* (2nd ed.) New York: Routledge.

hooks, b. (1994). *Teaching to transgress—Education as the practice of freedom.* New York: Routledge.

James, C. (1990). *Making it: Black youth, racism and career aspirations.* Oakville, Ontario: Mosaic Press.

Lee, E. (1985). *Letters to Marcia.* Toronto: Cross Cultural Communication Centre.

Lee, E. (1994). Taking multicultural anti-racist education seriously: An interview with Enid Lee. In *Rethinking our classrooms: Teaching for equity and justice* (1st ed., pp. 19–22). Milwaukee, WI: Rethinking Schools.

Lee, E. (1993). *Twice as good to go half as far.* In *Career equity for youth.* Toronto: Guidance Centre, Ontario Institute for Studies in Education, Training manual handout 14.

Lewis, S. (1992). *Letter to the Premiere.* In *Stephen Lewis report on race relations in Ontario* (pp. 1–37). Toronto: Government of Ontario.

Li, P., & Singh Bolaria, B. (1988). Race and racism. In *Racial oppression in Canada* (2nd ed., pp. 13–25). Toronto, Ontario: Garamond Press.

Lorde, A. (1984). *Sister outsider: Essays and speeches.* Freedom, CA: Crossing Press.

Lorde, A. (1995). Age, race, class, and sex: Women redefining difference. In P. Rothenberg (Ed.), *Race, class, and gender in the United States: an integrated study* (3rd ed., p. 446). New York: St. Martin's Press.

NAS. (2002). *Black Zombies* [CD]. Sony Music Entertainment Inc.

Smith, B. (1990). Racism and women's studies. In G. Anzaldua (Ed.), *Making face, making-soul/ Haciendo caras: Creative and critical perspectives by women of color* (pp. 25–28). San Francisco: Aunt Lute Foundation Books.

Smith, D. E. (1999). Writing the social: Critique, theory, and investigations (pp. 16–17). Toronto: University of Toronto Press.

Tatum, B. D. (1997). *Why are all the black kids sitting together in the cafeteria? and other conversations about race.* New York: Basic Books.

West, C. (1993). *Race matters.* Boston, MA: Beacon Press.

Winks, R. W. (1997). *The blacks in Canada: A history* (2nd ed.). Montreal: McGill University Press.

10

When White Students Write about Being White: Challenging Whiteness in a Black Feminist Classroom

Gary Lemons

Black feminist pedagogy embodies a philosophy that is a philosophy of liberation. Black feminism's major premise is the active engagement in the struggle to overcome the oppressions of racism, heterosexism, and classism, as well as sexism. . . . *[T]he Black feminist teacher artfully and skillfully interprets class interaction while never veering from the goals of liberation for humankind through the process of an analysis of oppressions* . . . [emphasis added].

Gloria Joseph

By centering education about race on Black women, the Womanist Thought course has allowed me to address the social history of racial ideologies. It has kept me focused on actual oppression, not within a theoretical framework, but in the lived experiences of Black women. . . . Theory without application is useless, and I fear that the danger in white people learning about race is that it will become just that . . . mastery of the theory. . . .

Nathaniel Meysenburg

My spirit has swelled with the scholarship of so many vital, explosive women.

Andrew Dahl

The words of the black women we have been reading have been exactly what I need. . . . They have offered me a vision of hope, healing and radical transformation. These qualities I need to keep close to my ear always—but especially now, during this time of imminent war [against Iraq]. . . .

Eleanor Whitney

Black Women at the Pedagogical Center

Can a single course on black feminism initiate a radical transformation in the racial/social consciousness of white students? The answer is an emphatic—"No!" Yet this is an ongoing question I have asked myself over the last ten years as a black professor teaching antiracism at a white, private liberal arts college in New York City. Year after year, I confront this question considering the likely possibility that from one semester to the next, there may be no students of color in any of my classes. As a teacher whose commitment to antiracist education is integrally linked to learning that promotes antisexism, I argue that "the classroom can be a critical location of resistance to advance the struggle against racial injustice—most strategically waged at the intersection of sexism, classism, and homophobia" (Lemons 2001, p. 1).

What happens in a course on black feminism where all the students are white (except for one woman whose skin color affords her the privilege of passing as white) and the professor is black and male? The answer to this question is the subject of this essay. My aim is to show that black feminist thought, as a social theory of liberation and pedagogical agent of social change, can be a powerful tool toward the development of critical race consciousness in white students. Those who embrace the notion that "black feminism's major premise is," in the words of Gloria Joseph, "the active engagement in the struggle to overcome the oppressions of racism, heterosexism, and classism, as well as sexism" may intellectually come to understand multiple oppressions as a distinct feature of black women's history in the United States, but on a deeper self-reflective level experience a liberatory understanding of it from within. Since first reading Joseph's essay some years ago on "Black Feminist Pedagogy," her soulful proclamation that the feminist teacher's vigilance about teaching is for the liberation of "humankind" has stayed with me. Her words have guided me in my work as a black male feminist, antiracist teacher.

I teach a course called Womanist Thought, its title inspired by Alice Walker's vision of a black feminist—as one who is "committed to survival and wholeness of entire people, male *and* female" (Walker 1983, p. xi). While the course focuses on the intellectual history of black women in the United States—from Maria Stewart's 1831 call for them to "possess the spirit of independence" (Stewart 1995, p. 29) to the diversity of thought among contemporary black feminist voices—it aims to emphasize its multidimensionality. Patricia Hill Collins has said,

[D]oing intellectual work of the sort envisioned within Black feminism requires a process of self-conscious struggle on behalf of Black women. . . . Reclaiming Black feminist intellectual traditions involves much more than developing Black feminist analyses using standard epistemological criteria. It also involves challenging the very terms of intellectual discourse itself. (Hill Collins 2000, p. 15)

White students studying the intellectual tradition of black feminists as a catalyst for self-examination must empty out their "invisible knapsack[s]" (to borrow a phrase from Peggy McIntosh). In the process, they begin "challenging the very terms of intellectual discourse itself"—particularly that which reinforces a mind/body split. Writing about the kind of intellectual work my students do in Womanist Thought offers a strategic moment for me to reflect on the power of black feminist pedagogy as a critical launch site for antiracist education. When feminist antiracist teaching is linked to pedagogy of composition that privileges autobiographical writing as a strategy for enabling students to connect social theory with personal empowerment, intellectual labor becomes a catalyst for *self-liberation*.

As an essay on the transformative power of black feminist pedagogy, this chapter is not meant to offer a detailed study of black women's intellectual tradition. Rather its aim, as stated earlier, is to show the overall impact that teaching black feminism can have in a college classroom where all the students are white. Privileging their voices in the discussion that follows, I foreground their thoughts about the course (at the beginning and end of the semester) to formulate my own assessment of its effectiveness in combating racism and white supremacy. I simultaneously engage how sexism, classism, and homophobia interconnect to the students. Womanist Thought compels students to confront these issues through personal self-examination, a key element in the writing strategy employed as they critically analyze black women's writings in the course. It not only challenges *whiteness* as a racial signifier of power, privilege, superiority, and the complex web of social relations it enacts, it also requires that students personally take on their own internalized racism. Teaching black feminism to white students pushes them to recognize what it means to be *white* in a culture of "white supremacist capitalist patriarchy" (bell hooks).

As a backdrop for my discussion, certain details about the course become relevant. Quoting from the course syllabus, I refer to its "rationale" statement:

When Alice Walker conceived the term *womanist*, she claimed an autonomous space that would signify with specificity and power the differences that define the politics of feminists of color. Foregrounding the nuanced relationship between gender, race, and sexuality—she asserts that womanist describes "[a] woman who loves other women, sexually and/or nonsexually. Appreciates and prefers women's culture, women's emotional flexibility . . . and women's strength." It is, however, the gender-inclusive conception of womanism that makes it a revolutionary standpoint [for women *and men* of color and all white people, *female and male*] . . ."womanist" is one who is "[c]ommitted to survival and wholeness of entire people, male *and* female." *Thus, while womanism is conceptually identified with feminists of color, it speaks across gender and race boundaries.* [emphasis added]

Summarizing the course objectives I say that the course aims

to survey the major works of womanist thought primarily to understand the standpoint and theoretical foundation on which the feminisms of Black/women of color represent themselves; to understand the problematics of feminist thinking produced by Black women in relation to the struggle against patriarchy, sexism, and homophobia within communities of color; *to think through the transformative implications of womanist thought not only for Black/people of color but all people who struggle against domination whether it be rooted in sexism, racism, classism, or any force which aims to dehumanize.* [emphasis added]

Readings for the course come from two primary texts: *Words of Fire, An Anthology of African-American Feminist Thought*, edited by Beverly Guy-Sheftall, and Patricia Hill Collins's *Black Feminist Thought*. An indispensable text in black feminist studies, *Words of Fire* provides conceptual clarity and continual substance in my attempt to offer a historical survey of black women's nonfiction writings. It affords students an amazingly visceral experience of and engagement in the dynamic evolution of black feminist thought and the diverse standpoints represented in the women's ideas that characterize it. Noting this point as one of the book's main features, Guy-Sheftall writes in the preface:

The women included here are also not a monolithic band with similar worldviews or the same conceptions of "feminism." . . . Sometimes their feminist discourse is autobiographical, controversial, visionary, understated and subtle, but more often it is hard-hitting and strident. Some authors are passionate and angry, others more cautious and indirect. . . . They share a collective history of oppression and a commitment to improving the lives of black women, especially, and the world in which we live. (Guy-Sheftall 1995, p. 15)

The fact that the women in this stunning volume "share a collective history of oppression and a commitment to improving the lives of black women, especially, and the world in which [they] live" is what makes it such a powerful text to teach and catalyst for the development of students' feminist consciousness.

The humanist vision set forth in the readings from *Words of Fire* is echoed by Hill Collins's sense of her task in *Black Feminist Thought* (2nd edition). As a complementary secondary source for the course, it offers students interpretive insight into the texts from the anthology while giving them an incisive critical context for understanding Black feminism as social theory. Hill Collins states,

> For African-American women, critical social theory encompasses bodies of knowledge and sets of institutional practices that actively grapple with the central questions facing U.S. black women as a collectivity. The need for such thought arises because African-American women as a *group* remain oppressed within a U.S. context characterized by injustice. . . . Black feminist thought's identity as a "critical" social theory lies in its commitment to justice, both for U.S. Black women as a collectivity and for that of other similarly oppressed groups. (Hill Collins 2000, p. 9)

Immersing white students in black women's intellectual tradition through the works of Guy-Sheftall and Hill Collins kept the course focused on the social contexts of black women's thought, while foregrounding their strategies of liberation. What remained clear in the course readings during the term is the notion that black female liberation is inextricably linked to the struggle for human rights. For white students in the Fall 2002 session of Womanist Thought, many of whom were active in campus organizing during the term against war with Iraq, the history of the black feminist movement served as a source of inspiration, for students committed to social justice.

When White Students Embrace Womanist Thought: Looking at the World Through a Black Feminist Lens

> As a white woman, I can attest, first hand, for the clarity that comes from looking at the world through a black feminist lens. I've discovered that there is an uneasy balance between being completely ignorant of, or simply refusing to acknowledge one's own privilege, and being over ridden with guilt for the injustice that is out of your hands. Now I am comfortable owning up to the privileges that I have. I am accountable for them, but I do not think they are deserved, and so I will pool the resources that I have access to and use them against this [oppressive] system.
>
> Tyler St. Jean

Antiracist teaching linked to pedagogy for social justice promotes a more radical agenda for the feminist classroom. While the Fall 2002 Womanist Thought course was not racially diverse, white students enrolled in the course as an elective for a variety of different reasons, all connected to a desire to study race. From firsthand accounts of students that follow, I provide a critical framework to reflect on the effectiveness of black feminist pedagogy in a white classroom. As stated in the beginning, black feminist thought functions as the crucial centerpiece in my approach to antiracist education. It enables white students to confront *whiteness* at a deep, heartfelt level—while personally engaging its interconnection to issues of race, gender, class, and sexuality.

Technically speaking, Womanist Thought is not a composition course. However, as a teacher who believes that well-conceived writing strategies enhance any course where critical thinking is taught, I make writing an integral tool of learning in all my courses. Students wrote a lot in Womanist Thought—two critical analytical papers every week during the term (maintained in a portfolio format).[1] Of the writing requirements, two were pivotally important not only in mapping the development of critical thinking but also for charting the evolution of racial consciousness. At the beginning of the term, each student wrote a "rationale statement"—a short paper assigned after the first class meeting in which students stated the reason(s) they chose to take this course. During the next class, they read them aloud sharing the differences (and similarities) that brought them together. As the last writing requirement for the course, students completed a take-home "final (self-)examination." The exam consisted of one question: "What does it mean to be "white" just having completed a course on black feminism?" Considering my insistence that critical self-interrogation drive class discussions all semester long around issues of white privilege, I had gained a certain measure of faith in the students' ability to respond with astute candor. I not only knew this would be an appropriate end-of-the-semester question, but also believed that the students would produce some amazing responses.

Revisiting the students' rationale statement, I discovered that on one level they were keenly aware of themselves as white people. This awareness figured significantly in their reason(s) for taking a course on black feminism. Generally speaking in the first writing assignment, however, most of the students acknowledged little familiarity with writings by black feminists. And, while many of them were conscious of themselves as white people, they all claimed a need to push beyond the boundaries of their existing racial comfort zone and knowledge about black women's intellectual tradition. Interestingly, some overtly expressed the idea that studying black feminism would help them gain a deeper racial understanding of themselves. Darragh, for example, a white woman student who wrote of a desire for a "safe place" to talk about race, considering the fact that when I have discussed race in the past I've been criticized by both black and white friends. . . . I have selected "Womanist Thought" because I hope it will allow me to ask the questions I've been told I shouldn't ask and maybe even those I've been afraid to ask. . . . I ask myself why is my "safe place" to talk about race a room filled with white students?

Darragh's question about the lack of racial diversity in the class speaks to a previous question she posed about her choice to attend a majority white college. Eugene Lang is a "white" (private, i.e., expensive) college. While students of color make up 26 percent of its student population (approximately 750), it appears (actually seeing students from underrepresented groups on a day-to-day basis at the college) that the numbers are much lower. In ten years of teaching at Lang, I rarely have more than two or three students of color in my classes. This is generally the case for most of my classes. More often than not, the fact is that many of the classes at Lang are all white, from what other colleagues tell me. Courses on race at the college are few. Courses about race and feminism are even fewer.

My classes are popularly known as "race" classes. For white students (with or without racial consciousness) at Lang who want to study race, my classes offer the possibility of doing so. I never promise that my classes will provide a "safe" place to talk about race. Most students enrolling in my courses already know this through word of mouth. I have no illusions about teaching race as a black man at a white school. Challenging white students to question white privilege and their relation to white supremacy and racism (from a black feminist standpoint) will not, in most cases, place one in the running for a "teacher of the year" award. Having students (white or of color should there be any) share their rationale statement in class allows space for their desire(s) to be acknowledged publicly. Students sharing personally at the beginning of the term tell me where they are (intellectually and emotionally) in relation to the course topic and where they want to go with it. One of my initial tasks is to help them open up more about what they want to learn—with the hope that they will feel compelled to embrace the liberatory ideology that characterizes black feminist thought.

Having students revisit their first writing assignment of the course at the end of it provides them with an autobiographical context in which to reflect on the personal, social, and political implications of their initial decision to enroll in the course—as white people. As students think back on it, the process (taking into consideration all the writing they have done during the term) allows them to chart their own individual intellectual, critical, and emotional development through the course. Throughout the semester while teaching this course, I tried to imagine how the presence of students of color might have altered it. As stated before, I continually drew attention to my presence as the only acknowledged "black" person in the classroom (who also happened to be the teacher). Teaching the class as a black man, I worked to affirm white students' desire to engage black feminist thought, while challenging them to interrogate white privilege and the lack of racial diversity in the college. No one can say with surety what difference the presence of students of color might have made in our classroom, but I do know with some certainty that these white students opened themselves up to the transformative possibilities in studying black feminist thought. In the space of this essay, it is impossible, however, to capture with fine detail all that students wrote in either the rationale statement or the final (self-)examination.

In the past, when writing about my work as a feminist antiracist in the classroom, strategically it has been important to me to include student voices for two reasons—(1) to illustrate the effectiveness of teaching autobiographical writing focused on self-reflection linked to composition for critical social consciousness and (2) to demonstrate the viability of antiracist teaching founded on black feminist thinking, as has been already stated. Having students write about themselves in relation to the course at the end of the semester is critically necessary to understand its impact on them. Having white students write about being white after a semester of studying black feminist thought makes perfect sense to me. Nearly all of the responses (fourteen papers) had to do with the students' arriving at a deeper level of race consciousness where *whiteness* represented a signifier of power, privilege, and the myth of racial superiority. While every student in some way spoke about being white in a black class, there were certain ones whose perspectives stood apart from the others. Rather than expressing guilt for being racially privileged because of their skin color, these students looked within to question how the self-critical knowledge of being white had come through the study of black feminists' interrogation of white supremacy. Commenting on the reality of an all-white class and the impact of womanist thought on it, Kate said,

> This has been a unique class. Unique first of all because it is a class on black feminisms wherein all the students are white. But it is also unique because many of us came to the class, if not knowing anything about black feminists, at least having had some experience with thinking "that way" ("thinking black," as Gloria Joseph put it). In fact, I feel that one of the most important things I've learned this semester is that thinking "that way," or having a womanist-centered philosophy is beneficial not just to people of color, but to white people too; not just to women, but also to men.

About his relation to being white, male, straight, and the questioning of such privileges, among others, Seamus declares:

> I cannot return to an academic, ideological, philosophical, spiritual, political, and . . . educational system that is centered around young, rich, straight, white, Christian males. . . . The questions that I found throughout the course far outweigh the answers (so goes great education). But some of the critical questions that I will never again need to hesitate or shy from when answering are these: What right do I have as a white male to study feminism, black studies, or identify as a feminist antiracist? Why study black women? And what can I ever know about their experiences?

Having studied black feminism in an academic setting that empowered him to engage this knowledge, Seamus gained a new sense of confidence as a white male—not only challenging his racial privilege but also the normalized power of his gender and sexuality.

Another white male wrote candidly about his need to connect theory with practice, eschewing the notion that race could be studied as social theory without a student having to grapple with its implications in one's everyday life. He makes a powerful case for an approach to studying race that merges the social, political, and personal. Having read some writings by black feminists, bell hooks among others, Nathaniel (a white male who attended a majority black high school in Pittsburgh, Pennsylvania) says:

> I began the course in Womanist Thought stating that it is interesting to question why a white male would want to even begin thinking about black feminisms and the struggle of black women. Through the course of the semester this question has been answered many time over, and in many ways. [Before this course] I had yet to discover that centering black women at the place from which ideas around race, gender, and class intersect would change my perspective on the world. . . . I cannot confront my own whiteness in a theory based way. Doing this would negate the existence of racism that I myself have internalized. When I read the works of Patricia Hill Collins, Audre Lorde, Ida B. Wells Barnett, Anna Julia Cooper, and many other black feminist writers, I learned not only about experiences within this system. As a middle-class white male, I live with the ability to at any instant step into everything that the classist, racist, patriarchy has to offer me. . . . But it is the writing of these women that keeps reminding me that the costs of my ignoring the [existing] power structures are too high. It is these women who encourage me to reject whiteness. *It is also these women who have engaged me in a deeper understanding of what my being white is in relationship to their being black.* [emphasis added]

Nat (his preferred name) acknowledges the transformative power of black feminist social consciousness illustrated in the women's texts he studied in class. Simultaneously, he (like Seamus) becomes more socially aware of the power of whiteness he possesses in relation to black women's experience of sexism and racism.

For some white students, however, black feminist thought compelled them to look within where internal complexities of racial identity had remained hidden from external view. They speak about a profoundly deep process of self-reclamation through an intense interaction and inner reaction with the writings of black feminist women. Sharon (a white-looking Jewish woman visiting student from Sarah Lawrence) wrote about moving from a theoretical understanding of race to one connected to the painful process of questioning white skin privilege, "passing," and reclaiming her racialized Jewish identity in this course as a means of fostering a deeper commitment to antiracist activism:

> I [had] never thought of race because I was white. Wasn't I? This is where I was wrong . . . I wasn't. And I never have been. It wasn't until Womanist Thought that I began to deconstruct what [my] identity as a Jewish woman meant to me. . . . I had never contemplated why I didn't wear my Star of David to school, why I hated my dark hair and dark eyes, why I insisted that they were hazel and not brown. . . . The politics of passing have been with me since I sprouted pigtails, from the day I learned that it was ugly to be a Jew, that it was about being Blonde (because all good Christians, all good Aryans are Blonde. . . . I wanted to assimilate; I wanted society to consider me beautiful. . . . In reading the [works] of these women [black feminists], in reading about their struggle and their strength on the path to self-love, I found myself compelled to follow. These women have taught me to love myself, despite what I thought I knew, despite what I was taught. Anti-Semitism, just as racism, teaches self-hate. I have come to realize that while I "passed" for white—I am not white. That I have denied much of my culture and heritage, coming from a place of shame . . . of my history and have in essence denied who I am. And it is in reading these women that I have learned . . . to begin the loving of myself—all parts of myself. . . . I am learning to live up to these incredible women who have taught me more about myself than any white woman, any middle-class woman, any Jewish woman, any queer woman, any woman, period, has ever attempted, let alone succeeded.

Another "white" looking woman in class, Bianca, publicly claimed that she, too, had been passing but that the primary texts we studied in *Words of Fire,* of so many black feminists and their struggles to speak out in spite of multiple oppressions facing them, had inspired her to awaken from a deep sleep, questioning critically ways she had racially assimilated and the "lies" such practice perpetuated in her daily life. Suggesting that she is "haunted" by the spirits of black feminists in their words, she now "keep[s] [her] eyes open at all times"—more vigilant of the ways oppression operates in the lives of black/women of color:

> I came to Gary's class a little confused. I'm neither white nor black, but have changed my hair color and dressed to pass as white. . . . How could I call myself critically conscious while I sat quiet [in the past] when a woman or person of color was disrespected. I feel as if I [have been] let out of a box of lies and I have been awoken. The essays written by women of color [we read] have honored me with their lessons and ideas. They have helped me to keep my eyes open at all times. Sometimes I feel a bit haunted by their presence, as if I just want to forget it and just live in a fake reality where everything is fine and equal. They are always there, though, with their words reminding me that the struggle for women, especially women of color, is far from over. I used to feel sorry for women of color but now I feel sorry for the people who do not care to understand the struggle of women of color. The book *Words of Fire* should be a required text. It taught me more about American history than any other book ever has. This was a book of heroes, a book that gave me inspiration for living my life. This a book that engaged my spirit, my mind and my heart.

For some white students in class, as the two women above profess, "whiteness," race privilege, and white supremacy had not entered their consciousness in a visceral way. They were blind to the idea of racialization, a common characteristic of whiteness in which white people are oblivious to how it feels to be raced.

As stated, a second thematic pattern surfaced in the final self-examination pointing to the emotional and spiritual transformation students experienced. They not only tap into the emotional current of their racial anxieties connected to a fear of dialogue on race, but also the internal upheaval such conversation might cause. In the writings of black feminists, they found the courage to speak about inner revelations. Amy, for example (a rather quiet and soft-spoken white woman), wrote about coming to consciousness about white identity through black feminism as similar to a spiritual awakening. Reflecting on the shift in her racial consciousness from the beginning of the semester to its end, she states,

> I came as a white girl, the "whitest white girl I know," [from her rationale statement] but I am certainly not leaving as such. Throughout my journey, the beautiful and [painstaking] words of many women of color [we read] such as Elise Johnson McDougald, Maria Stewart, Barbara Smith, Beth E. Richie, Sojourner Truth, and Margaret Alexander have lingered with me, especially in my heart well after I finished reading their texts.

Amy speaks about how painful the process of understanding racial privilege as a white woman can be. On the one hand, reflecting upon feelings about the internal upheaval the course was causing her, she laments not having known earlier in the semester how deeply black feminists were affecting her everyday life. On the other, getting in touch with the empowering effects of their writings, she could own the "linger[ing]" experience of them. Among her peers, Amy's experience was not unique. One of my aims for the course was to create a classroom space conducive to students' desire to come to terms (in her/his own way) with the challenges of race, gender, class, and sexuality black feminism posed. Writing afterward about an apparently difficult class session, Amy states:

> I went home that night beyond confused, beyond lost, disgusted with myself and humiliated. My once simplistic life of a sheltered and oblivious suburban white girl was being obliterated, and as painful as it was, it was also incredibly liberating. I didn't realize it then, but I was breaking the mold of the society which I was raised in, and ultimately raised me [with regard to] "white privilege." . . . This class (Womanist Thought) was more than a textbook-lecture kind of class; it tapped into spirituality, deep into my spirituality. I felt like a snake that was shedding her outer layer of skin. . . . I learned more about myself in this class, than I have on my own in the past twenty-one years. Spiritual awareness cannot be acquired through a textbook or a lecture, but rather in a safe haven that embodies a warm and open roundtable discussion.

Amy wasn't the only white woman to talk about the impact of black feminism and the emergence of critical race consciousness as having the force of spiritual revelation. One of several student leaders/activists in class who had spent the semester organizing on campus against war with Iraq, Darragh passionately wrote about the inspiration of many of the black feminists named above but also added the names of bell hooks, June Jordan, Michele Wallace,

> and many others [who] have left an everlasting impression on [my] soul and heart. Reading about and understanding the intersecting struggles and oppressions that black women have faced and continue to encounter, and their many acts of resistance in response, has encourage me to continue down my own personal path of struggle. Their bravery and strength push me onward. They tell me to continue my resistance and fight. Their words test me to push my boundaries of "safety." Their resilience and determinacy in the face of oppression . . . provide a precedent for me. I am no longer the person I was before I heard the words of these inspiring women. Before their words were unleashed onto my soul, I was afraid to talk about race because I was fearful of who I was or who I might be. I'm not ashamed to say that I actually cried before the first day of class because I knew it was going to be challenging for me. The challenge has proved to be the most important one in my life. These women have unfastened my spirit and allowed me to search within. I have come to terms with the fact that I am on the margins as well.

While Darragh, like many of the other white students, found a political connection with the black women feminists they read in the course that enlivened them spiritually, others gained strength from womanist thinking to act courageously in the face of personal adversity. Another woman, Jennifer found personal strength in Audre Lorde's words on the necessity of voice and breaking silence about oppression. In her final self-exam, Jennifer discussed her decision to enrol in Womanist Thought in spite of having to "justify to others why [she] chose to study black feminism." In a culture of white supremacy, where simplistic identity politics forecloses on the possibility of our transgressing racial boundaries, she also had to confront the question: "Who do [you] think [you are as a white woman taking a course such as this]?" It is, however, her thoughts about the pivotal importance of studying the work of black feminist women and its impact on her personal life. Determining to leave an abusive relationship, Jennifer writes:

> Personally I have gone through a very trying time, overcoming an emotionally abusive relationship with a partner of a different culture [who] left me feeling riddled with guilt and confusion because I wouldn't shut up and give [in to his] control. . . . To be stultified and stifled and passive and submissive, when I have so much to say and do. Reading the work of these many brave and incredible women, I found empowerment and voice enough to walk away with my head held high, removing the guilt from my mind and leave without a doubt in my heart. . . . Audre Lorde changed my life [through her words in such writings as] "Transforming Silence into Language and Action" to "Uses of the Erotic." Lorde spoke differently to me than any other writer, poet, woman, warrior ever had before.

Reading statements like the one above, among others, is profoundly humbling for me. Throughout the semester, it was generally clear in the students' responses to the readings that there was a deep respect for the endeavor we had undertaken. Having taught this course two times before with *Words of Fire* and *Black Feminist Thought* as the core texts, I already knew the writings they contained possessed the power to transform student consciousness. In previous times when the course was offered, in one there were a few students of color (one black male), along with two white males. The other, with only six students, was composed of all white women (the few women of color who enrolled dropped the course after the first session with the complaint that the class was "too white." That class never recovered from the absence of those women of color. Frankly, I think the white women students were angry that they left, feeling as if they had been rejected, summarily dismissed. Those feelings infected the work we did for the remainder of the term. One white woman student continually resisted the idea that she should have to feel some emotional connection with the women or the ideas she was studying. In retrospect, I believe her response arose from a complex inner struggle around my being a black man teaching the course, her own paralyzing guilt around her race and class privilege as an elite white woman, and her desire to collapse critical differences between the ideas of white feminist women she had studied in the past and the critique black feminist women in the course posed against racist practices in the history of feminism in the United States. I have come to expect that white students, as well as students of color (female and male) will challenge my position as a profeminist black male teacher. Writing elsewhere about the problematics of my identity in the classroom, I state:

> When I teach, students come to know that—regardless of the particular subject matter—my pedagogical strategies are linked to the idea of education as a holistic practice where mind, body, and spirit come together to project a vision of social change. Self-actualization as a key piece in the feminist positionality I construct in the classroom means that feminism enables me to move radically against the grain of patriarchal manhood and masculinity. (Lemons 1996, p. 264)

Throughout the semester, to no avail, I challenged her and the other white women to become more personally engaged in their response to the texts, to make a critical link between the "personal" and the "political," but the level of resistance was so intense that the course became a battleground between gender (represented by white women) and race (me and the "attack" black feminist women had launched against them). Needless to say, the course ended up being (for the white women and myself) uninspired, overly academic/"objective," emotionally, intellectually, and spiritually sterile—one of the worst classes I have taught.

How would a black woman feminist have dealt with the situation? Feminist black women professors who encountered white female resistance in the classroom with whom I talked suggested that an intersectional approach to feminist critique of gender oppression is an inherently volatile subject especially for individuals who possess unearned privilege—whether they are white, male, middle-class, and/or heterosexual. Having intellectually accepted the challenge of the feminist methodology I employ, the reality of its pedagogical performance is always potentially fraught around the complex interrelating dynamics of race, gender, class, and sexuality in the actual context of the classroom. Given that the majority of my students are white females, race and gender issues tend to be more contentious than issues of class and sexuality—mainly because of similar backgrounds and progressive attitudes. Teaching in almost exclusively white female classrooms over the years, I have come to know that the white female classroom in which black feminism is the subject will always be charged with racial tension. It can't be avoided.

Having white students engage the issue of racism in feminism from an autobiographical standpoint, for example, moves the discussion from the theoretical to the personal. More often than not the students discover that much of their anxiety in studying black feminism is predicated on a fear of being politically incorrect—that they may be accused of being racist for holding certain stereotypical beliefs about black women. Creating a class-room environment that promotes honest dialogue about white myths of black womanhood is the first and most difficult step in teaching black feminism in a white classroom. When white students begin to comprehend that they play a strategic role in advancing the vision of black feminist lib-eration, they come to know that black feminism is a humanist project for all people's liberation.

Black Feminism Is for Everyone, Being White and Talking B(l)ack: When White Students Write in Solidarity with Black Feminists

The idea that white people have a place in black feminist thought and that it can be a critical source of political empowerment for white students is a theme echoed in most of the final (self-)examinations. This articulation represents a profound moment of clarity in the students' understanding about the impact studying the writings of black feminists had had on them during the semester. "Black feminism is for everyone," declared Anna (a white woman in class who maintained that her knowledge of black women's historical struggle against often insurmountable hardship helped her overcome great personal adversity during the semester). The willing-ness of white students in this class to embrace black feminist thought in their personal lives is not only a testament to its liberatory power but its capacity as an agent of inner healing.

What made the writing in this class different from its predecessors has to do with the fact every student from the beginning of the semester openly expressed an intense desire to study black feminist thought, and throughout the term remained open to the possibilities of it as a transfor-mative personal, social, political, and spiritual project. It was clear to me after hearing students read their rationale statements when we began the course that what they were expressing emanated from the same source—a deep yearning to learn from black feminists toward a discovery of some-thing unknown about themselves as white people in relation to ideas of social justice. The willingness of these white students to write such forth-right candor, honesty, and emotional vulnerability about their initial de-sire prepared them to (help me) create a course in black feminist thought that would challenge (in varying ways) the mind, body, and spirit of every one of them. Having formulated rationale statements rooted in personal desire linked to a knowledge of its social implications, the students reasons for choosing Womanist Thought would develop into the critical foundation for what they would ultimately write at the end of the course. From this writing it quickly becomes apparent that the kind of intellectual, spiritual, and ongoing self-critical work they hoped to do in the course had come about.

Looking back to the first writing assignment, to underscore this point, I refer to one of the most poignant rationales. It came from Andrew, one of the white men in class who rarely spoke during the semester. His words spoke with searing passion about his feelings of dispossession as a gay man, dealing with the death of family members, and his desire "to learn from African American women" with the hope that "their stories . . . may in the end lead [him] to understand [his] own." Boldly he proclaimed,

> I am compelled because I am Queer, and because of that may taste at times the bitter distillation of the dispossessed, the cast aside and the thrown away. I am compelled as well to come to grips with the complexity and at times the guilt I hold in my privilege, born of European blood, Male, my ability to pass, unquestioned. I yearn to understand fully, if possible the duty, right, pain, and possibility of my skin that is heavy with connotations. I am as well compelled spiritually; I feel guided to know of such things, as though those who have fallen around me [a reference to the deaths of his mother, an uncle, and close personal friends] are tugging me towards some destination I can't see and perhaps yet shouldn't. . . . I am taking this class because it seemed like a class I naturally should take. . . . What I hope to learn from African-American women above all, I guess, are their stories, ones that may in the end lead me to actually understand my own.

Reading these words again reminds me how courageous Andrew was. The power of his candor shared in the first days of the term are mirrored in the unrelenting frankness of Anna's disclosure in her final (self-)exam and helped me to understand how deeply she had internalized the spirit of the black women studied in Womanist Thought. The blistering reality of her words penetrate my consciousness, as they bear witness to the universality of suffering eased by the hope in the healing words of another. Anna writes about how the words of black feminist writers in the course gave her (as a victim of sexual violation) "the strength, the tools, and the vocabulary" to fight sexual violence against women:

> In the beginning of the course I was very interested in the subject matter . . . but I don't think the actual concept of black feminism resonated so deeply within me until I experienced the ultimate practice of patriarchy—rape, about a month into the course. I now understand the dehumanization that many black women have

faced before me, and their stories have shown me that I still have hope. This [should] not have to happen again to any women, and will never happen again to me. [Historically], rape was [potentially] an everyday experience for black women, and still is for some. . . . This class, and these remarkable women [Black feminists read in class] have given me the strength, the tools, and the vocabulary to recognize why there are so many oppressions that all women face, what others are doing to fight against these oppressions, and what I can and must do.

Anna's will to go forward in the face of great personal adversity experienced during the course was catalyzed in her personal application of black feminist thought. For me, as a teacher committed to pedagogy of liberation, this is precisely where the viability of black feminism lies in the classroom. Anna, like the other white women and men in Womanist Thought, came to understand that its value as a course did not rest solely on intellectual competence in reciting the words of black feminists but, rather, about a fundamental willingness to embrace intellectually and *personally* the theoretical and political framework of their work. Comprehending her individual experience of oppression as a white woman within a larger system of domination in which racism and sexism is an ongoing feature of black women's daily lives, as well as the lives of other women of color, is something that Anna had not fully understood when the course began. Possessing the knowledge that her struggle as a white woman must be politically linked to that of black women and other women of color, she becomes a strong advocate for a key tenant of black feminism—a belief in coalitional politics.

In the preface to the second edition of *Black Feminist Thought*, Hill Collins reasserts the centrality of the experiential (i.e., everyday lived experience) not only as a crucial location for understanding black women's oppression and their response to it but the possibility for the existence of a critical connection between individual and group political consciousness. In this edition, she has articulated these ideas within a larger transnational vision rooted in coalitional politics. She notes,

I initially wrote *Black Feminist Thought* in order to help empower African-American women. I knew that when an individual Black woman's consciousness concerning how she understands her everyday life undergoes change, she can become empowered. Such consciousness may stimulate her to embark on a path of personal freedom, even if it exists initially primarily in her own mind. If she is lucky enough to meet others who are undergoing similar journeys, she and they can change the world around them. . . . *Reading Black women's intellectual work, I have come to see how it is possible to be both centered in one's own experiences and engaged in coalitions with others. In this sense Black feminist thought works on behalf of Black women, but does so in conjunction with other similar social justice projects.* [emphasis added] (Hill Collins 2000, p. x)

On a deeper insight into black women's intellectual tradition, Hill Collins comes to realize that coalition strategizing must be a central feature of its political project. As Guy-Sheftall authoritatively demonstrates in *Words of Fire*—through the more than fifty black feminist voices represented (including members of the "Combahee River Collective," who coauthored the groundbreaking and often anthologized essay "A Feminist Statement")—black women's struggle against multiple oppressions has always been rooted in an inclusive vision of liberation. Indeed, this was the ideological foundation on which white students in the course were able to build a framework of solidarity between their individual struggles (whether personal, political, social, or spiritual).

White students writing about the transformative power of black feminist thought in their lives underscores the universality of its appeal as a liberatory theory for social change. Reading their writings during the semester, I have come to believe that we shared a common desire—that in black feminist thought we would find a place to ground our beliefs in social justice. Like many of the white students in Womanist Thought, I had longed to connect my commitment to antiracism with feminist movement for the equality of women, as well as the struggles to end heterosexism and homophobia. Black feminism is inherently liberatory for all who suffer injustice. Theorizing an end to the multiple oppressions of black women, it lays the groundwork for a social movement that includes everyone. Black feminist thought has a universal appeal. In powerful yet poignant words, this is precisely what white students wrote about at the end of the semester. Like Anna, I too found in the stories of the black feminist women we studied and those of her peers the "strength, tools, and vocabulary" to defend my right to teach "for the liberation of humankind," as Gloria Joseph so eloquently proclaimed the pedagogical mission of black feminism to be.

Teaching and Writing from the Head to the Heart: Mapping White Desire

As stated at the beginning of this chapter, teaching in a majority white classroom at Eugene Lang College over the course of ten years is not new for me. It is the norm. A year ago, I taught *Womanist Thought* to a class of all white women. This time around, my strategy was different. From the first day of the semester to the end, I continually drew attention to two things: (1) that I was the only self-acknowledged person of color in the classroom and (2) that I was a "black" male teacher. None of the students (mostly middle- and upper-class, some acknowledged gay and lesbian) took issue with me (as a male) teaching a course on black feminism. Although I thought white female students in class (ten of fourteen) might take issue with my being a man as in "a black woman feminist would have been more appropriate in politically correct PC terms," none of them (including the four white males) posed it as an issue (not suggesting, however, that it shouldn't have been).

During the term, we consistently addressed the class's racial makeup—why were there no students of color in the room? Given the fact that Lang has very few students of color, on that level alone (and considering students' of color divergent curricular interests), we could justify their absence in the room. Nevertheless, it was always clear to us that this was a white class with a black male teacher. In light of these always potentially troubling race and gender realities, we moved forward. I am almost certain that, as white students in a "black" course (feminist or not), they experienced some degree of relief that there were no students of color in the class—particularly black women. Except for myself and various times I might interrogate things said in class, there was no ongoing "racialized" pressure in the room to inhibit white students from speaking freely.

My experience teaching courses on race in a majority white classroom has been that when students of color are in the room, white students are generally more inhibited, less talkative, and often resistant to engaging in discussions about race. (This too is another subject entirely.) Clearly student-to-student dynamics in the white classroom is far less charged with issues of voice and silence when race is the subject and students of color are not in the room, although I must honestly say that the classroom space lacks a kind of racial kineticism. In other words, in the racially homogenous white classroom (particularly one in a liberal institution), my experience has been one associated with the myth of whiteness as inherently cold, lifeless, uninspired—soulless. Yet my experience teaching antiracism through black feminism leaves no doubt in my mind that precisely because the subject matter in and of itself *is* a kinetic site where intellectuality and politics of the body and spirit are inextricably linked, a pedagogy of antiracism based on black feminist thought possesses the power to transform the racial consciousness of white students.

When white students embrace the idea(l)s of black feminism, they enter into a mind, body, spirit alteration. I know this from witnessing how (self-)critically conscious the students in this course became in a single semester. I am not suggesting for one moment that one course in black feminism is the racial cure for the white student yearning for critical race consciousness. I am, however, maintaining that for some white students who have never really explored white identity, white supremacy, and white privilege, black feminism opens the possibility for radical self-transformation not only toward the attainment of antiracist consciousness, but the conviction of political activism that calls for an end to white supremacy.

At Lang College, students (required by the administration) evaluate professors' performance at the end of the semester. Although the document addresses or seeks to ascertain our pedagogical competence, it is not designed to judge my performance as a teacher of antiracism. I believe that in a majority white university the study of whiteness linked to antiracism is essential. I also know that teaching antiracism in such an environment is inherently difficult, particularly because the topic of racism in a liberal white institution is not generally engaged with candor from my standpoint as one of a few teachers at the college who overtly teach antiracist studies. The official "teacher evaluation" form affords me little qualitative information to determine how effective my pedagogy is in promoting the need for antiracist consciousness. This is why having students write a final (self)examination works as a strategic tool for assessment beyond the requirement of the administration.

At the end of the course, it would not be naive of me to suggest that every student came to understand that the history of feminism for black women in the United States has never been about gender alone, nor would it be an unfair generalization to assert that each came to a deeper, more intimate self-knowledge—writing about what it means to be white studying the intellectual history of black feminists. But, importantly, what most, if not all, discovered was the power of writing that speaks "from the head and to the heart." They came to identify with the same yearning for freedom and justice they found in the intellectual tradition of black feminism—that it functioned as a critical catalyst for the production of an impassioned statement of personal desire about the need for white people to confront the privileges of whiteness, while being inspired by the feminist struggle of black women to living public lives committed to social justice and equality for all peoples.

Note

1. Quotations from class writing assignments in this essay have come with permission from the following students, whose commitment to black feminist pedagogy not only required them to confront the history of institutionalized, multiple oppressions faced by Black women—but also rigorously, emotionally, and spiritually challenged them to lay bare their own internalized issues of race, gender, class, and sexual domination. Their willingness to write "from the head to the heart" lies at the core of my belief in

the transforming power of Black feminist thought. Thus, I extend a heartfelt thanks to—Andrew Daul, Kate Englund, Matthew Hamilton, Anna Keye, Seamus Leary, Amy Mack, Nat Meysenburg, Bianca Nejathaim, Jennifer Pincus, Darragh Sheehan, Tyler St. Jean, Mona Weiner, Eleanor Whitney, and Sharon Zetter. Through your own passionate "words of fire," I have come to hold on a bit tighter to my conviction that antiracist feminist education is liberatory for all humankind.

References

Guy-Sheftall, B., (Ed.) (1995). *Words of fire: An anthology of African-American feminist thought.* New York: New Press.

Hill Collins, P. (2000). *Black feminist thought.* New York: Routledge.

Joseph, G. (1995). Black feminist pedagogy and schooling in capitalist white America. In B. Guy-Sheftall (Ed.), *Words of fire: An anthology of African-American feminist thought* (pp. 465, 469). New York: New Press.

Lemons, G. (2001). Education as the practice of racial healing: Teaching writing against racism. In S. Haber (Ed.), *The academic forum* (p.1). Jersey City: New Jersey University.

Lemons, G. L. (1996). "Young man, tell our stories of how we made it over": Beyond the politics of identity. In K. J. Mayberry (Ed.), *Teaching what you're not: Identity politics in higher education* (p. 264). New York: New York University Press.

Stewart, M. (1995). Religion and the pure principles of morality, the sure foundation on which we must build. In B. Guy-Sheftall (Ed.), *Words of fire: An anthology of African-American feminist thought* (p. 29). New York: New Press.

Walker, A. (1983). *In search of our mothers gardens.* San Diego: Harcourt Brace Jovanovich.

11

Reconceptualizing Our Classroom Practice: Notes from an Antiracist Educator

Grace Mathieson

> Our challenge, and it must be a collective challenge, is to transform educational systems as we know them today. One reason that the challenge must be a collective one between Aboriginal Peoples and Canadians, is that it is only in this way that we can break the patronizing, parochial and colonial nature of our educational relations. We must expose and denounce the racism.
>
> (Monture-Angus 1995, p. 96)

> All of us educated in the mainstream, no matter whether we grew up in the Caribbean, North America, Britain, or Africa, have been educated from a colonialist perspeective which has taught us to either disregard or disrespect the majority of non-White peoples on earth. . . . It is axiomatic that we reconceptualize what we teach and how we teach.
>
> (Henry 1998, p. 67)

This chapter discusses how black feminist perspectives can be used to transform Eurocentric curriculum and pedagogical practices.[1] I write this chapter as a white woman, an educator, and an antiracist activist. I also write as a single mother of two teenage children who are students in the educational system. I cannot separate these two parts of myself as I write, for they give me my voice and are the driving force that determines who I am and what I do. And as I write, I draw on the knowledge of black feminists and other antiracist activists to create a space of social transformation. They point out that this space can only be created by the resistance to systems of domination, the decolonization of people's minds, and the creation of a transformation pedagogy. Like Patricia Monture-Angus (1995) and Annette Henry (1998), I encourage educators to resist systems of domination by transforming the classroom into a space of social and racial justice. This transformation cannot happen unless we are able to deconstruct the normalization of whiteness and to ask ourselves, as Nora Allingham (1992) does, "How can an education which teaches, implicitly and explicitly, that one culture, one religion and one colour deserve the most and the best, be good for anyone?" (p. 1). All children need opportunities to learn about the knowledges, histories, and perspectives of diverse cultures and peoples, and to develop an awareness of the historical racism that exists in Canada and in the world. We can no longer deny, dismiss, and ignore how an oppressive educational system affects students of color.

Although I have taught many different subjects and grades, for many years in the elementary school system, I have not always taught from an antiracist perspective as I do now in my grade five class. Like many other white people, I remained unaware for many years of how issues of race and racism affected my life. I grew up in an all-white, male-dominated family, lived in a white, working-class neighborhood, and attended all-white schools. Submerged in a world of whiteness, I absorbed racism in my formative years, through the education I received, the movies and sitcoms I watched on television, and the conversations of family and friends. As a teenager I watched the unfolding of the civil rights movement in the 1960s and felt a solidarity with the black struggle against segregation. I remember my sister and I doing the dishes after the family meal and singing civil rights protest songs and listening to the inspiring speeches of Martin Luther King Jr. and Malcolm X. I consumed books in the library to do with slavery, segregation, and the black struggle for justice. As an undergraduate university student in the 1970s, I became involved with social justice issues—the protest against the Vietnam War and the women's movement, for example. I explored what it meant to grow up as a working-class female in a patriarchal society. Yet it wasn't until some twenty years later, during the 1991 Persian Gulf War, that I began to develop "critical consciousness" about racism and was pushed to reflect on the ways that race, racism, and whiteness shaped my life and the broader social reality.

At that time, I joined a volunteer group of people, some white and some Middle Eastern, who were outraged at the U.S. attack on Iraq and deeply disturbed by the way racism was so easily drawn on among the populous to enable the United States, Canada, and the Western world to achieve their imperialist goals. Over a two-year span we developed a high school resource kit on the Persian Gulf War titled *Issues of War and Peace* to expose the lies, rhetoric, and destruction to the Iraqi people and land. The kit provided an alternative perspective and was a very critical look at the way the media manipulated public opinion and silenced the voices of Iraqi people. I worked with a Palestinian woman on the antiracism section of this kit, which from the beginning was fraught with tension and confusion. Because no one in the group, neither white nor person of color, possessed a complex knowledge and analysis of race and racism, constructing an antiracism discourse became a difficult task that we simply were not equipped to tackle. Furthermore, we lacked a critical understanding of the role of white people in antiracism work and of the ways in which we experienced our lives differently based on our race. We were unaware of the significance of our racial positioning—of the privileged position whites had of entering and exiting the antiracism discourse at will, as opposed to people of color who "lived their race" every day of their lives. Although we were grappling with issues of domination, white privilege, and white supremacy, they were not clearly understood by us at that time. For example, the term white supremacy was a term most of us had only encountered to describe white supremacists who promoted hate crimes, and we didn't want to use the term for fear that teachers would be "turned off." Continual disagreements and discord among members of the group led to the eventual exclusion of the antiracism section of the kit.

I left the group, feeling rejected and discouraged, yet I had gained a strong determination to understand these issues on a deeper level. Sometimes painful experiences can change us and this was very much the case with this experience. It marked the beginning of my personal transformation and commitment to educational change and antiracism classroom practice. Driven by a need to bring clarity to the confusion and questions around issues of race, racism, and whiteness, I returned to university as a mature student a few years later to study at Ontario Institute for Studies in Education at University of Toronto (OISE/UT) in the Department of Sociology and Equity Studies.

Tremendous diversity exists within whiteness—ethnicity, culture, religion, class, gender, sexual orientation, ableism, as well as other axes of difference intersect and overlap in complex ways. These social categories determine our identity and sites of power so that we experience our whiteness in varied, complex, and contradictory ways, yet our common task as whites remains to cast our gaze on our whiteness. Whiteness has been that unexamined, elusive part of ourselves that has remained very much taken for granted, unquestioned, and normalized. Often, we define ourselves in terms of our ethnicity and equate ethnicity to race (Sleeter

1996) so that we do not see ourselves as having a racial makeup at all. However, if we continue to remain unconscious of ourselves as racial beings, of our race privilege and power, we will continue to live our lives in oppressive ways. When we unmask our structured position of racial advantage, we can no longer hold that racism is not about us. We begin the process of unraveling the many ways that we are implicated in an unfair system based on historical conditions that explain the unequal distribution of power and resources. As we gain an understanding of how whiteness structures our individual lives, and our reality, then we, as white educators, can apply this knowledge to our antiracism classroom practice.

Being connected to white histories of colonialism and imperialism and having been schooled, both formally and informally, within a Eurocentric worldview, I agree with Becky Thompson (1997), a white antiracist educator, that there is a feeling of living a double life—of being white and benefiting from privilege, on the one hand, and opposing the ideology of whiteness in education, on the other. Yet, I recognize that it would be less than honest to think that whites who are doing antiracist work are any less affected by our white privilege. Our positionality requires us to not only recognize our privilege based on our racial location but also our white racism, because no matter how much we as antiracists fight white racism, we cannot escape being white and, thus, being accorded the inequitable distribution of resources and power by racial group. As Scheurich (1993) stresses, it is necessary to remind ourselves that "it does not matter whether we are a "good" or a "bad" white; all whites are socially positioned as whites and receive social advantages because of this positionality. No individual white gets to be an exception because of his or her antiracism" (p. 9).

Antiracist educators, such as George Dei (1996) in *Theory and Practice: Anti-racism Education*, Sherene H. Razack (1998) in *Looking White People In The Eye: Gender, Race, And Culture in Courtrooms and Classrooms,* and Annette Henry (1998) in *Taking Back Control: African Canadian Women Teachers' Lives and Practice* show us how race, ethnicity, culture, class, gender, ability, and sexuality influence the dynamic of the classroom, creating a space where we can learn a more complex reading of the world if we are able to hear these different voices and perspectives. We can enrich our teaching practice and build the academic success of our students by drawing on the knowledge the students bring to the class and introducing subjects and resources that reflect these knowledges and that can be woven into the curriculum we teach. The classroom is a space where there are many possibilities to learn in different and more enriching ways. Students come into our classrooms with their own experiences, communities, histories, and ways of seeing the world. Crucial to the academic success and empowerment of students is the link between knowledge production and identity. Students need to see that schooling is about them. This requires becoming conscious of the multilayered silencing and exclusion of the stories, experiences, and histories of the minoritized, including gay, lesbian, and bisexual youth, that exists in our educational institutions and of the destructiveness of this monocultural approach for all youth. By retaining a focus on whites and on men, we overlook the roles so many have played and continue to play in our society. This shortcoming continues to be addressed by educators and activists. Monture-Angus (1995) asserts that she experiences negative feedback from some of her white students when she presents an aboriginal point of view. She relates that she is criticized by these students for not being objective and is told that she is presenting opinions and propaganda, and not law to these students. A Eurocentric perspective, by contrast, is not challenged in the classroom because it is institutionalized as the "canon" of academic knowledge; it is legitimized as rational and reasoned truth.

bell hooks (1989) points out, "There must exist a paradigm, a practical model for social change that includes an understanding of ways to transform consciousness that are linked to efforts to transform structures" (p. 118). As members of the dominant group we carry the legacy of racism with us and although we may be conscious that we are not responsible for our historical racist roots and that racist thought and ideology are not something we invented, we need to critically self-reflect on the ways we are affected by and possibly invested in the very ideology of whiteness we oppose. At the same time, we need to understand how whiteness operates as a hegemonic force in our schools to oppress, exclude, and silence the knowledges, experiences, and histories of people of color and aboriginal peoples. When we engage in a dynamic process of deconstructing Eurocentric hegemony and decolonizing our own minds, we are rethinking schooling and finding ways to transform our classrooms. We know that we cannot change the overall structure through our everyday teaching practices and, as one of my professors frequently mentioned, the antiracism work that one teacher does in one classroom can be undone by another teacher in another classroom. Yet, in spite of this, antiracist educators recognize the power we have in the classroom to make a difference in our students' lives. As Paulo Freire (1997) states, "We have to believe that if men and women created the ugly world that we are denouncing, then men and women can create a world that is less discriminatory and more humane" (p. 315).

Current educational policies and practices have increased the emphasis in schools on Western scientific knowledge. It is crucial, that we challenge, not only the narrow focus of the dominant curriculum that is negative and demeaning to the minoritized but that we also deconstruct the dominance of the scientific paradigm within schools, which only sanctions knowledge that involves those things that can be objectively proven. George Dei (1999) asserts that it is only through Western examination and interpretation that subjugated knowledges receive legitimization. He states:

> Asian, African, Aboriginal cannot become legitimate, because according to Eurocentric definitions they could never become scientific. The only way to "science" is through whiteness. Thus, the process of demarginalisation of the ideas of the "para-normal," the "new-age," "homeopathy" and "astrology" are achieving popular currency and study by moving away from the centre of indigenous knowledges and belief systems towards the periphery of Western science. (p. 23)

Most educators still do not understand that racism in schools is not so much about racist intent as it is a study of the racist effects of a white-dominated school system. The curriculum by the selection of books and the course of study values and validates the perspective of the dominant, which impacts negatively on students of color. Students will perceive the value of their race and their ethnicity through what they see reflected in or omitted from the curriculum. For example, many teachers continue to focus on the contributions of the classical composers to music, considering this to be the "real" music curriculum, while ignoring the roots of jazz in black America, or traditional aboriginal drumming. Despite the fact that educators and activists have been addressing these issues for many years, there is still resistance to incorporating an antiracism practice. Many of us are still more comfortable using words like diversity, inclusivity, and cultural sensitivity when we discuss issues of oppression rather than words like racism, domination, subordination, and oppression, which speak more directly to power inequalities.

As educators we must speak honestly and with passion to engage students in critical discussion about our world. We must focus on allowing students their own voice—a voice that represents who they are—female, male, lesbian, or gay, poor, black, aboriginal, disabled. Engaging in change can make education, as Paulo Freire (1997) describes it, "the practice of freedom":

Education either functions as an instrument that is used to facilitate the integration of the younger generation into the logic of the present system and bring about conformity to it, *or* it becomes "the practice of freedom," the means by which men and women deal critically and creatively with reality and discover how to participate in the transformation of their world. (p. 53)

If we are to engage in education as the practice of freedom, then we must unravel Eurocentric hegemony, and resist the pressure to conform to the ideas, values, and perspectives that drive the status quo. If our goal is to allow all students to reach their potential, to stay engaged in the educational process, and to develop as critical thinkers, having a sense of pride and esteem in who they are, then we cannot view ourselves as the disseminators of a neutral body of knowledge and information working on behalf of the state but must interrogate power and privilege and the crucial role played by racism and whiteness. And if we are driven by a vision to create a more just and humane world, then what is called for is nothing less than a radical rethinking of our role as educators and of schooling, beginning with an interrogation of our own selves.

Black Feminist Theory

Black feminist educators and critical theorists understand the importance of promoting an oppositional worldview to bring about change in society and in education. As bell hooks (1990) describes it, "How do we create an oppositional worldview, a consciousness, an identity, a standpoint that exists not only as that struggle which also opposes dehumanization but as that movement which enables creative, expansive self-actualization?" (p. 15). Black feminists have constructed an alternative body of knowledge, grounded both in their collective history of oppression and their struggle to envision and create an Afrocentrism that reflects their political commitment to constructing positive African-centered worldviews. Black feminists have long advocated the need to articulate a black feminist standpoint that speaks to their own particular history and experiences, while simultaneously acknowledging the rich diversity and difference among themselves.

When bell hooks wrote *Ain't I a Woman* in 1981, she found that not only was there very little written about black women's experiences, but that racism and sexism were so entrenched that their experiences were dismissed as insignificant and unworthy of scholarly attention. Most works in existence at that time were written by black males or white females and distorted black women's stories and experiences through racist or sexist assumptions. Placing black women's experiences within a feminist context, then, addresses the issue of authentic voice and power—black feminists want to tell their own stories and unravel the negative effects that both race and gender have had on their past and present lives. Audre Lorde reminds black feminists of this diversity when she states "that unity does not require that we be identical to each other" (1991, p. 94). As a black lesbian poet and writer, she attests to the oppressive dimensions of heterosexism and homophobia, rooted in fear of difference, and argues that these forces work like racism to oppress black lesbians and operate to separate and divide black feminists. She challenges black feminists to begin to confront their homophobic thoughts and behavior.

In Canada, black history has not yet been established as a legitimate field of historical inquiry as it has in the United States (Bristow et al. 1994). That slavery and segregated schools existed in Canada, for example, are still not widely known among Canadians, and although black communities date back four hundred years, their historical presence has been largely omitted from the face of Canadian history. This leaves the erroneous impression that blacks are relative newcomers to our country. Furthermore, because Canada has been seen as a haven for runaway fugitives from the United States, an aura that Canadians are morally superior people to their southern neighbors has been constructed. The myth is that we are not a racist society like the United States. The national image we have of ourselves as a multicultural society serves to hide the deep racism that has run through this country since its conception—we are a mosaic, while the Americans are a melting pot. The idealism of multiculturalism that enabled racial and ethnic groups to preserve their heritage was viewed by many minorities, angry and frustrated by systemic racism, as a smokescreen that masked their lived inequalities and struggles, experienced socially, politically, and economically. The blanket of silence that exists around issues of race and racism in the Canadian context continues to be huge and is only recently being pried open and exposed. The Japanese internment during World War II, and the establishment of residential schools for aboriginal peoples, are examples of racist state practices that have been devastating in their impact on these populations and have recently received national attention.

Like their sisters to the south, the experience of black feminists in Canada has been one of erasure and silencing, as the black presence has been ignored and/or distorted by history texts written by white men. More recently, black women's experiences have been included in texts by white feminists, as they have attempted to write themselves back into history, however, their work is marked with distortions and omissions and does not accurately reflect the black female experience either. Peggy Bristow et al. (1994) report that Mary Ann Shadd Cary is not accorded the recognition she deserves as the first woman publisher and editor of a Canadian newspaper in the 1850s, nor is Addie Aylestock recognized as the second Canadian woman to be ordained as a minister in 1951. In the past decade, these exclusions and distortions have been addressed by black women writers, who are writing their own feminist history and like African American feminists, want to show how both gender and race shaped the lives of black pioneer women. In *We're Rooted Here and They Can't Pull Us Up* (Bristow et al. 1994), six African Canadian women research the history and accomplishments of black women in Canada and report that there is in fact, thus far, an unacknowledged tradition of writing in the black women's community that has been overlooked. Beginning with Mary Ann Shadd Cary who in 1852 wrote *A Plea for Emigration to Canada West*, they cite numerous black women who, although not necessarily writing from a feminist perspective, were nonetheless writing black women's history.

Black feminists know that their histories and experiences have been and often continue to be silenced and undervalued in the educational curriculum. White and male have long stood for what constitutes the normative in schools. Although pedagogies that affirm multiple worldviews are needed as a means of engaging all children, incorporating an African-centered pedagogy is an example of one approach to breaking down this narrow and hegemonic position. An African-centered pedagogy promotes the development of a critical consciousness, so that history and structural power are analyzed within intersecting social locations, while at the same time promoting the development of an African worldview and legitimizing African knowledge. Both are necessary components to providing a healthy ground for students' pride and esteem to flourish and grow. Yet even within the context of an African worldview, it is easy to fall into privileging the male perspective over the female experience. When we do this, we continue to oppress on the basis of gender. In addition, when we draw from African American history and ignore the African Canadian experience, we feed into the myth that racism is part of the American experience, not the Canadian, and at the same time we fail to recognize the accomplishments and achievements of historical black figures, who surmounted the forces of racism and sexism in our own country. In both cases we do our students a disservice.

This past February, two of my grade five students, both African Canadian boys, made presentations at the City Hall's Black History Month

Closing Ceremonies. They researched and wrote reports on the life and accomplishments of Frederick Douglass and Rosa Parks. Our main speaker for this event was Adrienne Shadd, a writer and researcher from Toronto who is related to Mary Ann Shadd Cary, the first female editor of a newspaper and outspoken abolitionist. Adrienne Shadd's presentation highlighted the accomplishments of Mary Ann Shadd Cary and other black Canadian feminists—strong, articulate women who dedicated their lives to ending slavery. She also spoke about the Canadian civil right's movement. As she spoke, I reflected on my own antiracism classroom practice, and became aware of how easy it is to forget that we have a rich history of resistance to racism, right here in our own country. At that moment, I adjusted my own focus and made a mental note to find out more about both the abolitionist movement and the civil rights movement in Canada, and to work to incorporate more of the Canadian experience into my antiracism classroom practice.

If we want to strengthen our antiracism classroom practice, then, we must pay attention to the ways that both race and gender shape our own lives. Beverly Tatum (1999) states that although we all have multiple identities, "some dimensions of our identities are reflected more saliently than others—a distinction made apparent by the energy we invest in their examination" (p. 60). As a black woman, she explains, she has invested more time in thinking about what it means to be black and female, in that order, than what it means to be heterosexual, able-bodied, and middle class. This, she continues, is because these parts of her identity are most often reflected back to her as significant in the eyes of others. bell hooks (1981) relates that the forces of racism and sexism have been inseparable determining forces in her life. Yet, unlike black feminists, most white educators have invested little time in thinking about what it means to be white because it is reflected back to us by others as normal. To be white is to be Canadian, the standard, the universal measuring stick by which all others are measured. What we fail to understand, however, even though black feminists have been telling us for decades, is just how oppressive this is for those who fall outside of the parameters of whiteness.

The British writer Hazel Carby (1997) states that "the existence of racism must be acknowledged as a structuring feature of Black women's relationship with White women" (p. 46). Carby, argues that black women need to tell their own "herstories" through their lived realities and experiences of oppression, and that white women must write from their own experiences and acknowledge how they are simultaneously oppressor and oppressed. By doing so, we explore the interconnections between the forces that shape our lives and the forces that shape black women's lives; this, in turn, is key to shaping our respective worldviews. This understanding and perspective also shapes the relationships of black students and their white teachers. It is essential that we as antiracist educators understand the history of racism and how it has shaped black-white relations over the decades, placing white in a position of privilege and power over black. When we become aware of the power dynamics, we can change our perceptions of white as privileged and explore how white positionality affects the social construction of our knowledge, our understandings of ourselves, our world, and our perception of the racialized "Other." When we acknowledge that we speak, think, and act from a privileged location, we break through white as normative to decenter white, male authority—we can then grapple with how as white women we can oppress women of color.

When we deconstruct white positionality, we unmask notions of liberal individualism that function to cover up power differences and maintain the status quo. bell hooks (1992) states that whites "have a deep emotional investment in the myth of 'sameness,' even as their actions reflect the primacy of whiteness as a sign informing who they are and how they think" (p. 167).

Through the ideology of individualism, many whites tend to interpret racism as an individual belief rather than an institutional system supported by a collective worldview. Thus, it is common to hear whites proclaim that we are all racist, meaning that we all have prejudiced attitudes. While the prejudiced attitudes of individuals cannot be denied, it is at once a denial of difference and of domination and feeds into the erroneous belief that equal opportunities exists. The common statement among whites, "We do not see color," is part of this myth of sameness. The proclamation "We do not see color" also functions to hide power differentials. Not long ago, the local Hamilton Board of Education Teachers' magazine, *The Apple*, published an article written by a white educator, highlighting Black History Month activities. Students created posters, wrote poetry, and made collages featuring aspects of black history. Along with the article was a photograph showing this teacher and a multiracial group of students holding a banner that proudly proclaimed, "We do not see color!" In a society determined not to see color, this proclamation speaks not to the unity of the students, as I think perhaps was the intention of this teacher, but to the color-evasive and power-evasive ideology of whiteness. The oppressiveness of the statement "We do not see color" lies in the fact that it tries to obliterate difference that arises from historical contingencies. It is at once a denial of difference and of domination. In other words, if whites do not register color, they also do not register white privilege and power, nor the historical legacy of racism (Rodriguez 2000). When the historical legacy of racism is erased, it can then be maintained that we are all on an even playing field.

Driven by a collective vision and a shared intellectual and political commitment, black feminists work together in racial solidarity to develop black women's standpoints that oppose the unjust practices and ideas of the social hegemony. Patricia Hill Collins enthuses that "without a collectivity or group, there can be no critical social theory that aims to struggle with the realities confronting that group" (1998, p. xvii). Many black feminists attest to the strength and determination of black women to give back to the community, to use their agency to create viable alternatives that reflect their Afrocentric worldviews. Heidi Safia Mirza (1997) states, "Valorizing their agency as subversive and transformative rather than as a manifestation of resistance, it becomes clear that black women do not just resist racism, they live 'other' worlds" (p. 270). She points to the strategy black women in England have used to do this—the creation of black supplementary schools. The organization of these schools is a grassroots effort led mainly by black women who want to resist mainstream schooling and provide an alternative way of being and knowing for black students—a place where blackness "becomes the norm" (p. 273). Their collective efforts are building social support networks that reflect the values, ideals, and visions for redefining their world.

As educators, we can participate in building links between schools and black communities. For example, an African Canadian friend of mine is a yoga instructor who is working with black youth in her community. She approached me about a Yoga for Youth program in my school. She heard that yoga was being used in California with at-risk black youth. Yoga strengthens the body and teaches breathing techniques and meditation that strengthen students' abilities to concentrate and control anger. After a visit to the school to explain the benefits of yoga to both students and their parents, she began teaching yoga classes to ten- and eleven-year-olds in the gym after school. Through storytelling and discussions, she stresses Afrocentric ideas; and through her program, she is building links with students in the school and the community.

As black feminists retell their own history, and work to overcome obstacles of racism and sexism in their own lives and in the lives of their children, they are transforming their lived realities. Working collectively, they are creating African-centered worldviews that enable their children and students to connect to a curriculum that is motivating and reflects the concerns, values, and struggles of black people within a political and historical dimension. As they work to break down systemic silencing, they are "claiming the marginalized and devalued space of Black womanhood not as one of tragedy but as one of creativity and power" (Hill Collins 1998, p. 128). As white, antiracist educators we have a lot to learn from black feminists. We need to listen to their stories, to their perspectives, and to their histories. We need to hear what they have to say, not only about their own lives and experiences but about the oppressiveness of white women, and of our power to silence. We need to acknowledge that we can be simultaneously oppressed and oppressors. When we impose our ideas, when we do not listen to the silenced voices, and when we speak for all people, we are acting in oppressive ways. As white antiracist educators we need to engage in the dual process of deconstructing Eurocentric power and decolonize our own minds, as we strive to live our lives and teach our students in more antiracist and liberatory ways.

Decolonizing the Mind

> Critically examining the association of whiteness as terror in the black imagina-
> tion, deconstructing it, we both name racism's impact and help to break its hold.
> We decolonize our minds and our imaginations. (hooks 1992, p. 178)

Working from an antiracist perspective as white educators involves re adjusting the Eurocentric lens from which we view the world. It involves unlearning and relearning how to see, hear, and read the world. We need to ask ourselves if we can recognize racist ideology when we hear it in conversations, when we see it in movies, or read it in newspapers. If we can't recognize it in our everyday lives, we won't be able to recognize it when it emerges in the classroom, in the conversations of our students, in the films we view, and in the textbooks we use. If we can't identify it, then we can't confront it and it will continue to perpetuate in our classrooms. Not only do we as teachers need to decolonize our thinking, we need to teach our students to decolonize theirs.

All of us who are white, even those of us who strive to be antiracist, are affected by racist assumptions and thoughts. Becky Thompson (1997) contends that we are in fact "antiracist racists" because we receive un-earned privileges due to our whiteness, yet we are striving to become con-scious of our racism and oppose white supremacy. We need, as bell hooks asserts, to "decolonize our minds and our imaginations." The first step in this process is to deconstruct our assumptions and viewpoints so we can better understand how racism and whiteness affect us as whites and affect racialized Others. In this way, we may be able to understand our own complicity in an oppressive system. This insight is not meant to induce feelings of guilt or paralysis; it is meant to encourage us to open up to critical self-reflection.

In this process, it is important that we understand how black women and black students see us as white women and white educators. bell hooks (1992) argues that whites have been "socialized to believe the fantasy, that whiteness represents goodness and all that is benign and non-threatening" (p. 340). By contrast, she asserts that, in the black imagination, whiteness is often associated with terror, "a power that wounds, hurts, tortures" (p. 340). hooks states that there is a "profound psychological impact of white racist domination" (p. 340) experienced by blacks in response to the legacy of white domination. Whites' inability to conceive of this terror, she holds, is itself an expression of white supremacy. White oppression extends beyond black-White relations. Patricia Monture-Angus, an aboriginal law professor, had to rush her eleven-month-old son to the hospital when he fell and broke his arm. She was accused of child abuse by the doctors and separated from her son for eight days. When she explained to them that she was a law professor, she was laughed at by the doctors and questioned as to how frequently her husband beat her.

When we actively engage in the process of deconstructing racist ideology, so prevalent in the popular media, and become aware of how we are affected by it, we begin to decolonize our minds. As we encounter situations that cause us to reflect critically on our emotions, reactions, and inner conflicts, our consciousness expands, our awareness increases, and we reject harmful ideology and are more able to understand complex realities. Movement occurs as we shift our perspective and deepen our understanding of ourselves and come to terms with the ways we have been invested, often unconsciously, in the ideology of whiteness. The racist construction of the black male as an object of both terror and desire in the popular press has its historical roots in colonial discourses used to keep the black male in subjugated positions. Gabriel (1998) states that this image "resonates deepseated fears and anxieties within the psyche of white America" (p. 19). I remained unconscious of this racist construct until I personally experienced the fear of the black male. This incident happened a number of years ago when one afternoon I entered the small enclosed cubical outside of the bank to use the bank machine. A young black man was there, with his back turned to me withdrawing money. Standing behind him, for one short moment, I froze with fear as I realized that we were alone and a feeling of certainty that I would be robbed overtook me. I was greatly relieved when he walked past me and exited the building. After withdrawing money, I exited and walked past the parking lot to see this same man getting into his car along side of his wife and two young children. The contradiction between my perception of this person as a criminal and the reality of him as a family man, the father of two young children, stunned me. I looked long and hard at him in an attempt to imprint this image of him as a family man on my mind. I was flooded with emotion at that moment. I was angry at myself, and ashamed at the same time. I was seized by a desire to deny this experience, to disown it. Yet, surfacing even stronger was a need to know where this experience was rooted, and how it could be part of my psyche. I thought about the black men that I knew who were caring, sensitive individuals, devoted to their wives and children and how the image of the black male as threatening, menacing, and evil unexpectedly emerged from seemingly nowhere and paralyzed me with fear. This was a transformative event for me because it was a moment when I was pushed to think through the pervasive way that racism affects all of us, and to come to terms with the power that racist images have on our psyche, and on our social and collective unconscious.

As white educators we need to understand the power relations that exist in society and how these power relations have caused and continue to cause harm. Although the content of racist ideology has changed significantly since the days of colonization and slavery, its function remains the same: to justify and perpetuate economic exploitation and political inequality based on color. To decolonize our minds is to understand how these power relations work. Issues of race, racism, and whiteness are complex and deeply embedded in our everyday lives and social and political fabric. Rodriguez (1998) poses the question, "Do you really think it is possible to step fully outside of the history of racism, to remove ourselves from the way this history has inscribed itself on our bodies and in our very speech acts?" (p. 43). Clearly, we can't. We can critique, challenge, and deconstruct harmful ideology when we encounter it in ourselves and in the media and teach our students to do the same. We can also do this by drawing on black feminist thought and other antiracist ideologies. By doing so, we are actively engaging in a more democratic and liberatory classroom practice.

Both hooks and Rodriguez ask educators to rise to the occasion and reconceptualize a new curriculum that is inclusive and that challenges taken-for-granted Eurocentric and male-centered paradigms. To embark on such a project, I believe it is necessary to assess how we are situated in the colonial discourse and to ask ourselves in what ways we can engage in the transformative process of decolonizing our minds. We all choose different ways and avenues to engage in decolonization. I have chosen black feminist theorizing as an entry point for my learning and teaching.

Rethinking the Curriculum: Notes into Action

Mother of Brown-Ness
EARTH-MOTHER,
Mother of all our brown-ness,
Hands clasped with arms
stretched round the world
Cuddle me closer, warm upon your breast
Slumberous, sweetly, darkness at rest.
Wake me to living and loving;
Scatter my dreams into the ethereal air.
Mother of brown-ness surround me
Deep in your sweet loving care.
Margaret Walker (1993)

After teaching middle school students for many years, I decided two years ago to teach younger students and accepted a position as a grade five teacher at a public school, located in the north end of the city—a lower economic area with many immigrant families and a high percentage of students of color. I looked forward to working with younger students and to the challenge of developing an antiracism curriculum and to creating a classroom that fostered respect for differences based on race, religion, language, gender, class, sexuality, and so on. Almost immediately, I began to mull over ideas in my mind of how to deconstruct the ideology of racism with younger students. I wanted students to not just learn theory but to critically reflect on what they learned so that they could apply new learnings to their own lives. As I began to work with the grade five students, I was conscious that my antiracism practice was privileging a male and mainly American perspective. I took on the challenge to make the curriculum more inclusive and to strengthen the focus on the Canadian context. I did this by infusing a black feminist perspective and a stronger antiracist feminist perspective into my everyday work.

Accomplishing this was much easier than I initially anticipated. There are many good resources available, and while there are teaching expectations to be met, there are no stipulations on the resources that can be used to meet these objectives. For example, a writing expectation is to have students write a nonfiction report based on information they take from nonfiction books. I have purchased nonfiction books on black history for my own classroom use so that all students can research one black historical or contemporary figure. Among many books that are available are the following: *Rosa Parks and the Montgomery Bus Boycott* by Teresa Celsi, *Mary Ann Shadd: Publisher, Editor, Teacher, Lawyer, Suffragette* by Rosemary Sadlier, *Brown Girl in the Ring, Rosemary Brown: A Biography for Young People* by Lynette Roy, and *A Picture Book of Sojourner Truth* by David A. Adler. These women are examples of strong activists who were able to overcome obstacles and leave a mark on history. While learning how to write a nonfiction report, students also learn of the struggles and history of black women.

Another learning expectation for grade five students is to identify a writer's or character's point of view. For this exercise, my students use *The People Who Hugged the Trees* by Deborah Lee Rose, based on a legend from Rajasthan, India. The legend tells the story of Amrita Devi and several hundred villagers who were the first tree huggers to protect their forests nearly three centuries ago. The students learn that the story is told from the village people's point of view. To explore another point of view, I ask, "What would be different about the story if it was told from the point of view of the Maharajah?" We discuss the fact that Amrita is the heroine of the story and if the story were told from the perspective of the Maharajah, then he would be the hero of the story, and we would hear about his beautiful palace and his need for more wood. From his point of view, the villagers might be seen as unreasonable troublemakers, rather than brave people trying to protect their environment. By developing a power triangle that places the village people at the base of the triangle and the Maharajah at the apex, the students can see how the power structure of this society works. Once the students understand perspective and point of view, I introduce the concept of nonviolent protest and show that even though the villagers were poor, they used their collective power to oppose the Maharajah's army. This story is a good link to issues of nonviolent resistance and to times in history when people have used their collective power to resist and change unfair state laws and practices. We study Gandhi, Martin Luther King, and Rosa Parks during our unit on government, when we explore the theme of protest and resistance in more depth.

To bring in the perspectives of aboriginal students, we have studied the novel, *Indian Summer,* by Barbara Girion. In this story a white family moves to Woodland Reservation in New York State for the summer. The two girls in the story become instant roommates but not instant friends. Problems and conflicts unfold between them, based on their perceptions of each other's differences. While discussing the plot, setting, and characters, I also introduce to the students the history of colonialism, so that they can begin to understand how racism has worked in Canada and in the United States. We discuss the European conquest, the taking away of land from aboriginal peoples, and the setting up of reservations. We explore racist stereotypes and look at how these racist images work in the media. Students are also introduced to aboriginal beliefs—most notably, respect for the environment. When the novel is finished, an aboriginal guest speaker is invited to the class to discuss issues such as aboriginal spirituality, the Indian Act, and residential schools in Canada.

I have found that teaching poetry is an effective way to present the work of talented, articulate black authors—Maya Angelou, Margaret Walker, and Langston Hughes—and to teach students to express themselves through this form. During the year, the students write rhyming couplets, limericks, and diamonte poems in which they reflect on and express their own identity and culture. Before they write, however, we look at the different ways a student can express his/her identity and then discuss how gender, race, culture, religion, language, and class shape their sense of self. We take time to play with word combinations that express heritage and race. For many of my students this is an opportunity to explore their diverse heritage, a very new experience. A student born in Guatemala, for example, might express her/his identity as Latina/o, Central American, Latin American, and Canadian. For many students this was an opportunity to explore their diverse heritage. One student wrote that she was French Canadian, African Canadian, and aboriginal; an aboriginal student identified by saying, "I am Onieda, I am Mohawk." Other students expressed that they were of Cambodian, Vietnamese, or Chinese heritage. For the white students, this exercise seemed strange, as they simply said that they were Canadian. I tried to help them deconstruct this category by pointing out that I was a white woman, of British heritage and a Canadian. They then identified themselves as white Canadians, which can be seen as the taking of small steps toward politicizing whiteness and challenging its normality.

Exploring issues of racism through film has been very meaningful with grade five students. *For Angela*, a very powerful film that speaks directly to racism, is based on the real-life experience of a racial assault against an aboriginal mother, Rhonda Gordon, and her young daughter, Angela. While waiting at a bus stop, Angela and Rhonda are verbally attacked by a white male high school student, who attempts to amuse his friends as he hurls racial taints and slurs at them. The racial assault does not stop as they board the bus, while his friends respond with laughter, the passengers on the bus, visibly uncomfortable, witness this assault in steely silence. Angela cuts off her braids that night, no longer wanting to be seen as aboriginal. Rhonda, tired of the relentless onslaughts and the negative affects on Angela, goes to the high school and with the assistance of the principal finds the main perpetrator. She confronts him in the principal's office and makes him listen to the devastating affects his actions have on Angela.

It is important to allow students time to discuss their feelings after the film. There are excellent suggestions in the after-viewing guide, some of which I draw on for my discussion. We begin by reviewing the emotions felt by Rhonda, Angela, Ian, Ian's friends, the bus driver, and the passengers on the bus. Then we explore Ian's actions and possible motivation for doing what he did. I make a connection between power and gender by asking the students if the racial assault would play out the same if the perpetrator was a female and the victims were male. Most students are quick to respond that they don't think it would; they think that a teenage girl would not assault a father and his son in this same way. We discuss the fact that Angela and her mother are victimized on the basis of both gender and race. The silence of the bus driver and the people on the bus does not go unnoticed by students and they wonder why they do not act to stop Ian. Students also feel that the bus driver should have intervened in this situation and the police should have been contacted. In our discussion we identify a stereotype as an untrue idea, prejudice as a negative attitude, and discrimination as acting on untrue ideas and negative attitudes, and we explored concrete examples of each. We look at how racist ideas, individual behaviors, and systemic practices are linked to these definitions. Students quickly mentioned slavery, Jim Crow laws, segregation, and residential schools as examples of systemic racism that we have studied.

During Black History Month, we have an opportunity to explore the Underground Railroad and the role black women played in this movement. In "The Lord Seemed to Say 'Go': Women and the Underground Railroad Movement," Adrienne Shadd (1994) documents the tremendous obstacles women faced when escaping to the North via the Railroad between 1815 and 1865. In addition, she explores both the formal and the informal networks set up by black women to aid escaping fugitives. These personal accounts and stories are brought to life and given voice. There are untold stories of courage and determination shown by black women in working for freedom. Shadd argues that Harriet Tubman, who is synonymous with the Underground Railroad, is only one of many women who resisted slavery and took part in the networks to help the fugitives. By bringing black women into focus, Shadd makes them the subject of her own history.

Moving Forward

Recently, I attended a literacy in-service at my school and was delighted that a story titled "Stubborn Mary Shadd," by Karen Shadd-Evelyn, was used as an introductory activity. This story, in the grade four *Collections* series, is a biography of Mary Shadd, the first Canadian editor and abolitionist. A grade four teacher, a white woman, sitting beside me stated that this was a story that she would never use with her students because there was too much history that needed to be taught before students could understand the story. Probing her reluctance to teach this story, I asked if she would be willing to attend an in-service on the Underground Railway. I pointed out that she had four African Canadian girls in her class, to which she responded that she had five students from Kosovo. "What about them?" she asked. She argued that she could not privilege black history and ignore everybody else's history, and in addition, she reasoned there wasn't time to teach black history. Yet the question we as educators need to ask ourselves is, "Whose perspective and history is being privileged? When we remain oblivious to the needs of black students and other students of color, and treat black history as separate from the mainstream, and when we exclude it, are we not then perpetuating racism?

Our students are not "mere consumers of knowledge" (Freire 1997, p. 315) and our role, as educators, is not to simply dispense more and more information. Furthermore, we can no longer hide behind the guise of multiculturalism, with its emphasis on cultural awareness, and the creation of "feel-good stories" that function to prop up white supremacy and whitewash and obliterate racism. Deconstructing power and privilege in classrooms with students is critical to their development as thinking, knowledgeable, caring, and ethical individuals. Doing antiracism work may not seem easy in the wake of a very conservative movement in education by government, yet we must take a stand and work against the grain, for there is no middle ground in antiracist work (Dei 1996). For white educators, this work involves an interrogation of whiteness, beginning with ourselves and our commonsense assumptions about our school system as being neutral, fair, and equitable for all students. When we deconstruct whiteness to understand how it functions as a system of domination, both outside and within ourselves, and engage in a critical and reflexive process of interrogation, then we can use this knowledge to contribute to transformative educational agendas and practices. We can teach our students to both decolonize their minds and to develop critical consciousness, and thus "achieve a deepened awareness both of the sociocultural reality that shapes their lives and their capacity to transform that reality" (Freire 1985, p. 93).

Note

1. A shorter version of this essay was first published in *Back to the Drawing Board: African-Canadian Feminisms*, edited by Njoki Wane, Katerina Deliovsky and Erica Lawson (Toronto: Sumach Press, 2002).

References

Adler, D. (1994). *A picture book of Sojourner Truth.* New York: Holiday House.

Allingham, N. (1992). Anti-racism education and the curriculum: A privileged perspective. Keynote address to Wards 10 and 11, Toronto Board of Education, January 31, 1992.

Benson, R., Bryan, L., McDonell, W. Newlove, K., Player, C., & Stenson, L. (1997). *Collections: Building community.* Scarborough: Prentice Hall Ginn Canada.

Bristow, P., Brand, D., Carty, L., Cooper, A. P., Hamilton, S., & Shadd A. (1994). *"We're rooted here and they can't pull us up": Essays in African Canadian women's history.* Toronto: University of Toronto Press.

Carby, H. (1997). White women listen! Black feminism and the boundaries of sisterhood. In Mirza, S. H. (Ed.), *Black British feminism: A reader.* London: Routledge.

Celsi, T. (1991). *Rosa Parks and the Montgomery bus boycott.* Brookfield, CT: Millbrook Press.

Dei, G. J. S. (1999). The denial of difference: Reframing anti-racist praxis. *Race Ethnicity and Education, 2,* 17–37.

Dei, G. J. S. (1996). *Theory & practice: Anti-racism education.* Halifax: Fernwood Publishing.

Feelings, T. (1993). *Soul looks back in wonder.* New York: Puffin Books.

Freire, P. (1985). *The politics of education.* New York: Bergin & Garvey.

Freire, P. (1997). A response. In P. Freire with J. W. Fraser, D. Macedo, T. McKinnon, & W. T. Stokes (Eds.), *Mentoring the mentor: A critical dialogue with Paulo Freire* (pp. 303–29). New York: Peter Lang.

Gabriel, J. (1998). *Whitewashed.* London: Routledge.

Girion, B. (1990). *Indian summer.* Toronto: Scholastic.

Henry, A. (1998). *Taking back control: African Canadian women teachers' lives and practices.* Albany: State University of New York Press.

hooks, b. (1981). *Ain't I a woman: Black women and feminism.* Boston: South End Press.

hooks, b. (1989). *Talking back: Thinking feminist,thinking black.* Boston: South End Press.

hooks, b. (1990). *Yearning: Race, gender, and cultural politics.* Boston: South End Press.

hooks, b. (1997). Representing whiteness in the black imagination. In R. Frankenberg (Ed.), *Displacing whiteness: Essays in social and cultural criticism* (pp.165–79). Durham, NC: Duke University Press.

hooks, b. (1992). *Black looks: Race and representation.* Boston: South End Press.

Hill Collins, P. (1990). *Black feminist thought: Knowledge, consciousness, and the politics of empowerment.* New York: Routledge.

Hill Collins, P. (1998). *Fighting words: Black women and the search for justice.* Minneapolis: University of Minnesota Press.

Johns Simpson, M. (1993). *Official guide for teaching "For Angela."* Montreal: National Film Board of Canada.

Lourde, Audre.(1991). I am your sister: Black women organizing across sexualities. In Makeda S, (Ed.), *Pieces of my heart: A lesbian of colour anthology*. Toronto: Sister Vision Press.

Markey, S. (Coordinator) (1996). *Issues of war and peace: A resource kit for high school teachers and students*. Hamilton: The Iraqi Children's Art Project.

Mirza, H. S. (1997). Black women in education: A collective movement for social change. In *Black British Feminism: A Reader* (pp. 268–77). London: Routledge.

Monture-Angus, P. (1995). *Thunder in my soul: A Mohawk woman speaks*. Halifax: Fernwood Publishing.

Razack, S. (1998). *Looking white people in the eye: Gender, race, and culture in courtrooms and classrooms*. Toronto: University of Toronto Press.

Rodriguez, N. M. (2000). Projects of whiteness in a critical pedagogy. In N. M. Rodriguez & L. E. Villaverde (Eds.), *Dismantling white privilege: Pedagogy, politics, and whiteness* (pp. 1–24). New York: Peter Lang.

Rodriguez, N. M. (1998). Emptying the content of whiteness: Toward an understanding of the relation between whiteness and pedagogy. In J. L. Kincheloe, S. R. Steinberg, N. M. Rodriguez, & R. E. Chennault (Eds.), *White reign: Deploying whiteness in America* (pp. 31–62). New York: St. Martin's Press.

Rose, D. L. (1990). *The people who hugged the trees*. Hong Kong: Roberts Rinehart.

Roy, L. (1992). *Brown girl in the ring: Rosemary Brown, a biography for young people*. Toronto: Sister Vision: Black Women and Women of Colour Press.

Sadlier, R. (1995). *Mary Ann Shadd: Publisher, editor, teacher, lawyer, suffragette*. Toronto: Umbrella Press.

Shadd, A. (1994). The lord seemed to say "Go": Women and the underground railroad movement. In P. Bristow et al., *"We're rooted here and they can't pull us up": Essays in African Canadian women's history* (pp. 41–68). Toronto: University of Toronto Press.

Scheurich, J. J. (1993). Toward a white discourse on white racism. *Educational Researcher, 22*, 5–10.

Sleeter, C. (1996). White silence, white solidarity. In J. Garvey & N. Ignatiev (Eds.), *Race Traitor* (pp. 257–65). New York: Routledge.

Tatum, B. D. (1999). Lighting candles in the dark: One black woman's response to white antiracist narratives. In C. Clark & J. O'Donnell (Eds.), *Becoming and unbecoming white: Owning and disowning a racial identity* (pp. 56–77). Westport, CT: Bergin and Garvey.

Thompson, B. (1997). Home/work: Antiracism, activism and the meaning of whiteness. In M. Fine, L. Weis, L. C. Powell, & L. M. Wong (Eds.), *Off white: Readings on race, power, and society* (pp. 354–66). New York: Routledge.

Walker, M. (1993). Mother of brown-ness. In T. Feelings (Ed.), *Soul looks back in wonder*. New York: Puffin Books.

12

The Xinachtli Project: Transforming Whiteness through Mythic Pedagogy

Carlos Aceves

The Mexicans practiced a purification at the end of every fifty-two years in the belief that it was time for the world to come to an end. I have scarcely heard of a truer sacrament, that is, as the dictionary defines it, "outward and visible sign of an inward and spiritual grace," than this, and I have no doubt that they were originally inspired from Heaven to do this.

Henry David Thoreau, *Walden*, p. 56.

At the center of the Aztec calendar is a human face. Perched between his lips is an obsidian dagger. His head is symmetrically outlined by symbols. Most Mexicanos who look into the piercing eyes of the Sun Stone see something they know but have difficulty articulating. The language of this ancient text is now unknown to them, deprived of its use for nearly four hundred years. The message from those who came before us is lost yet frozen within this monolith.

I have asked this question often to many among my people: Look at this calendar. Is it part of who you are? I ask. Inevitably the answer can be summarized as:

"Yes, but I cannot read it. I don't understand what it says."

They are expressing a dilemma articulated by all who have been colonized and have not recovered their history, their indigenous roots confined as museum pieces and academic interpretations by the very society that systematically repressed this knowledge. Part of what Mexicanos are saying when reluctantly accepting a historic tie to the face of the Tonal Machiotl (Aztec calendar) is "It's my face but it looks foreign to me. Part of me is not understandable to my psyche." Another implication is racial in nature. The face in the calendar is an indigenous face, but how can it be mine if I am no longer indigenous?

These questions reflect an internal conflict within a people affected by five centuries of European colonization. Reclaiming this face would be an act against the mental colonization Mexican people internalized during the three hundred years under the Crown of Spain, under the colonizer, under whiteness. It is tantamount to proclaiming that Mexicans are a millenary not centuries-old people. When I initially attempted to proclaim that it was my face looking at me from the Sun Stone it was strictly as a reaction to my awareness of living in a society dominated by whiteness where my own culture was not validated. At the time I did not yet understand the language of the conglomeration of symbols in the Aztec calendar or the philosophy behind it. My actions against this oppression were motivated by anger, in part at the Europeans for having made me illiterate in the indigenous language of my people and for the genocide against my people. It is now known that "(in) Mexico there were close to 25 million people in 1500. By 1600 only 1 million native Mesoamericans were still alive" (Carrasco, p. 129).

The cultural pride that ensued was useful for a time and fueled my motivation for political struggle through the Chicano Movement. Eventually I came to understand that without knowing what this ancient document said, what words lay in this stern face looking at me across the centuries, my liberation could not be complete. My first journey into Mexico in 1983 initiated me into a series of meetings and developments of relationships with individuals who were keepers of this ancient knowledge through the oral tradition. My identification with the face of the Tonal Machiotl began to transcend racial identity, gradually influencing my realization that without being able to see the universality of my existence I would be doomed to live a life confined within externally imposed boundaries. Eventually I internalized an idea fundamental to my work in mythic pedagogy: the Aztec calendar is model of practical kinship with Creation.

In the classroom we present the face of the Sun Stone as the face of humanity, a face observing the sky and recording the evidence of its cyclical movements. Realization of this universal human exploration of the sky does not hinder but rather enhances the ethnic identity Mexicano students may find in the mythic history of this commonly recognized symbol of Mexico. As they learn to daily change the dates along with the Gregorian calendar and understand the astronomical facts recorded in its symbols, the Sun Stone comes alive empowering the children with critical but affirming eye to their indigenous history. They discover the scientific knowledge recorded in its concentric rings, such as the orbit of the Earth, the cycles of Venus and the moon, the great alignment of the Morning and Evening Stars with the Pleiades. As they lay on our large replicas of the Tonal Machiotl they re-experience the ancient plotting of the universe and diagram their own place in Creation.

Reclaiming my indigenous Mexican identity began fully in 1990 when a group of concerned Chicanos convened a meeting in Phoenix, Arizona to initiate a project in public schools. The goal was to sensitize young Mexican Americans to their indigenous roots. These concerned activists had concluded that to exalt the fusion of cultures that had created contemporary Mexican society was a denial of a colonization process. What historians portrayed as a marriage between a Spaniard and an Indian was more of a rape than a marriage. This view stripped Mexican and Chicano people of their indigenous identity. Any liberating effort based on this assumption could not fully address the root causes of Chicano failure in public schools. Therefore a program was proposed that would allow students of Mexican heritage to claim their millenary history while at the same time enabling them to transcend the boundaries placed on their culture by Western society. It was called the Xinachtli (Sheen-ach-tlee) Project, from a Nahuatl (Aztec) word meaning "germinating seed" (Godina 2003).

Three years prior, Mexican anthropologist Guillermo Bonafil Batalla (1987) in *Profound Mexico: A Denied Civilization* had made a similar analysis. He described Mexico as living two realities, the "reality" of the Mexican image promoted by the government and media and the one lived by the vast majority of the population. The first he labeled as fictitious. The second was actual but living in an almost underground fashion. Most Mexicans live a Mesoamerican reality stringently denied by the superstructure that governs the country. In other words, while the people live an indigenous identity, those who hold political and economic power attempt to impose a European image. Batalla found this detrimental for two reasons. It caused in the people a kind of cultural psychosis and inferiority complex by looking and living a brown life but having to pretend to be white. There are constructs in Mesoamerican cultures that can be used as models to create a social life in Mexico that does not rely on the systematic destruction/exportation of natural resources but rather builds on the indigenous history of its people and their mythic component.

As one of those who met in Arizona, I realized that Mexican indigenous culture has been presented as something that is dead, frozen in time, a museum piece that has no relevance to our current existence. Like Batalla, the members of the Xinachtli Project agreed that as long as our indigenous identity remained mummified, we would always fall prey to the psyche of dependency and low self-esteem. In 1995 I returned to the elementary school in Texas where I had been "educated" to begin implementing the Xinachtli Project in the classroom.

Beginning with the Personal

My childhood experiences at Canutillo Elementary began in the summer of 1960. Not knowing any English, I entered into an institution where all of the teachers, the principal, and the school nurse were white and did not speak Spanish. Only the janitors, bus drivers, and cafeteria personnel were Mexican. They did speak my language. I quickly learned the skin and linguistic characteristics of those who "rule" and those who are ruled. Reinforcing this state of affairs were rules forbidding the use of Spanish in or outside the classroom, rules that were enforced with detention, slapping of the hand with a ruler, or visits to the principal's office for paddling. Overt racism was something condoned. On many occasions, I remember teachers making racist comments about blacks and Mexicans without reservation or fear of official reprisal.

The Chicano Movement and other activist reforms of the late sixties and seventies changed that. In doing so, one question had been left unanswered. It was a question I asked myself as a student of Canutillo Elementary, and as a militant of the Movimiento. Whenever I currently ask it of my students (they are all of Mexican descent) in the classroom, there is an obvious reaction of discomfort.

Why am I brown?

This question, and the inability of these Mexican youngsters to answer it, is important. What lay beneath the rule against speaking Spanish was a more subtle and powerful message. To use Batalla's words, an entire civilization has been denied. This denial placed my childhood friends and me in a forked-road dilemma. Should we adhere to an identity we did not understand and that was pronounced as irrelevant by the majority society? Or, should we begin adopting a fictitious identity, pretending to be white. For Chicanos this "passing" is almost contingent upon denying the obvious that is internalized by an extension of that important question.

If I'm white, why am I brown?

It took a great mental effort to avoid the answer. In embracing a false image I fell prey to a psychological conditioning to be "oppressed." My academic success in high school could not be accounted for as the exclusive result of my own endeavors for it was dependent on a denial of me. My own doubts and distortions led to a distancing from the ability to be free because any achievement came with St. Peter's predicament: denial. I felt like the chimp in the Michael Crichton (1980) novel (*Congo*) that was taught sign language by humans. This chimp spent so much time with humans that he did not identify as a chimp. When asked to describe his own kind in sign language, he signed, "black things" (p. 66). As Freire (1970) states: "The oppressed having internalized the image of the oppressor and adopted his guidelines, are fearful of freedom. Freedom would require them to eject this image and replace it with autonomy and responsibility" (p. 29).

Through the struggle in the Chicano Movement I began to be purged of my internal colonization and made ready to answer yet another variation on the question. If I'm not white, why am I brown? I am an indigenous person was my answer. As many of us began embracing an indigenous identity most of our brethren felt we were betraying or denying the "Spanish side" of ourselves. The Chicano Movement had been until then based on mestizaje as an ideology that viewed Mexicano/Chicano people as a culmination of a hybrid becoming a cosmic race. This idea was borrowed from José Vasconselos (1925), architect of Mexico's educational system after the Mexican Revolution of 1910.

The Native American scholar Jack Forbes (1973), on the other hand, saw mestizaje as an ideology of colonialism to divide indigenous people. A mestizo was not a "cosmic" being but basically an Indian who could speak and dress like a European. The term anoints people with a slightly higher social status because as mestizos they are "part white." Forbes saw the idea as a divisive tool of colonialism.

In the 1950s Mexican American civil rights organizers, in a vain attempt to end racial discrimination against Chicanos, struggled to have people of Mexican ancestry legally declared "white" by the courts. In many states this racial status still exists for the so-called Hispanic population. Early in the Chicano Movement, Forbes warned its militants not to fall prey to this thinking.

European imperialist thinking has denied Native Americans the right to possess large (mass) nationalities. The anthropologists and colonialists generally have decided that Indians are tribal forever. Whereas other peoples have had the right to merge tribes together and form large nation-states, Native Americans become something else whenever they leave their village (Forbes 1973, p. 199).

Xinachtli as Indigenous Culture and Pedagogy

When a culture attempts to mold another culture, the children of the subjugated culture are placed in the dilemma of having to divorce themselves from the reality of their parents through the self-destructive condition of self-shame. This scenario places the children of the dominating culture in the position of needing to oppress their counterparts as a means of maintaining their own self-esteem, a situation that is illusory and self-destructive to both.

To counter the ill-effects of this condition, well-intentioned multiculturalists might encourage, even exhort, these children to have pride in their cultural roots. Children of the dominant group are in turn encouraged to find tolerance and understanding for the minority culture. But pride is a chair with three legs, it may hold you up for a while, but eventually you will fall.

While it is important for minorities to be proud of their heritage, the defensive posture posed when a particular culture becomes "centric" to the curriculum restricts the children's creative potential. Culture is not something frozen in time but a dynamic process, ever evolving. If indigenous culture is going to be valuable as pedagogy, it needs to give students a means of achieving critical thinking, academic skills, egalitarian values, the ability of self-knowledge and knowledge of the social and natural world. Without this we would not be dismantling the imposed identity of colonialism but rather perpetuating the internal mental colonialism under an indigenous title. Without interaction based on mutual respect and free of the burden of oppressed-oppressor relationship, people condemn themselves to a schizophrenic cultural mode. Children, as with all people who achieve an internal liberation, must be able to see themselves as universal as well as particular beings. The ideology of "cultural pride" exalts their value as particular but not universal, for in having to "defend" and "preserve" a culture they feel bound to its boundaries and the idea of "changing or altering" it puts their efforts of pride and preservation in peril. It is merely an extension of "my country, right or wrong." Freire (1970) analyzed that the central problem is this:

> How can the oppressed, as divided, unauthentic beings, participate in developing the pedagogy of their liberation? Only as they discover themselves to be 'hosts' of the oppressor can they contribute to the midwifery of their liberating pedagogy. As long as they live in the duality in which to be is to be like, and to be like is to be like the oppressor, this contradiction is impossible . . . they must perceive the reality of oppression not as a closed world from which there is no exit, but as a limiting situation which they can transform (pp. 30–31).

My participation in the Xinachtli Project depended largely on whether the program could empower the children with the ability to transform their worlds. In the meaning of the term "xinachtli" came the first clues that transformation would be an integral part of the project. As mentioned, Xinachtli is a Mexica (Nahuatl-Aztec) word that means "germinating seed." Xinachtli is the moment when a seed bursts. "According to Mesoamerican cosmogony, such an occurrence is a moment when a seed is neither seed nor plant, but represents a moment of infinite possibilities." (Godina 2003).

Through my research I found an interesting connection with a German mystic, Rudolf Steiner (1924). In his work, *Agriculture*, Steiner argues that the creative potential of seeds lies in their ability to enter a period of chaos containing an infinite number of possibilities just before they become their respective plants. This concept, and Steiner's lectures demonstrating its application to German farmers, is credited with having saved that country's agriculture. Without a doubt this philosophy later influenced Steiner in the 1920s when he created a school that integrated academic learning with egalitarian principles and spirituality. The schools and their process spread and today, like Montessori, Waldorf education schools dot the globe.

Steiner's ideas of seed reproduction and the cosmogony of the term *xinachtli* are very much in line with the new scientific discoveries of the theory of chaos, which presents all systems in the universe as ever changing through the creation of order from randomness. (Gleick 1989). I interpreted these connections as pointing to the universality of the Mexican indigenous concept. Xinachtli became not just the project's title but its ideological essence.

Each individual's experience is by its very nature xinachtli. Just as a seed needs to have a moment of endless possibilities so that the flowering of a new plant is a creative act and not simply replication, so too a human life needs this chaos of possibilities. Within the xinachtli moment everything is possible. Children come to the world with a strong, even threatening, creative power. Derek Bickerton, professor of linguistics at the University of Hawaii, contends that children are probably responsible for the creation and recreation of language and cites the development of Hawaiian Creole, a language of a highly sophisticated grammar that includes combination of Chinese, Japanese, Korean, Portuguese, Hawaiian, and various Spanish dialects that have merged into a single language within the span of one generation. Bickerton asserts that this new language

... simply had to be the work of children, crowded together jabbering away at each other, playing ... It requires a different order of respect to take in the possibility that children make up languages, change languages, perhaps have been carrying the responsibility for evolving language from the first human communication to the twentieth century speech. (Thomas, 1974, p. 287)

Current research finds the potential of the mind in early childhood more complex and extensive than previously thought (Goldbeck, ed. 2001). I wanted very much to embrace a pedagogy that embraced this tremendous creative potential.

Xinachtli and the Role of Myth

Myth is a commonly shared experience across cultures. This symbolic reconstruction of the world was the final juncture in connecting indigenous culture with practical pedagogy. The function of myth is to experience the totality of humankind in relationship to the world via a symbol or story that is true but not necessarily factual. Renowned mythographer Joseph Campbell (1949) writes:

[I]n his life-form the individual is necessarily only a fraction and a distortion of the total image of man. He is limited as male, female; at any given period of his life he is again restricted as child, youth, mature, adult, ancient. . . . Through ceremony and myth such as marriage, burial, installation, and so forth we translate the individual's life crisis and life deeds into a classic, impersonal form. . . . generation of individuals pass like anonymous cells of a living body; but the sustaining, timeless form remains" (p. 382–3).

Childhood, more than any other stage of our lives gives us the opportunity to fully experience the multiple realities of our existence through a metaphorical expression of the world. It is a unique opportunity for children to use the mythic process in their developmental education. When children are asked to "fly" they simply unfold their arms like a plane or superhero and off they go. As adults we are likely to follow the request by the clarification "you mean pretend to fly." It is not that children are unaware of their limitations, they simply have a natural ability to transcend them.

During his years of observing his daughter, Tara, Sobel (1991) discovered a plethora of mythic interactions between Tara and her environment. What children possess, and what most adults have lost or forgotten, is the ability to interact through symbolic drama with their environment. Tara's mythic interactions did not hinder her grasp of reality but allowed her and her observing father to discover the universe in new and even magical ways.

In this early writing, Campbell already suggests a myth as a valuable tool to transcend our social limitations. In later years through his interview with Bill Moyers (1988), he expanded on this value saying "there is a fourth function of myth, and this is the one that I think everyone must try to relate to—and that is the pedagogical function, of how to live a human lifetime under any circumstances (p. 31)." For me this statement meant I had found the link between myth and using an indigenous identity as a liberating pedagogy. Those seeking liberation need to transcend the understanding of reality as imposed by the oppressors and the prejudices created by their thinking. I read Campbell to mean that myth facilitates this transcendence. Take for example Carrasco's (1990) description of Mesoamerican ritual. He writes of a continual process of "world making, world centering, and world renewing." Ceremonial centers were organized so that "elites, warriors, captives, traders, farmers, poets, and commoners could experience this cosmovision and participate in its nurturance" (p. 52). This process can be applied to helping students to experience democratic dialogue and to critically analyze reality.

In the Xinachtli Project we use the Tlahtokan or Speaking Circle. This activity is introduced in a series of stages that reflect Carrasco's world making, centering, and renewing. From the beginning we use a symbol for centering the circle. Sometimes it is a candle, which is lit at the start of each session; other times it is a replica of the Aztec Calendar. Each child then creates a totem such as decorated stick, a painted rock, or feather. The Tlahtokan is opened with the children placing their totemic items in a circle around the center symbol. Our dialogue is usually regulated by a "talking stick," which gives its holder the "authority" or turn to speak. Shelly Kessler (1990) organized a similar process for Crossroads Schools, a Santa Monica, California private school. There high school students were required to attend a daily class called "mysteries" in which students used the process of "council" for interactive dialogue. While the Crossroads program focuses mainly on social studies, in the Xinachtli Project Tlahtokan we cover all subject areas including mathematics and science.

Another way we participate in "world renewal" is by placing a circular box within the Tlahtokan parameters. Each quadrant of the box is painted with the primary colors (red, white, black, yellow). As a follow up to lessons and discussions about feelings, children write about a recent memorable incident and the feelings it produced. As they sit around the "emotions box" they share their writing, fold the piece of paper, and deposit it in the box. Each quadrant has an opening through which the children can deposit their "feelings." Periodically we dig a hole outside and carefully "burn" away the deposited feelings. We explain that traumatic emotions are released in the smoke while good emotional experiences are enhanced by the fire and shared with the universe.

Elements of the Mythic Process

The elements of myth are many but the process may be divided into four basic elements. There are: Deification, Truth, Harmony, and Mystery. This process is not linear, nor do the elements fall in a progression but are integrated into a common whole.

Initiation of the mythic process does not begin with any one of these but with a desire to give some spiritual expression to our interaction with natural phenomenon (Eliade 1975). The expression of the mythic process as pedagogy lies in taking action first without worrying about the meaning behind it. Meaning is a value judgment that comes later upon finding comfort in the product of deification or to a group establishing customs, institutions, or rites. Mythic pedagogy's point of departure is process designed to validate a child's need to explore and express herself mythically.

Deification

Creation of deities, inherent in the spiritual expression of phenomena, is carried out by individuals and groups every day in spite of their theological or technical sophistication. Some deities survive longer than others but they are products of a need to give humanlike form to a natural phenomenon for the purpose of establishing a relationship with that phenomenon. This mythic creation allows the relationship to transcend time and the restrictions imposed by self-perpetuating social systems.

Main deities initially revolve around the four elements: water, air, earth, and fire (Hopkins 1969). The deification of earth into Mother Earth (Tonantzin Tlali) promotes a different relationship with nature than simply thinking of the earth as a "planet." Deities are as much a personification of God in nature as they are of ourselves (Hartshorne 1948). Myth is not religion even though religion often makes use of myth. The mythic process need not be tied to a belief in God or as a proselyte of religion, which would make it incompatible with the democratic value of separation of church and state.

Children express their creation of a deity when they acquire an invisible friend or discover that a monster is living under their bed. In this sense the Sesame Street Muppets are deities that provide a forum for the instruction and entertainment of young children. Modern day psychotherapy has incorporated forms of deification when patients are asked to "rescue and reassure their inner child" (Bradshaw 1991). Metaphors and dramatic play that seemingly have no connection to a psychological condition are used to release a person from a mental obsession.

Many of the symbols of Mesoamerica are deities. In the classroom children learn how they express the natural phenomenon they embody. Through writing, drama, and the symbolic interaction of a circle, students conduct a dialogue with these entities under a school-approved policy of pretend play. Links with actual historical experience and metaphorical analysis are provided by the teachers. In this manner they understand how Quetzalcoatl discovered corn by becoming an ant, founded the Toltec Civilization, became the Morning Star, and lives in us today as a symbol of our rational thinking. They explore how his twin, Tezcatlipoca, is irrational thought and the necessity for Xolotl (sholotl) as their hidden brother negotiates their relationship through dreams, fantasy, and humor. Scientifically they learn that Quetzalcoatl is the face of Venus in the morning, Tezcatlipoca is her face in the evening, and Xolotl is Venus during her disappearance from the night sky.

Truth

Truth is often viewed as a commodity to be owned, usually by those in power. The mythic process views truth as something residing in the totality of a situation or phenomenon. Without being able to perceive its totality we are unable to perceive its truth. Upon acknowledging this limitation we transcend it by embracing the idea that we can have a vision of truth, not the truth itself. We further this with our commitment to be seekers of truth and learning to respect the limited perception of ourselves and others. Myths are true but not factual. They carry visions of truth. Myths are able to transcend our limited perception without rejecting the ideal of truth because they are metaphorical expressions of the experience of becoming "one" with an event or phenomenon.

In the Native American tradition a vision is transformed into a kind of community visual textbook through the creation of ritual based on the narrative of those who received the vision. In the Xinachtli Project, truth as an element of the mythic process is embodied in the use of a ceremonial circle. Children are often reminded that anything placed within the circle is only partially perceived and that validation of the "total" truth is dependent on unifying the perceptions of all that sit around it.

Harmony

Death and destruction are not usually associated with harmony; peace and prosperity are. While we may relate the absence of conflict to the state of harmony, quite the opposite is true. Harmony is actually a process of balance more in the context of the Daoist notion of the unity and struggle of opposites. Conflict is an integral part of harmony—that is the way things even out, the way consensus is reached, the way Creation evolves. The attitude we have about conflict determines to a large extent if we achieve harmony or not. Viewing conflict as something bad leads to behavior that tends to resolve conflict through domination or avoidance. When conflict is seen as a useful tool for achieving harmony we can enter into a relationship that avoids domination and seeks growth through consensus.

On a very practical level life is a journey toward death. At each step of our lives, death eats away at us through accident, disease, aging until we must give away the totality of our being. Western society handles this contradiction with the attitude that death is something to be conquered through medical science and a subject to be avoided. The mythic process embraces death through rituals, deities, and an attitude that death is an ally of life. The death of living things replenishes the Earth's fertility.

The mythic process projects harmony as the ability of letting go, of being able to voluntarily give away parts of ourselves, not as a tragic act but one of renewal. In the Xinachtli Project this ability is taught through the use of the emotions box, whereby feelings (good and bad) are released through the fire. We also use death deities, especially in the celebration of Día de los Muertos (Day of the Dead), the Mexican three-day festival when the departed are remembered through the use of comedic play, rhymes making fun of death, and the creation of altars with food and candy offerings for the souls of our loved ones. Valleno and Marin (1989) demonstrated that children as early as four and five have a healthy understanding of death and that they are not traumatized by the subject as is often thought in Western education.

In the process of Tlahtokan (Talking Circle), children also learn to embrace the conflict of opinion not by shouting someone down or interrupting them but empowering them to share through the authority of the talking stick. They learn to wait their turn to hold the stick and see it as a symbol of another's right to have their say, hopefully understanding that the urgency they have to share is just as urgent to another. Decisions are made by consensus rather than majority rule. Breaks between the gathering allows for more personal dialogue, even gathering of pertinent information. Consensus requires negotiation of conflict, the art of compromise through participatory not elective democracy.

Mystery

Native American scholar Jack Forbes (1974) observed that the fundamental difference between Western thought and indigenous culture is the "white man's" inability to accept mystery. It is the acceptance of mystery, Forbes pointed out, that is the cornerstone of Native American spirituality. Mystery is basic to the mythic process because it allows for the asking of questions that have no answers. Western thought values questions by their possibilities to be answered. The mythic process views the ability to say, "I don't know" not as a surrender to ignorance but to our human limitations in order to transcend them.

Is the universe infinite? We can assume that it is or it is not, but given our human limitations we will never know. What is the validity of asking such a question? Because the question, not the answer, is a confrontation of our place in the vastness of Creation, a confrontation that inspires our intuition, creativity, awe, and respect for that which is beyond us. Perhaps the best inducement to creativity is "we don't know, so let's imagine."

When will I die? What is love? Is the world going to end? Does God exist? Is there life after death? How many stars are there in the sky? Asking such questions raises an important element to human life: the validity of faith. The need to believe, even in what we know. Mystery points out our frailty within Creation; it is the policeman that arrests our self-righteousness where we mistake strength for faith. Mystery is the realm of possibilities, our gateway to go beyond our limitations; a gateway than can be opened mythically. Mystery favors a personal view of the Creator as opposed to a prescribed one. It fosters respect for the theological views of others. When mystery is removed from religion we enter the realm of the faithful versus the infidels, the Christians against the pagans. Respect of personal vision is integral to mythic pedagogy.

Within the circle of the Xinachtli Project the subject of religion arises. Roughly one third of the population in Canutillo is of a born-again faith, which squarely puts them into conflict with the traditional Catholic population. This conflict is manifested in the children when we touch on this topic. The born-again verbalize that the Catholic children are "going to hell" while the Catholic children get defensive countering with "no es cierto, no es cierto (not true)." These encounters are wonderful opportunities to use the component of mystery. What is more intriguing about this situation is that support of the project is expressed by both Catholic and born-again parents who approve learning about their Mexican heritage despite its obvious ritual-based activities.

Resouces and the Significance of Political Struggle

The viability of a project that uses indigenous culture via the mythic process necessitates the availability of learning resources that are grounded in indigenous culture. In the towers of academia much of the information concerning Aztec culture is based on the interpretation of that civilization by the very people who destroyed it. Fortunately there has been a groundswell of neo-indigenous intellectuals and cultural workers who are giving us a new view of ancient history, philosophy, and culture. Among them are the founders of Universidad Nahuatl, an independent institution of higher learning in Ocotepec, México, which teaches Mesoamerican culture from the indigenous viewpoint through collaboration and alliances with area traditional keepers and indigenous communities.

Martha Ramirez, a U.S. citizen who emigrated to Mexico from California in search of her roots, and Mariano Leyva founded this university shortly after Leyva had been elected deputy under the Cardenista Front for National Reconstruction, a coalition of left-wing parties that first cracked the ruling PRI party's hold on power in the 1980s. Mariano Leyva is a veteran of Plaza Tlaltelolco in 1968 where the Mexican Army opened fire on a student demonstration, killing over three hundred. Martha Ramirez was a veteran of another demonstration violently repressed, the Chicano Moratorium against the Vietnam War in 1970 where journalist Ruben Salazar was killed. For many years they spearheaded Grupo Mascarones, a theatre group much like Luis Valdez's El Teatro Campesino. When I met them in 1990 our dialogue gave me useful insight into Mesoamerican history, culture, and language from an indigenous perspective. Their training as revolutionaries now made use of indigenous culture as an ideology for struggle, not just academic study.

Their work, the political opening for indigenous issues created by the Zapatista rebellion in Chiapas, and the academic work of Bonafil Batalla, Arturo Meza Gutierrez, and Tlacatzin Stivalet are creating a new atmosphere in which indigenous constructs in social cosmogony are being taken seriously. Their counterparts in the United States, Tupac Enrique, Heriberto Godina, Michael Heralda, and Mazatzin, are furthering the work as well. The resources they offer are available to anyone with an Internet search engine. Introduction of the project into public school would also have been impossible without the political reforms actualized by the Chicano Movement and those who forced the government to implement bilingual education.

For the last three years, teachers in the Xinachtli Project at Canutillo Elementary attend an intensive summer institute where we are exposed to this revival in the interest by Mexico of its ancient heritage. Drawing on personal experience and the availability of informational resources about Mesoamerica through an indigenous perspective, the elements and process of the Xinachtli Project are introduced as an integral component of the curriculum. Toward this endeavor we can summarize the components of Xinachtli in the school as follows:

1. While the information shared about Mexican indigenous culture uses all sources, we ground our presentations on the work of practitioners of the oral tradition and scholars who themselves based their studies on native individuals and communities.
2. Contemporary Mexican and Chicano culture, including food, customs, and beliefs, is presented as a direct extension of the nearly six thousand year old Nahuatlaca culture of North America.
3. The Nahuatl language is taught as a contemporary language and awareness is made of the more than three hundred words of Nahuatl origin in modern-day Spanish.
4. The Aztec calendar is taught, including keeping its days, weeks, months, and years along with the Gregorian calendar.
5. Mesoamerican symbols are presented as modes of knowledge, which the students are encouraged to manipulate to create their own symbols and stories.
6. Children are shown how the scientific process, the use of the five senses, and knowledge of the human body are reflected in Mesoamerican cosmogony.
7. Activities are done through the context of symbolic interaction via the mythic process and Mesoamerican ceremonial process.
8. Mesoamerican mathematics are an integral part of learning math and credited with having developed the concept of zero as a number and the use of pi as a geometric construct.

Project members hope to develop a curriculum grounded in ethnography and data that can be shared on a mass scale so that our primary goal, the development of a liberating identity, may be extended to other schools. To this end we are looking to the scholars on our advisory, all of whom are researchers at a university level, to initiate this activity. The experience at a west Texas school serving a large immigrant community whose poverty level qualifies its students for 100 percent free lunch program is potentially a treasure house of pedagogical information.

Mythic Pedagogy: A Process of Creating a Liberating Identity

That humans experience the world mythically is not a novel idea. The myth of finding an eagle perched on a cactus growing from a rock guided the Aztecs to build their capital in the middle of a lake. The several-thousand-year-old mythic symbol of Ying/Yang remains an inspirational shield for martial artists all over the world. Tomás Atencio (1976), known for his distinguished work in critical pedagogy at La Academia de la Nueva Raza in northern New Mexico, stated that "the role of myth to culture is that of a catalyst to a chemical reaction."

Conducting classrooms via a curriculum that assumes the constructs of the dominant (white) culture creates a stigma among non-white students and negates them from tapping into the constructs of their own culture. But pitting one cultural format against another (brown vs. white) through a "cultural pride" curriculum creates its own restrictions. Can we use the mythic process to consciously initiate a societal and personal transformation? Critical pedagogue, Henry Giroux (1990) alluded to this when commenting on the writings of black feminist writers whose use of myth is integral to their work: "The development of stories in this literature becomes a medium for developing new relations of solidarity, community, and self love" (p. 23).

La Llorona as Critical Pedagogy

A source of power of mythic stories is in their transcendence of time. This can be used to bridge the ancient with the contemporary while creating a valuable lesson. Take for example the story of La Llorona (The Weeping Woman). The legend is familiar to Mexican and Chicano children. It tells of a single woman with children who wants to marry a man whom she has fallen madly in love with. The man expresses a desire to marry her but cannot accept her children, which are not his. The woman throws the children into the river in an attempt to keep the man. He then rejects her for committing murder. She runs back to the river to rescue her children. In vain she searches but never finds them and is then condemned to roam the river forever crying for her children.

This tragic love story is one that was five hundred years in the making. Leon-Portilla (1971) cites that three years just prior to the arrival of the Spaniards, the people of Mexico City would hear a woman crying for her children. The Medicine People told chief Moctezuma it was the wail of

Coatlicue (an Earth deity) crying for her children whose pain and suffering would soon turn the waters of Lake Texcoco red with blood.

Upon the arrival of the "conquistadores" the relationship of Hernán Cortez, commander of the Spaniards expedition, and Malintzin, a woman captive from a Nahuatl village in Veracruz, shaped the legend even more. For the supposed love of Cortez, Malintzin helped the Spaniards defeat the Aztecs. Not only did Malintzin witness the savagery of the colonizers destroy Mexico City and the waters of Texcoco turn red with the blood of her brethren but much later saw her only son by Cortez, Martín, garroted by the Spanish Inquisition. An area of 18 million Mexicans dwindled down to less than 1 million. The lost children of La Llorona were now fully identified. To this day Mexicans will call a traitor a Malinchista just as a Yankee uses the term Benedict Arnold.

Storytellers like Rodolfo Anaya (1984) use history as basis to rewrite the tale, others like Joe Hayes (1987) use more contemporary versions to identify it with their locality. What all versions have in common is that they embody the story of the Mexican people at different levels, some of which are universal. Anyone familiar with the story can relate it to the woman in the midwest of the United States who placed her children in the trunk of a car and let it sink into the river believing this would insure her relationship with her lover.

Chicano children's ability to put the legend in a modern context was exemplified when we introduced the myth to a fifth grade class. First, we told the historically based version (Malintzin and Cortez) without alluding connection to the story of La Llorona. As we were telling the story they recognized it immediately. "It's the story," they began whispering. When we finished our historic tale we asked if anybody had heard it before. They all said , "It's La Llorona."

Among the children there were different versions of the story, but all with the same plot. What they all agreed on was that you could hear La Llorona at night down by the local river. Even though they agreed that the story happened somewhere else, at night La Llorona was a local phenomenon. Here she becomes a deity useful for invoking critical dialogue.

We asked them to compare and contrast each version given. What ensued was an exploration of meaning at three levels: psychological, sociological, and historical. One student, recalling a recent discussion of the Columbus Quincentenary, said, "That's one reason we had a hard time deciding it was good that Columbus came. If we say yes, we're rejecting the Indians and if we say no, we're rejecting the Spaniards. It kind of like what La Llorona had to decide."

"It doesn't matter," said another. "It's right if we side with the Indians because the Spaniards did wrong to kill them and take the land. La Llorona knows she did wrong, that's why she cries."

"But in a way she did right because she did what she had to get what she wanted," added another, "She was a strong woman even if she was wrong."

Still another said, "It's just like when my mother divorced my father. I thought it wasn't right to tell my father to leave, but that's what she wanted. But it hurt us very much."

"Yes, I feel like La Llorona's children when my father and mother fight," another responded. "And if they get divorced, it will be like getting dumped in the river."

"La Llorona was wrong, she killed her children. It's never right to kill anyone, especially your own children," one child contended.

"But it happens," said a girl who in earlier discussions had revealed her parents are separated and that "my mother just cares about what she wants. If I complain, she beats me and it's my father who is trying to get me away from her for that."

We can see that this dialogue was interactive, creative, critical in analysis, met the existential needs of the students, and authenticated Mexican culture not only through historical references but in finding universal themes of societal conflict. It would not take much to stir the dialogue toward other issues related to the role of women in society. For example, why is Llorona not satisfied with her role as a mother but needs to be a wife. Who sets the rules for either of those roles? Can those expectations be changed, how, and by whom?

Presentation of this story seems to divide boys and girls into opposing camps. The girls are generally more sympathetic to Llorona than the boys. Work on this article had made me realize how much this story lends itself to a constructive dialogue about the plight of women in society and will encourage the teachers involved in the project to use it as such.

Xinchatli: *Nehuan Ti Nehuan* or *In Lakech*

While the multiculturalist idea that the United States is a salad bowl rather than a melting pot is a lofty one, it still places minority cultures as stagnant icons competing with a majority social structure that is flexible and evolutionary. White children are not "required" to put on the attire of their Pilgrim ancestors to celebrate their heritage but mariachis and ethnic dances by minority children are seen as promoting cultural diversity in the classroom. There seems to me to be an underlying current of inequality in this situation where one group is limited by its own history while the other is free simply to be.

Nehuan ti nehuan in the Nahuatl (Aztec) language or *in lakech* in Mayan is a Mesoamerican greeting. Simply translated it says "I am you are I." This acknowledgment of mutual reflection between human beings sets forth a tone of mutual respect through mutual identity regardless of age, color, or creed. Any pedagogy that does not enable, teach, and foster this notion, with or without the greeting, cannot empower its constituents to see their own universality and find the common ground of mutual respect and equality with others, especially with members of a group who have inherited the spoils of colonial conquest of their ancestors.

Xinachtli, more than anything else, is based on fermenting this notion in children. Pride in racial identity must not replace the personal with the accidental. The personal is universal, natural, and innate in all human beings. The accidental is that by chance our souls emerge in a body of a certain color, taught a particular language, raised in specific social environment. What guides our work is not the effort of introducing children to information about their indigenous heritage, although that is an important component of the project, but rather a process through which they can gain deeper understanding of their present, enhance their academic learning, and place their history within a universal context where being part of an ethnic group is a reflection—not a separation—of their humanity.

Transpersonal theoretician Ken Wibler (1986) tells us that men and women "want the world because they are the world, and they want immortality because they are in fact immortal. But instead of transcending their boundaries in truth, they merely attempt to break and refashion them at will. They are caught in trying to make their earth into a substitute heaven, not only do they destroy the only earth they have, they forfeit the only heaven they might otherwise embrace" (p. 338).

Surrounding the face in the Aztec calendar is a conglomeration of symbols representing the universe and its cosmic motion. Our indigenous traditional tells us that the person in the middle is not only recording the natural cycles of Creation but realizing that humans are a reflection of the universe. In the middle of the Sun Stone, humanity is finding her reflection in the Cosmos from which she came from. With this awareness of the integration of the general with the particular, humanity becomes conscious of our dynamic role. Colonization has made us shun that Aztec face because of its indigenous features. To fully embrace it as our own we need to recognize that is not only our indigenous history that ties us to it but the nature of our humanity as well. In this way we can understand that we are a world of brothers and sisters, divided only by the barriers that we allow others to impose upon us, not by the design of Creation.

Nehuan ti nehuan.

References

Atencio, T. (1976, April). *Community education model of La Academia de la Nueva Raza.* Paper presented at a meeting of the Chicano Studies Program, University of Texas at El Paso.

Anaya, R. (1984). *The legend of La Llorona: A short novel.* Berkeley, CA: Tonatiuh Publications.

Batalla, G. B. (1987). *Mexico profundo: Una civilización negada.* México, D.F.: SEP.

Bradshaw, J. (1990). *Homecoming: Reclaiming and championing your inner child.* New York: Bantam Books.

Campbell, J. (1949). *The hero with a thousand faces.* Princeton, NJ: Princeton University Press.

Campbell J. (1988). In Flowers, B.S. (ed.), *Joseph Campbell with Bill Moyers: The power of myth.* New York: Doubleday.

Carrasco, D. (1990). *Religions of Mesoamerica.* San Francisco: Harper & Row.

Crichton, M. (1980). *Congo.* New York: Ballantine Books.

Eliade, M. (1975). *Myths, dreams, and mysteries: The encounter between contemporary faiths and archaic realities.* (P. Mairet, Trans.): New York: Harper & Row (original 1957).

Freire, P. (1970). *Pedagogy of the oppressed.* New York: The Continuum Publishing Company.

Forbes, J. (1974). *Native American spirituality.* A paper presented to faculty and students at the University of Texas at El Paso.

Forbes, J. D. (1973). *Aztecas del norte: The Chicanos of Aztlan.* Greenwich, CT.: Fawcett Publications.

Giroux, H. (1990). The politics of postmodernism: Rethinking the boundaries of race and ethnicity. *Journal of Urban and Cultural Studies, 1*(1), 23.

Gleick, J. (1989). *Chaos: Making a new science.* Penguin USA (reprinted 1998).

Godina, H. (2003). *The Xinachtli Project website [http:www.uiowa.edu/~xin13/].* University of Iowa Department of Education.

Golbeck S. L. (2001). *Pscyhological perspectives on early childhood education: Reframing dilemmas in research and practice.* Mugar LB 1139.22 (p. 79).

Hartshorne, C. (1948). *The divine reality: Social conception of God.* London: Yale University Press.

Hayes, J. & Trejo, V. (1987). *La Llorona: The weeping woman.* El Paso, TX: Cinco Puntos Press.

Hopkins, W. E. (1969). *Origin and evolution of religion.* New York: Cooper Square Publications.

Kessler, S. (1990). *The mysteries sourcebook.* Santa. Monica, CA: Crossroads School, Human Development Department.

Leon-Portilla, M. (1971). *Vision de los vencidos.* México: UNAM.

Sobel, D. (1991, Fall). A mouthful of flowers: Ecological and spiritual metaphors from early childhood. *Holistic Education Review, 4* (3).

Steiner, R. (1924). *Agriculture.* (George Adams, trans. 1958). London: Biodynamic Agricultural Association Rudolf Steiner House.

Thomas, L. (1974). *A long line of cells.* New York: Book of the Month Club.

Thoreau, H. D. (1875). *Walden or Life in the woods.* New York: Barnes & Noble, Inc. (reprinted 1993).

Valleno, R. & Marin, M. I. (1989). Children's understanding of death. *Early Childhood Development and Care, 46,* 97–104.

Vasconselos, J. (1925). *La raza cósmica.* Universidad de Varsovia, Centro de Estudios Lationamericanos (out of print).

Wilber, K. (1986). *Up from Eden: A transpersonal view of human evolution.* Boston: Shambhala Publications.

AFTERWORD

Taking It into the Classroom

Judy Helfand and Virginia Lea

Editing this book has been an interesting and informative journey for the two of us. We have come out of the experience with a renewed commitment to identifying race and transforming whiteness in the classroom. We have been educated by the culturally diverse pedagogical forms that our contributors propose to enrich antiracist, critical multicultural classrooms. We have grown personally in relation to the lessons that the contributors have learned in their lifetimes about rethinking their own whiteness. We have been moved to imagine alternatives to our current ways of knowing and teaching in our classrooms. And we have also found support for continuing and strengthening many of our current classroom practices. In what follows, we both offer short reflections that illustrate some of the insights that each of us has taken from our contributors to transform whiteness in our classrooms—a challenge that we meet with renewed enthusiasm as a result of editing this book.

Virginia's Reflections

As part of the Multicultural Pedagogy course that is a prerequisite for the Elementary Education credential program in which I teach, I ask my students to brainstorm what they mean by whiteness. Although the prospective teachers in my course are almost all white, female, and middle class, the responses from a small group of them include many of the aspects of whiteness addressed in this volume. These individuals recognize that whiteness is subject to change to meet the goals for which it was developed. They recognize that whiteness as a system was not constructed consciously, but at the same time they see that some of the parts were deliberately conceived to preserve their authors' privilege. They also see this process continuing today.

While I have been impressed by the ability of some of my student teachers to name, in abstract terms, the practice of whiteness in the world, when asked to identify how race and whiteness play out in the classroom, almost all my student teachers are flummoxed. The specific, everyday forms that whiteness takes as part of curriculum, teaching practices, and the structures within which classroom communication and activities take place are opaque if not invisible to most of my student teachers. They also have a hard time recognizing the cultural scripts—philosophical and ideological—that they draw on in their quest to become teachers. These scripts often fit so well with the practical instantiations of whiteness in the classroom that they feel they are swimming in familiar and benign water, to use Maxwell's terms. Indeed, it is in naming the ways in which whiteness plays out in the life of the classroom that the contributors to this volume have made such a valuable contribution to my knowledge.

In what follows, I offer a selective and simplified description of some of these philosophical and ideological scripts along with an example from our contributors that has helped me to rethink this potentially imperial way of thinking, feeling, believing, and acting as it is applied to the classroom. As some of the contributors point out, many educators have a hard time recognizing the dominant philosophical and ideological scripts that have shaped what goes on in the classroom and influenced how they define the educational process.

These ubiquitous American philosophical and ideological scripts are well described by Gerald Gutek (2004) in his book, *Philosophical and Ideological Voices in Education*. Idealism is the first philosophical script that Gutek addresses. Idealism is an ancient philosophy that claims the existence of universal forms of knowledge that may be known through reason. Through their own education, teachers are supposed to be able to come to knowledge of the "truth" and help their students to come to the same understandings. Idealism is a philosophy that legitimizes ways of teaching and learning in the light of existing "truths," and because these knowledge forms are seen as "truths," their proponents believe they may legitimately colonize the classroom. This imposition may be seen as the practice of whiteness.

In her chapter in this book, Strobel argues against this form of colonization. She draws on Mikhail Bakhtin in pointing out that: "We will never know who we are just by looking at the mirror . . . we must allow other people to tell us who we are from their own locations and positions. And from there create dialogue. Create Art. Create Love" (p. 45).

Realism is the second philosophical script. Realism only validates ways of knowing in the classroom that can be evidenced through rational, "scientific" means. In challenging this claim to legitimate knowledge, Aceves offers us "mythic pedagogy." Engaging the whole child—mind, body, and spirit—and including all children, mythic pedagogy calls on multiple ways of knowing. Aceves writes:

> What guides our work is not the effort of introducing children to information about their indigenous heritage, although that is an important component of the project, but rather a process through which they can gain deeper understanding of their present, enhance their academic learning, and place their history within a universal context where being part of an ethnic group is a reflection—not a separation—of their humanity (p. 275).

American nationalism is an ideological script that paints a selective picture of the United States. This picture leaves no room in the curriculum for more than a cursory glance at colonial and postrevolutionary U. S. socioeconomic, political, legal, and cultural practices such as the genocide of Native peoples, the slavery of Africans, and the indenture, wage slavery, and economic oppression of thousands of people from all ethnic backgrounds. In other words, it excludes the experiences of oppression of people of color and low-income people upon whose backs the wealth of the United States was built.

Drawing on black feminism, both Mathieson, and Lemons offer us antidotes to this nationalist paradigm, the one for the fifth grade, the other for the college classroom. They contribute a rich set of resources for rethinking the whiteness at the heart of public and private school curricula, and helping students to develop identities based on fair and just relationships.

Classical liberalism asserts the importance of the individual, of entitlement to freedom from government intervention, and economic progress through free market competition. In the classroom, this often amounts to an inordinate emphasis on competition over cooperation and inclusion, of independence over the challenging process of creating harmony through the winds of conflict and tension. Both Christensen and Aceves offer us pedagogies that promise to introduce students to alternative way of being in the world. In Christensen's own words:

> Using the Circle Teaching methods and techniques allows a student to work within a protected environment of a small group of equals that provides opportunity to speak and discuss and learn from peers while utilizing choices during

learning and teaching. Circle Teaching also encourages creative inclusive activities as each student uses his personal skills in teaching the learning materials. (p. 189)

Conservatism emphasizes traditional, Eurocentric norms and values over a rethinking of alternative ways of living together in the United States and the world that might disrupt hierarchy and serve all people equitably. In the classroom, conservatism entails reproducing Eurocentric knowledge, as well as preserving traditional ways of expecting students to participate in and conduct themselves in the classroom. For example, students may not speak unless they raise their hands, and emotion has little place in their academic study.

In their efforts to disrupt this hierarchy, Hallam and O'Brien offer the reader practical ways of allowing all students to bring their diverse ways of thinking, feeling, believing, and acting into the classroom so that they, as well as students who embody traditional ways of being, may have access to a rich experience.

In my Multicultural Pedagogy and Social Studies courses, I offer several experiences to help student teachers begin to see the what, the how, and the why of whiteness, enriched and reinforced by the contributors to this book. We talk in a circle about the chameleon forms that whiteness takes. We undertake simulations, read and write poetry, watch videos, and search out currents from the mainstream mass media that reinforce whiteness. The student teachers juxtapose their readings of black feminist, indigenous, and other narratives with adopted classroom texts to gain an alternative perspective on history, the classroom, and the world in which they live. They consider other pedagogical forms, communication styles, and participation structures that allow access to the educational process to all students. Perhaps most importantly, they simultaneously explore the what, the how, the why of their own whiteness by writing personal narratives and offering responses to each other's stories as part of a cultural portfolio.

My student teachers begin their Multicultural Pedagogy course by experiencing what for many of them are fresh culture shock experiences in order to develop their own capacity to empathize with the intense emotional strain and cultural dissonance that school brings about in many of their students raised outside of the mainstream. Student teachers continue with a mini-"Funds of Knowledge" project (Moll, et al. 1992) by going, *as learners,* into the families of students from cultural backgrounds with which they are unfamiliar. We prepare student teachers to change roles with parents and community, opening themselves up to the possibility that community and ethnic knowledge is as valuable as traditional academic knowledge. Culturally relevant knowledge requires placing the students' lives at the center of any educational project, and offering new and rewarding experiences for the families and students (Freire, 1970/1993).

It is my hope that by offering these opportunities to my student teachers and inviting them to contribute their own contributions and changes to our program, we can interactively acknowledge and rethink our whiteness. Allowing my student teachers to have real voice in my classroom has powerfully impacted my own whiteness. I look forward to continuing my own journey of transformation with hope for our collective future, in spite of the global imperialism at work at the beginning of the twenty-first century.

Judy's Reflections

In attempting to transform whiteness in my classroom at a community college where I teach American Cultures, I begin by making pedagogy visible to the students through short articles and a description of my own practices. Although classroom norms usually go unnoticed and unnamed, when called upon to think about them, most students can easily describe elements of a "normal" classroom. Christensen's chapter on Circle Teaching left me even more committed than before to reforming the physical space so students sit in a circle, even when this is challenging. We talk about the reasons for this in class and also for the frequent furniture moving required to flow into small groups and back to the whole throughout the class period. We also address the likelihood of uncomfortable feelings, including anger and fear, in being asked to participate in one's own learning in new ways. Aceves's chapter on mythic pedagogy and O'Brien's on anger reinforced my desire to find ways of talking about the need for emotion and spirit alongside reason and intellect and of continuing to use experiential and reflective activities that ask students to pay attention to deeply held messages, memories stored in the body, surfacing feelings, and connections to ancestral voices. Nervous about leaving students adrift in unfamiliar waters, I try to reassure them by provide academic endorsement for violating classroom norms. For example, they may read essays on pedagogy from bell hooks (1994) *Teaching to Transgress* and excerpts from Elizabeth Minnich (1990) *Transforming Knowledge*.

As many of the authors in this collection make clear, we need to assemble multiple voices and perspectives in constructing knowledge. Lemon's chapter on bringing black feminist voices into classrooms with a majority of white students through texts reassured me that students can still engage with perspectives of those from social locations different from their own even when those bodies are not physically present. And as clashing stories fill the room, I find myself returning often to an insistence on using both/and thinking, asking students to try and hear accounts that differ from one's own experience not as refuting that experience, but as adding a new perspective. In her discussion of Western dualisms, Strobel demonstrates the long-term possibilities of rejecting the either/or thinking we are steeped in—and provided me with hope for dialogue as a process.

In what languages are these multiple perspectives given voice? Language took on more importance for me as I engaged with Featherston and Ishibashi and then Hallam as they explored the myriad ways in which academic norms requiring "standard" English deprive those who do not speak white, middle-class English of their authentic voice. As a result, I added a new section on language to my syllabus and have started finding a variety of spoken word recordings to use in the classroom in addition to written narratives.

These are some examples I was able to draw easily to consciousness in thinking about how what I absorbed in reading these collected authors is coming with me into the classroom. I know their words and ideas and passions are operating on me in other ways I have not yet identified as well. In her chapter in which she names race and racism as a problem in Toronto schools, Bullen reminded me of the dedication and extra effort required of black teachers to simply do their job. Recognizing the privilege I hold as a white, middle-class teacher, I end this book editing project with a renewed commitment to continuing to name race and racism in the schools, and continuing to educate myself to new ways of identifying race and transforming whiteness in the classroom. I will continue the conversations begun between these pages as I work with other educators to forge an antiracist pedagogy devoted to the practice of social justice.

Our Hope

As the authors in this book imply, pedagogical practices, ways of participating, and ways of expressing emotion are not neutral but they can become antiracist, equitable, and thus inclusive, meeting the needs of all students in the process. They can contribute to the transformation of whiteness, even though whiteness does indeed have a dynamic face. It constitutes the symbolic and cultural scripts, and the economic advantages that best serve people who make decisions in our world. But by vigilantly recognizing the practical and ever shifting face of whiteness, we can take actions to transform it in the ways we self-identify, communicate, organize relationships, and interpret knowledge and texts in our classrooms. It is our hope that this book has made a contribution to this process.

References

Freire, P. (1970/1993). *Pedagogy of the oppressed.* New York: The Continuum Publishing Co.

Gutek, G. L. (2004). *Philosophical and ideological voices in education.* Boston: Pearson Education.

hooks, b. (1994). *Teaching to Transgress: Education as the practice of freedom.* New York: Routledge.

Minnich, E. K. (1990). *Transforming knowledge.* Philadelphia: Temple University Press.

Moll, L. C., Amanti, C., Neff, D., & Gonzales, N. (1992, Spring). Funds of Knowledge for teachers: Using a qualitative approach to connect homes and classrooms. *Theory into Practice. 31*(2), 132–141.

Contributors

Carlos Aceves, 49, teaches first grade bilingual at Canutillo Elementary School in west Texas. He holds a B.A. in journalism and an M.Ed. from the University of Texas at El Paso. He has been an activist in education since age sixteen through such organizations as the Movimiento Estudiantil Chicano de Aztlan (MEChA), the Global Allaince for Transforming Education (GATE), and the Xinachtli Project.

Pauline Bullen completed "A Multifaceted Study of Institutional Racism In the Toronto Public Educational System: Perspectives of a Black Educator" in August 2000 for her masters thesis. Pauline is currently a Ph.D. candidate at the Ontario Institute for Studies in Education at the University of Toronto, Canada; she is also a teacher/guidance counselor at a Toronto High school with a large population of "inner city" youth. Through her various publications and activism, Pauline has become known in the Toronto school community as a strong advocate for youth, especially for those black youth who are the most disenfranchised within the school population.

Rosemary Ackley Christensen, Mole Lake and Bad River Wisconsin Ojibwe educator, teaches at the University of Wisconsin, Green Bay. Born on the Bad River Reservation in Wisconsin, she received her Ed.M. from Harvard University in 1971, completed the the course work and doctoral work for a Ed.D, with a concentration in Educational Policy and Leadership in 1999. Her dissertation is entitled: *Anishinaabeg medicine wheel leadership: The work of Dave F. Courchene Jr.* In addition to teaching, Christensen has had lengthy experience as an administrator, curriculum developer, planner, writer, researcher and Indian education advocate. She is a founding member of the National Indian Education Association, and in recent years worked with the Ojibwe language, writing and producing five units for family use. Her sons, Barry J. and Dane H. Christensen, live and work in North Carolina.

Elena Featherston is a teacher, multiculturalist, diversity trainer, writer, filmmaker, and grandmother. She is African American, Native American (Cherokee/Cree), and Scot-Irish. Her works have included *Skin Deep,* an anthology of women,s writings on race, ethnicity, and culture; a documentary on the life and works of Alice Walker (*Visions of the Spirit*), numerous articles, and trainings throughout the U.S., Canada and Europe with not for profit and profit corporations, government, academic, service, health, business institutions. As the founder of Featherston & Associates, she is a nationally recognized organizational development and diversity consultant known as a dynamic and inspirational presenter and facilitator.

Jean Ishibashi, a third generation Japanese American (often told how well she speaks English), is a noted oral his/her/ourstorian, videographer, community activist, and educator. She is a curriculum evaluator and developer who has taught Multicultural Education and Asian American Studies classes at UC Berkeley, Sonoma State University, and San Francisco State University. The founder of New Ways to Learn, a not-for-profit organization that establishes multicultural protocols to educate educators, Dr. Ishibashi is an antiracist, reflective educator who guides teachers in their efforts to develop rigorous cultural curricula that respects differences. Dr. Ishibashi is also an inspired mother and enthusiastic salsa/samba student.

P.J. Hallam's positive experiences with the Learning Record motivated her to earn a Ph.D. in literacy assessment from UC Berkeley. She is a research specialist at the Berkeley Evaluation and Research (BEAR) Center. Her current work centers on authentic assessment of teachers, through the Evaluating the Validity of Teacher Licensing Decisions project, cosponsored by the University of Michigan, the Interstate New Teacher Assessment and Support Consortium and the State of Wisconsin.

Gary L. Lemons holds a Ph.D. in English and American literature from New York University. He has held two NEH fellowships for college teachers and a Rockefeller Post-Doctoral Fellowship. He serves on the faculty of Eugene Lang College at New School University where he teaches courses on antiracist feminism, education, and cultural studies. He is the founding director of the Memoirs of Race Project. He has published widely on issues of race in education and the media, black feminist pedagogy, and is completing a book on black men and feminism.

Sherry Marx is an Assistant Professor of Secondary Education at Utah State University. A qualitative researcher, her areas of specialization include teacher beliefs, studies of Whiteness, and critical theory. Dr. Marx teaches courses in multicultural education and ESL education. She is a graduate of the University of Texas at Austin. Her dissertation won both the AERA Mary Catherine Ellwein Outstanding Dissertation Award for qualitative research and the AERA Division G Outstanding Dissertation Award. The chapter presented in this volume is based on her dissertation study.

Grace Mathieson is a teacher in the Ontario elementary school system. An underlying dissatisfaction with the school system and her teaching practice led her to return to university to study in the Department of Sociology and Equity Studies in Education at OISE/UT. Her personal challenge is to transform her classroom curriculum and practice so that it reflects her beliefs in social and racial justice. Although it is easy to be discouraged by the Draconian measures being applied to education by government, her passion and vision fuel her classroom work with young students, and she believes that white educators have much to contribute to rethinking education.

Kelly E. Maxwell, Ph.D., has been involved in intergroup dialogue for the past five years and in the higher education community for a decade. As a faculty member and Associate Director in the Program on Intergroup Relations at the University of Michigan, she teaches courses on intergroup issues including social identity, privilege, oppression and power. In addition, she trains students to facilitate intergroup dialogue on campus. Her research interests include policy and intergroup relations issues in higher education, particularly related to the critical examination of white privilege and its role in maintaining systems of inequity in education.

Eileen O'Brien received her Ph.D in sociology with a concentration in race and ethnic relations in 1999 from the University of Florida. She has published two books—*Whites Confront Racism: White Antiracists and Their Paths to Action* (Rowman and Littlefield, 2001) and *White Men on Race: Power, Privilege, and the Shaping of Cultural Consciousness* with Joe R. Feagin (Beacon, 2003)—and a forthcoming text-reader with Joseph Healey,

Race, Ethnicity and Gender (Pine Forge Press). She is currently a Visiting Assistant Professor of Sociology at the College of William and Mary in her hometown of Williamsburg, Virginia, where she resides with her partner, Kendall James, and their biracial daughter (and love of her life!) Kaya O'Brien-James.

Leny Mendoza Strobel is Assistant Professor in the American Multicultural Studies Department at Sonoma State University. She is the author of *Coming Full Circle: The Process of Decolonization Among Post-1965 Filipino Americans* (Giraffe Books). Her other writings have appeared in *Postcolonial Theory and the U.S.: Race, Ethnicity, and Literature* (University of Mississippi Press); *Filipino Americans: Transformation and Identity* (Sage Books); *Encounters: People of Asian Descent in the Americas* (co-editor, Rowman and Littlefield); *Filipino Writers in the Diaspora* (Anvil Press); *Amerasia Journal*; and *The Other Side*.

Studies in the Postmodern Theory of Education

General Editors
Joe L. Kincheloe & Shirley R. Steinberg

Counterpoints publishes the most compelling and imaginative books being written in education today. Grounded on the theoretical advances in criticalism, feminism, and postmodernism in the last two decades of the twentieth century, Counterpoints engages the meaning of these innovations in various forms of educational expression. Committed to the proposition that theoretical literature should be accessible to a variety of audiences, the series insists that its authors avoid esoteric and jargonistic languages that transform educational scholarship into an elite discourse for the initiated. Scholarly work matters only to the degree it affects consciousness and practice at multiple sites. Counterpoints' editorial policy is based on these principles and the ability of scholars to break new ground, to open new conversations, to go where educators have never gone before.

For additional information about this series or for the submission of manuscripts, please contact:

Joe L. Kincheloe & Shirley R. Steinberg
c/o Peter Lang Publishing, Inc.
275 Seventh Avenue, 28th floor
New York, New York 10001

To order other books in this series, please contact our Customer Service Department:

(800) 770-LANG (within the U.S.)
(212) 647-7706 (outside the U.S.)
(212) 647-7707 FAX

Or browse online by series:
www.peterlangusa.com